Higher Education for Everybody?

Higher Education for Everybody?

ISSUES AND IMPLICATIONS

EDITED BY W. TODD FURNISS

AMERICAN COUNCIL ON EDUCATION · Washington, D.C.

Contributors

WILLIAM M. BIRENBAUM
President, Staten Island Community College

ELIAS BLAKE, JR.
President, Institute for Services to Education

EDWARD J. BLOUSTEIN
President, Bennington College

ROGER E. BOLTON
Associate Professor of Economics, Williams College

MICHAEL CLEAR
Chairman, Academic Committee, and Senior Student, Washington
University

DON DAVIES
Associate Commissioner for Educational Personnel Development,
Office of Education, U.S. Department of Health, Education, and Welfare

FRANK G. DICKEY
Executive Director, National Commission on Accrediting

HEINZ EULAU
Chairman, Department of Political Science, Stanford University

ARTHUR S. FLEMMING
President, Macalester College

JOHN K. FOLGER
Executive Director, Tennessee Higher Education Commission

W. TODD FURNISS
Director, Commission on Academic Affairs, American Council on Education

LYMAN A. GLENNY
Associate Director, Center for Research and Development in Higher
Education, and Professor of Higher Education, School of Education,
University of California, Berkeley

v

SAMUEL B. GOULD
Formerly Chancellor, State University of New York

ANDREW M. GREELEY
Program Director, National Opinion Research Center, University of Chicago;
Professor of Higher Education, University of Illinois—Chicago Circle Campus

ROBERT W. HARTMAN
Research Associate, The Brookings Institution

TIMOTHY S. HEALY
Vice-Chancellor for Academic Affairs, City University of New York

VIVIAN W. HENDERSON
President, Clark College

CHARLES J. HITCH
President, University of California

A. J. JAFFE
Director, Manpower and Population Program, Bureau of Applied Social
Research, Columbia University

DAVID C. KNAPP
Dean, New York State College of Human Ecology, Cornell University

DOUGLAS M. KNIGHT
Division Vice-President, Educational Development, RCA

SCOTT W. MAC COY
President, Council of Students, College of Arts and Sciences, and Junior
Student, Washington University

WARREN BRYAN MARTIN
Coordinator of Development, Center for Research and Development in
Higher Education, University of California, Berkeley

JAMES L. MILLER, JR.
Professor of Higher Education, Center for the Study of Higher Education,
University of Michigan

PATSY T. MINK
Representative from Hawaii, United States Congress

DANIEL P. MOYNIHAN
Formerly, Counsellor to the President, The White House (until January 1,
1971); Professor of Education and Urban Politics, Harvard University

Contents

Foreword

As Sir Eric Ashby has noted, differences among national systems of higher education are heavily influenced by circumstances that are not always readily apparent to the casual viewer. In England, he has asserted, the weight of an institution's tradition is considerable, and an "inner logic" derived from long experience seems to guide expansion and improvement. The autonomy of English colleges and universities is such that drastic change may be more readily achieved by establishing new institutions than by attempting to modify existing institutions. Russia, on the other hand, makes a central political determination of the nation's manpower needs and then fits institutions as well as individuals into them. According to Sir Eric, the most important factor shaping the development of higher education in the United States has been student demand. With vastly increased numbers of young persons and a greater proportion of them wanting tertiary educational opportunities, it is no wonder that our nation is moving toward what is loosely described as "universal higher education."

This movement is gaining momentum without much public awareness of the issues and implications entailed. Political leaders make encouraging promises of advanced educational opportunity for everybody who wants it and can benefit from it, and all too frequently do not follow through in helping to provide the necessary allocation of resources. Professional educators, too, often give lip service to more education for virtually everybody and show an unwillingness to effect required modifications in the institutional status quo.

To help the higher educational community and all who have a stake in its further development gain a better understanding of the issues at hand and ahead, the American Council on Education chose "Higher Education for Everybody?" as the theme of its Fifty-third Annual Meeting. About a dozen basic papers were commissioned, numerous written commentaries on them were elicited, and hundreds of educators were drawn into discussions of these presentations. As Todd Furniss, the editor of this volume, has indicated, basic premises, practices, priorities, and leadership questions were all scrutinized.

This book highlights issues and implications that should be of deep concern to everyone who must share in the multitude of decisions to be made regarding the present and future of American higher education.

More than that, however, the outcomes have a very direct bearing on the kind of nation and world we and our descendants will find around us ten, twenty, thirty and more years from now. What the contributors to this book say is, therefore, of significance to considerably larger numbers of persons than were present for the Council's meeting in Saint Louis this past October. The publication of *Higher Education for Everybody?* is an effort to make that constituency as large as possible.

LOGAN WILSON, *President*
American Council on Education

Preface

IS UNIVERSAL HIGHER EDUCATION DESIRABLE? IS IT FEASIBLE? THIS VOLUME answers both questions affirmatively—but indirectly—through an examination of a variety of definitions of the term "universal higher education."

Surprisingly, the affirmative answers arise not out of a common set of premises nor out of a grand design within which some practices are found to be good and practicable and others are not. Instead, in the first section we see at least four quite different premises about higher education set forth by authors who, despite their differences, conclude that expansion of higher education is desirable and, under certain circumstances, may be feasible.

Some of these circumstances are elaborated in the second and third sections: admissions policies, considerations of quality, the fundamentals of reform, alternatives to traditional college instruction, new roles for adults as students, and the all-important financial and political questions, the answers to which, in the end, will determine whether the society will support universal higher education in any form.

The papers, commissioned for the 1970 Annual Meeting of the American Council on Education, make two additional conclusions inescapable.

First, higher education in the United States must make a long overdue effort to redefine "the college student." Today's working definition is based on an out-of-date stereotype—the full-time undergraduate resident in a four-year college. Yet some of the authors in this volume tell us clearly that we will not be able satisfactorily to broaden higher education's role until we look at our students as they actually are: some young, some older, some highly skilled, some wedded to nontraditional cultures, some intellectually far beyond introductory college work. Recognition of their real characteristics will call for the establishment of a variety of untraditional programs and, in turn, a reversal of the recent trend of the institutions that house them to become more alike.

The second conclusion is that such reform as is required by a redefinition of the student clientele will have to be made in the presence of continuing difficulties facing institutions and their leaders. One may observe pessimistically with Mr. Moynihan that college presidents are too occupied with immediate campus emergencies to devote much time and energy to reform. But, more optimistically, one may agree with the authors in the fourth section that what is to be done is clear and not impossibly difficult to accomplish.

The Council's 1971 Annual Meeting will be devoted to questions of financing expanded and diversified postsecondary education. The issues raised in this volume deserve the most careful attention as American higher education prepares for inevitable changes in the nature and extent of the support it can command.

To the authors in a collection such as this, an editor owes many unre-payable debts, which I happily acknowledge. In addition, I wish to express special thanks to members of the Council's Commission on Academic Affairs, Policy and Planning Committee, and Board of Directors, all of whom gave valuable suggestions about the nature of the meeting for which the papers were prepared. Miss Olive Mills, senior editor, and Mrs. Lilyan Kahn, administrative secretary, represent the many members of the Council's staff whose continuing help has been essential in planning and publishing this volume.

W. T. F.

PART ONE

PREMISES: *Higher Education as...*

Means

Process

Catalyst

Response

W. TODD FURNISS

Educational Programs for Everybody

Aᴅᴍɪɴɪsᴛʀᴀᴛᴏʀs ᴀɴᴅ ꜰᴀᴄᴜʟᴛʏ ᴍᴇᴍʙᴇʀs ᴏꜰ Aᴍᴇʀɪᴄᴀ's ɪɴsᴛɪᴛᴜᴛɪᴏɴs ᴏꜰ higher education are today having to consider the implications for their institutions of such slogans as "Universal higher education—a right, not a privilege," "Equal access to higher education," "Open admissions," and "Breaking the credentials barrier." These and similar slogans imply that the educational community collectively will soon admit more students than they now do, that the additional students will be different, and that new educational programs appropriate to their needs will be offered.

There is no collective American educational community, but rather several thousand essentially independent public, private, and commercial institutions, each with a set of educational programs finite in number, capacity, materials, facilities, and other dimensions. When pressure is applied, each institution must decide whether to change its set of programs to accommodate different kinds of students, or greater numbers, or both, and if so, what will be the nature of the revised set.

The alternatives available to administrators and faculty in making these choices are limited in three ways. First, any revisions must take account of benefits for all involved in the enterprise, even though the impulse for change may appear to require benefits only for the new student. Second, choices will be partly determined by "models" used in planning educational programs, each kind of model having its characteristic advantages and disadvantages for those involved in higher education. Before a model is used, its consequences must be appreciated. Third, any new programs must be based on an understanding of the relationship between occupational training and the functions of traditional liberal education lest programs promise more than they can deliver or deliver less than the beneficiaries have a right to expect.

After a brief note on definitions and the kinds of practical questions facing administrators, this paper considers the three limitations on choices under the headings "benefits," "models," and "liberal education," and then indicates some implications and alternatives suggested by the analysis.

Planners in higher education today are having to interpret the terms of the new slogans, particularly "universal" and "higher education," and to apply their interpretations to a host of practical questions.

There was a time when *higher education* could be narrowly defined as those academic and professional curricula leading to degrees in colleges and universities. Programs offered in trade schools, agricultural extension, proprietary technical and business schools, correspondence schools, employer schools, and the like were given other names: vocational and technical education, apprenticeship, adult education, and the like. These distinctions by location of the programs no longer apply. Each category of institutions has adopted some programs from other groups. Yet the term "higher education" continues to carry its aura of selectivity and prestige. As a substitute broad enough to cover all fields, "postsecondary education" lacks the aura and seems to do less than justice to adult and postgraduate education which logically are included.

Universal also creates difficulty. Literally, it stands for everyone. It carries the favorable connotations of "universal suffrage," but at the same time, it implies the notion of compulsory attendance associated with secondary education. Both the Carnegie Commission on Higher Education and the Federal administration have thus avoided the term and in its place put "equal access," qualified to include only those who wish education and are able to profit by it. As an initial working definition for educational planners, "Equal access to postsecondary education programs for those who desire them and are able to profit by them" is reasonably precise and will be used here. As a banner for a social movement, the label will satisfy no one.

Using this definition, faculty, administrators, and other program planners are faced with a number of tough questions, among which the following are typical:

- Should Ivy University, with admissions standards now set at a combined SAT of 1350, drop the figure to 800? Should it open a school of accountancy? Can the University Senate refuse?
- Should Greenbriar State University curtail its expanding graduate programs and open compensatory education centers in the neighboring urban communities?
- Should Meecham University's Continuing Education Program for Women require 30 semester hours of courses in the sciences, social sciences, and humanities as a prerequisite for a degree?
- Should Tom Wilson, who failed to go to college after high school, be given financial support if he wishes to return at thirty after holding a job? Should he be given degree credit for his work experience?

- Is liberal education, as it is now formalized at Dartherst College and similar prestigious institutions, a prerequisite for all who would aspire to the most highly rewarded occupations in society?
- Does the responsibility of the Curriculum Committee at Dillingham Technical Institute extend to helping the student develop a "life style" and "self-awareness" in addition to the skills and behavior necessary to the limited range of occupations for which he is being technically prepared?
- Should Calvert Junior College make liberal education the center of its programs for all its students?
- Are the courses in the catalog of Winship Municipal University best taken in an established sequence, or should the student choose what he wants when he wants it?
- Should racially integrated institutions require formal sensitivity training of administration, faculty, and students as part of the educational program?
- Should each state provide a range of educational programs within twenty miles of every potential student, or should it provide for moving students to comprehensive centers?
- What indices of success should the state legislature require of Algonquin State College to ensure accountability and economy in educating its students?

These apparently random questions are related at the most fundamental level: the experiences a student shall have in educational programs, that is, broadly, in educational activities and their settings. Let us look first, then, as the planner must, at the benefits that students and others expect from educational programs.

BENEFITS

Educational programs are means, not ends. They are established, modified, or eliminated in order to confer benefits and their nature is thus the concern principally of the beneficiaries.

There are two overlapping kinds of benefits to the student which may result from higher education programs. The first stresses ultimate improvement in his occupational and intellectual life resulting from changes in skill, knowledge, and attitude brought about by educational programs. For him, these benefits are all in the future. The other benefits derive from the setting where the educational activities take place. These benefits are all in the present.

The future benefits the student hopes for are often expressed as "an increase in options," although it is probably more accurate to say "better options." The number of options may be smaller because the changes resulting from educational programs may unfit him for some. And options once achieved may—in the light of newly developed attitudes—be considered unsuitable even though the graduate can perform their duties.

The other kinds of benefits to be achieved lie in the present. Some may accrue from pleasure taken in the activities themselves as the program unfolds. More may come from the setting in which educational activities take place, from its geographical location, the nature of its student body, the interaction among its students, and from its provisions for social activities. Institutions vary widely in the extent to which their programs foster these benefits, and students vary widely in their desire for them.

Social and commercial agencies derive benefits from educational programs to the extent that educational activities bring about changes in the skills, knowledge, and attitudes of others, not of themselves. To achieve these benefits, they establish and support institutions. As sponsoring agencies having relationships with administrators and faculty, there is not much difference among a commercial entrepreneur, a philanthropic or sectarian organization, and an elected or appointed organization. Whether they seek profits, prestige, workers to fill manpower needs, or protection from the ignorant and untrained, they provide support to the institution in return for changes brought about in students.

In this respect, institutions are agents of their supporting agencies, whose benefits they ensure by delivering those changes in students the agencies expect. But because institutions are also the means by which students get their benefits, they must take student goals into account quite as much as they do the goals of sponsors. And within the institution itself, faculty, administrators, and support personnel look for benefits that may have little or nothing to do with the benefits students or sponsors seek. Among them may be the opportunity to live in a congenial community and the chance to pursue professional interests.

This brief analysis indicates that the only relationship common to all beneficiaries is the changing of the student's skills, knowledge, and attitudes through an educational program. But changes in students are not the only or even the primary goals of some of the beneficiaries, who may have other relationships they consider more important. For example, agencies use institutions for research and service that have little or nothing to do with students, and often these functions have more attractive faculty benefits attached than do educational functions.

In this complex of relationships, the role of the institutional administrator is in part that of a filter, sifting out from the profusion of expectations of students, sponsors, and faculty those ingredients that might cause an explosion. His goal for the institution is its survival on the evident ground that without the institution students would not be changed and no party would benefit. Students who demand that the faculty's entire attention be on them, legislators who insist that the institution provide instant and successful compensatory programs for a region's undereducated, faculty who threaten to resign unless their class loads are further reduced: each of these is asserting its claim to benefits. The administrator, even though he may be fully persuaded of the propriety of each demand, will often be unable to accommodate them all simultaneously and in full measure.

It is in this context of sifting and balancing that the modification of an institution's program for a new, more "universal" clientele will be worked out.

MODELS

Considering the central aim of an educational program—to bring about changes in a student—it would seem wrong to insist that planners of educational activities become aware of common ways of thinking about systems and the consequences of such thinking. But today the devising of "systems models" is found at all levels of the educational enterprise. At the level of instructional and guidance activities—as the individual student encounters them—course syllabi, independent reading lists, and structured laboratory sequences are models of systems designed to bring about change and to test the extent of change. At the institutional level, the college catalog details the models of systems that categorize instructional activities into curricula leading to certificates and degrees. We see also systems of institutions, like the California state higher education system, with its subsystems of junior colleges, state colleges, and universities; such systems have been designed in several models. And finally, there are national systems, like the various sponsor agencies within the Federal government. The components of the educational encounters of a particular student are affected directly or indirectly by the ways the planners of these systems have developed their models. The following review is intended to introduce some of the issues raised by models as we think about higher education programs for everybody.

There are several classes of models in use in educational planning today. Common to all is an attempt to control variables in such a way that the outcome will be predictable and replicable. For example, a syllabus will attempt to coordinate student characteristics, subject matter, time, facilities, faculty characteristics, instructional and guidance methods, and setting so that not just one student but a succession of students will be changed in certain ways. The factors to be coordinated, in system terms, are the variables. The way each model handles the variables distinguishes it from the others.

At some levels of educational planning (notably in state systems and the Federal government) what Boguslaw calls "formalist models" and "heuristic models"[1] are used: the one attempts to account separately for every category of variable by identifying it and predicting the results of every variation, whereas the other establishes principles which will be used in response to the individual variations of the elements in the system. Far more characteristic of planners on campus, however, are "production models" and "ad hoc models."

Like a manufacturing program, the *production model* constructs a process that depends on certain kinds of raw materials and specific machinery for its ability to operate successfully. This has been the most common model in American higher education. The model has restricted goals, a limited number of activities, and a restricted student body. A school of medicine provides an example. Its goal is to produce 50 M.D.'s a year. To do this, it needs certain facilities, faculty with defined specialties, certain support personnel. And it needs a certain kind of student in predictable numbers. Given these, it can virtually guarantee its success in changing students.

The importance of "guaranteed success" is the key to the prevalence of the model and to its popularity with all the beneficiaries of education. Success must be both visible and measurable. Typing speed can be measured; bar exams can be passed; computers can be programmed; paintings can be displayed; farmers can adopt new irrigation techniques; and graduates can get employment that uses their new skills. The model's chief disadvantage is that its success may lead to the overproduction of increasingly obsolete products. The dangers to a production model are that it will have to take "unqualified students," or too many students to handle, or compromise on staff or facilities. These will overload the system or destroy it by trying to use raw material or machine parts that don't fit.

Although it is most easily identified with technical, professional, and vocational programs, the production model has also been used for traditional liberal arts colleges. The measures of success have usually been less directly quantifiable than those of professional and technical institutions, and more symbolic or longer range. The number of graduates admitted to postgraduate work is one measure often used; the scarcity of dropouts is another; the former undergraduates now in positions of influence is a third. But direct measurement of such institutional goals as "good citizenship," "awareness of self," "ability to think clearly and creatively about the problems of living in the modern world," is difficult if not impossible. The institution careful of its reputation for success on these mea-

1. Robert Boguslaw, *The New Utopians: A Study of System Design and Social Change* (Englewood Cliffs, N.J.: Prentice-Hall, 1965).

sures will ensure against obvious failure, at least, by selecting a familiar and homogeneous student body and resisting pressures to admit the unfamiliar. And it will increasingly turn toward the production of preprofessional students in the academic discipline, and away from the needs of the generalists among its students.

"Pure" examples of *ad hoc educational models* are far harder to find than production models. The ad hoc approach is, "Let us establish our system in such a way that we can respond to today's issues and needs. When we have responded, we will be a different system, but one still able to respond to the unknown of tomorrow. We will forego some of the advantages of replicability and predictability in return for flexibility—or sometimes, for survival." We find a few examples of the deliberate use of the ad hoc approach in those liberal arts colleges that have turned their backs on the preparation of disciplinary specialists in favor of fostering the hard-to-measure qualities of flexibility, creativeness, and intellectuality in their students. The approach is also central to student-run experimental colleges; and it is also used by a few new institutions—for example, Federal City College and the SUNY College at Old Westbury. Whether these will become production models it is too early to tell.

While one might expect to find pure examples in institutions which by law or lack of attractive power are unable to select their students, such as some of the larger public universities, it appears that the use of the ad hoc approach is only a temporary measure until a production model can be devised for any new and unfamiliar group of students who may appear. Pressures for measurable results are so great as to make stability a more important goal than flexibility.

The ad hoc approach is, however, often the only possible one for badly disrupted universities. Responses to events in the spring of 1970 on many campuses, including the cancellation of classes and the closing of institutions entirely, may provide "educational experiences" of great pith and moment, but it is safe to say that they were not preplanned for replicability and with an eye to demonstrating a measurable success in achieving the aims of the educational program.

The ad hoc model may be adopted under pressure or by choice. Its chief characteristic is flexibility, and therefore the possibility of both desirable and destructive innovation; its chief disadvantage is that its success cannot be guaranteed, either to its students or its sponsors.

The characteristics of educational programs—the actual encounters designed to change a student—are determined not only by a calculation of benefits but also by the ways in which those involved at the several planning levels design the models of which the programs are a part. At times, planners even at a single level may have to work with both production models and ad hoc models simultaneously, depending on the goals to be met and the variables that are accessible to their control. In providing programs for a more "universal" clientele, many administrators will be asked to accept the uncertainties of ad hoc models in place of the reliability of the safer production models.

Liberal Education

So far, this analysis has dealt almost exclusively with two special conditions prevailing over educational programs: benefits and educational models. It is time now to move to the nature of programs themselves and the changes they are designed to bring about in students.

Generally speaking, our postsecondary educational institutions have little difficulty in devising and conducting those activities that provide their students with the cognitive skills to participate in the occupations society requires. It does not really matter very much whether the student is chosen or is self-selected as long as he has the minimum of the attributes required for success in the program and sufficient motivation to carry him through. With these, the high school graduate in secretarial school or a computer-planning program, the medical student, or the accountant learning a hobby can all very likely have their aims satisfied. For them, money and time may be the only barriers to success.

Occasionally, there are problems apart from money and time. For example, even though the goals may be clear and both student and institution have agreed on them, effective techniques may be unknown. This appears to be the case with basic literacy, as in the administration's program called "The Right to Read." In other cases, the goal may not be defined clearly enough. For example, what is an appropriate program for occupations in environmental studies? In the past, programs in biological ecology have been devoted to the preparation of professional biologists, not environmental activists. And in still other cases, the program, although it may succeed in making changes, may not do so very efficiently, and thus strain resources.

With some qualifications, we may predict that "higher education for everybody" will be able to provide cognitive skills for all the occupations society values. The tough questions are going to be faced in deciding what should be provided of "liberal education," the kind of program that, in addition to cognitive skills, deals with behavior, attitudes, and the formation of a community with common values.

Traditional liberal education

Traditional liberal education sets four overlapping goals: (1) fostering individual traits beneficial to the student, such as confidence, dignity, aesthetic sensitivity, resourcefulness, adaptability to new conditions, and commitment (characteristics today included in the catch phrases "life style" and "self-awareness"); (2) fostering the acceptance of such social values as honesty and integrity in dealing with others, concern with their welfare, and acceptance of responsibility to work for the common good; (3) fostering the kinds of behavior thought to be appropriate to the occupations for which the student is being prepared; and (4) teaching the student the skills and knowledge appropriate for his success in each of these aspects of life, with emphasis on analytical techniques, and ability to generalize and synthesize.

To achieve these goals, conventional liberal arts colleges have developed educational programs that are models based on manipulating the variables of subject matter, community formation, and time. The subjects to be studied include both technical and vocational skills and knowledge and a range of topics dealing with our common heritage: the physical nature of the world, the arts, history, the character of individuals and societies, philosophy. Community formation is a function of bringing together student with student and student with faculty in both social and intellectual pursuits so that they may discover the commonality of their interests, develop respect for each other, and learn the social necessity for certain standards of behavior. Since the study of subject matter and the formation of stable communities take time, conventional programs are established to cover a period of years, and provide more time out of class (in residences, social activities, cultural events, etc.) than in class.

Changing values and behavior

This formula for liberal education presupposes much that the move to widen educational opportunity is challenging today. For example, it is clear that individual values as expressed in attitudes and behavior do change over time and in response to many kinds of stimuli, planned and unplanned. Planned changes use applications of the carrot and the stick (rewards and penalties), as well as the notion that moderately homogeneous groups will, without control, become more homogeneous. This is not the place to review the controversies among psychologists and sociologists respecting the ways behavior can best be changed, except to note that they vary as widely as the kinds of manipulation of the environment in B. F. Skinner's *Walden Two* and the deliberately nonthreatening discussion with a listener trained in psychiatry. In the first, it is assumed that the values and behavior desired are to be determined by someone else (supposedly benevolent), and in the second, that the individual is helped to develop the values and behavior he desires.

The traditional residential liberal arts program has, at least until re-

cently, assumed that its job was in large part to change or reinforce attitudes to the point where the behavior of its graduates would predictably
reflect the acceptance of a common set of values. To do the job, it has
used a multitude of carrots and sticks, environmental control, and counseling. Lately, its proponents have been far less certain than they once
were that its methods are the best: increasingly mindless competitiveness
for grades and the growing student reaction thereto have been indications
of trouble. And they have also begun to believe that the values to be
fostered need reexamination.

The first three goals of a liberal education listed above—self-awareness,
acceptance of social values, and development of appropriate occupational
behavior—are relatively easy to achieve when student, faculty, employer,
and the larger society are in agreement on what values and behavior are
suitable. Traditional colleges have long prepared a group that:

1. Uses intellectual techniques of generalization and analysis in making
   decisions rather than relying, for example, on magic or on emotional
   reaction to individual cases.
2. Values experience, expertise, independence, and resourcefulness.
3. Assumes competition, and rewards with money and positions of influence those who are both capable and willing to work hard.
4. Is self-consciously nonoppressive while valuing order, law, and predictability of behavior.

In the assumptions listed above lies a further assumption: that the best
rewarded occupations in society require not only certain definable skills
but also certain kinds of behavior if they are to be performed for the benefit of society. For example, the physician must use his judgment to do his
job satisfactorily. No society can prescribe what the physician observes in
a patient, what his diagnosis will be, nor what (within limits) will be the
best treatment. Yet few societies will favor the physician whose observations are eccentric, whose diagnosis is based on considerations other than
the welfare of the patient, or whose treatment is deliberately deadly. Although the society cannot prescribe all the specific actions of a physician,
it nevertheless can establish *standards of acceptable and predictable behavior* within which the individual physician has discretion. Furthermore,
since the physician must, to be effective, both behave correctly and establish confidence that he will behave correctly, he will be expected to adopt
inside and outside his practice some forms of behavior which are only
symbolic.

Quite obviously, minimum behavioral standards for the many occupations in our society vary vastly, just as do the skills and knowledge required. The reader may wish to test this assertion by analyzing the occu-

pational requirements represented in the jingle starting "Rich man, poor man, beggar man, thief."

Traditional students

When developed as a production model, the traditional liberal arts program has sought raw material that shows promise of being convertible to the desired finished product. Thus, it requires of its students a level of skill and knowledge that can be raised to acceptable levels in the time available; it has similarly sought students whose attitudes and behavior are sufficiently developed along promising lines so that the planned reinforcement will be possible; and, of course, it has sought students who can afford the necessary time.

If the production model is to work smoothly, the program must not admit students whose basic skills are at such a low level that they require more time than is available or whose native intelligence (however measured) is inadequate. It must reject those whose attitudes are more aberrant than the program can handle. And, since the model is based on time, it cannot accommodate those whose time is limited or can be given only in such scattered pieces that they cannot participate in the community development which is part of the planned program.

By contrast with the liberal arts program, most vocational and professional programs make the assumption that the student's attitudes and behavior are already suitable for the occupation for which he is being prepared, or at least that not a great deal of programmatic attention will have to be given to their reinforcement. These programs emphasize the development of skill and knowledge, often at a very sophisticated level. If a student's attitudes and behavior appear to be unsuitable for the occupation, he may not be admitted (for example, a medical student), or he may be dropped, or he may simply be left to discover the exclusion for himself when he tries to get and hold a job.

To ensure against inappropriate attitudes, most university professional schools limit admission to college graduates. But among those admitting high school graduates, including some business and engineering schools, many have in the past two decades incorporated in their curricula some of the offerings of the liberal arts college on the campus. Most of these complain, however, that the results have not justified the investment of time; yet they are reluctant to take on the job themselves by liberalizing their own offerings.

The "universal student"

The potential student population for "universal higher education," even if the definition is limited to "postsecondary education for those who wish it and can profit from it," is more diverse than a *strict* adherence to the requirements of either liberal education or vocational and professional educational programs can handle. Some of those who cannot be accommodated are suggested in the list of questions in the first section of this paper. For example, the traditional liberal arts college has no ready place for the student who must work outside the college community most of each day, the older student who cannot or does not wish to be part of a young community, the student whose skills are so deficient that special and time-consuming remedial programs must be provided, and the student whose purpose is to destroy the value system on which the college's program is based rather than to accept it. Professional and vocational education is not prepared to remedy deficiencies in basic skills, but only to develop ones for which the groundwork is laid, and it can do little to help students whose behavior patterns are inappropriate for the occupations they seek.

One might stop here and say that if the student does not fit into either traditional liberal or professional and vocational categories, he is not the proper concern of postsecondary education. He will have to seek to better his options by other means. To take this position is to exclude a good many potential students and to use the procrustean bed on others.

In fact, of course, the educational community has not taken such a rigid stand, and somewhere in the country there is probably a college and an academic program suitable for every variety of student. Public institutions and some private ones have admitted an increasingly diverse population. The larger public universities now admit to their undergraduate schools students at many levels of academic preparation, with very diverse attitudes and behavior patterns, and with wide variation in the time they can devote to class and academic community. Having admitted them, these institutions have discovered that if the students are to benefit new educational programs are required. Student and student-faculty communities ("the community of scholars") no longer form a homogeneous group: we have instead the hippies and the Jocks and the Black Student Union and the political action groups and the squares and moderates, as well as divisions based on the professions, such as the aggies and the medics. These coalesce and part from each other according to a seemingly endless series of issues or campus events, often led by or trailed by faculty who are almost as diverse in background and attitude if not in skill. Meanwhile, the administration, forced by the nature of the student body to take an ad hoc position, finds most of the faculty insisting that their own disciplines must be handled according to the strict requirements of a production model: the English Department doesn't really want 4,000 freshmen in English Composition, most of whom have no interest in or talent for what the department knows how to teach.

Because the very large universities cannot handle everyone, junior and community colleges and the smaller state colleges have flourished. Their programs are often easier to prescribe because their clientele, drawn from a single region and from less diverse backgrounds, is likely to be more homogeneous than the university's, and production model programs abound. But these institutions do not entirely escape the ad hoc approach for two reasons. First, they are dealing often with students for whom no program has been tried and tested, at least by the faculties they have employed. Second, if the students are aiming at those occupations that require the sophisticated skills and the attitudes and behavior of the traditional liberal arts graduates, these colleges may not have the time, facilities, staff, and predominant attitudes in the "community of scholars" to do the job. This is not to say that they do not do a job that may be socially valuable and personally very rewarding to the student: a community may be formed, predictable behavior may be assured, students may come to know themselves, and they may have moved relatively further in bettering their options than the standard middle-class student in the traditional college. It is worth noting that many of the predominantly Negro colleges fall into this category, as well as some avowedly "second-chance" colleges.

Some Implications and Alternatives

In view of this analysis, what might be done if the postsecondary population is to have the chance to improve its options across the board? What kinds of programs will have to be made available or invented?

Much might be accomplished within existing institutional forms. For those who have the time and the basic skills and attitudes, traditional liberal education *as a pattern* seems still to provide great promise: training in intellectual and technical skills, the reinforcement of attitudes by the study of common materials, and the formation of a community do work. Nevertheless, it should be evident that the details of the pattern must be varied according to the nature of the skills and attitudes the student arrives with. Thus, the simple imitation of a successful program at a highly selective college seems doomed to certain failure in a college unable to select its students, for two reasons: the imitator will discourage its students by setting distasteful standards or ones impossible for them to attain; or it will promise options that only a very few of its graduates will in fact have open to them.

If imitation of the standards promises failure, so does its converse, complete rejection. It is possible, in order to demonstrate "success," to set requirements for the improvement of skill and change in attitude in such a way that very little or no change actually takes place, and the student's options when he graduates are no better than when he entered.

Many for whom the four-year college program is inappropriate find satisfactory opportunities in trade, vocational, and technical training programs, and on the job. Particularly for the beginner, the barrier to success in these programs is not a deficiency in attitude or skill, or even a requirement of a massive block of time, but rather a lack of money, for there is seldom a subsidy for the vocational student until it is to his employer's advantage to have him retrain. If educational opportunity is to be widened, this lack must be corrected. Its costs would seem to be far less than financing four years in a liberal arts college for a student who does not need more than vocational training.

Among those for whom a four-year college program is inappropriate may be found the group identified by Kingman Brewster in his comments on involuntary attendance: attendance under coercion of the draft, of parental pressures, or of the need for a credential, and not because the college can add measurably to skills or attitudes. If these students are to be "freed," provision for their later educational needs should be considered, taking into account that, if they return, their accumulated experience and their altered circumstances will require different kinds of programs.

The alternatives suggested here leave a portion of the postsecondary population unaccounted for. Adults whose attitudes toward themselves, their work, or their associates prevent them from holding jobs; those with extremely low levels of skill; those who thoughtfully reject such socially approved values as competitiveness: can these be helped to better their options through conventional educational programs, or would other kinds of programs (therapy, apprenticeship, communal living) be more effective? Or should their "failure" be considered regrettable but inevitable?

THE FUTURE: AD HOC OR PRODUCTION MODELS?

Consideration of the benefits sought by students, institutions, and sponsoring agencies, of the advantages and disadvantages of production and ad hoc models, and of the elements of educational programs, suggests several conclusions. The American postsecondary educational community, ranging from technical schools through multiversities, has sought to provide production model programs whose results are easily measured and whose successes assure survival. Although often responsive to the manpower requirements of employers, the university has been slow in meeting new societal needs, the influx of new types of students, and changing needs of traditional students.

Ad hoc planning is seldom adopted voluntarily by either faculty or administrators because of the uncertainties of its results and therefore the dangers to continued support. Yet it offers alternatives in meeting the needs of an enlarged and, in part, untraditional student body, including those who because of age and circumstances have been wholly neglected in the past.

Today, many of our institutions have adopted ad hoc planning involuntarily and under pressure. Ad hoc planning does not mean necessarily the abandonment of all the familiar patterns of educational programing: the development of intellectual and technical skills, the formation of communities with shared values, and the fostering of independence and resourcefulness. It does mean a careful consideration of how these patterns may be adapted to students rather than how the students may be adapted to production programs that now exist. The adoption of ad hoc planning as institutional policy and a refusal to rely *solely* on the safety of production models offers the promise both of serving the beneficiaries and, in the long run, assuring the survival of the institution.

George Bernard Shaw's story of Eliza Doolittle and Professor Higgins, transformed into the popular musical comedy *My Fair Lady*, may help us to pull together many of the threads running through this analysis. The student, Eliza, comes to Higgins to get a new option: "I want to be a lady in a flower shop instead of selling at the corner of Tottenham Court Road. But they won't take me unless I can talk more genteel. He said he could teach me. Well, here I am, ready to pay."[2]

Higgins nearly drives her away; he has already recorded her dialect. But his friend, Colonel Pickering, feels sorry for Eliza and offers to be sponsor. In the form of a bet, he provides the promise of satisfaction and money to Higgins (the institution's benefits), and he offers to subsidize Eliza (student funds for the disadvantaged). He thus becomes the sponsor whose benefits are essentially philanthropic ones.

Higgins' system is a production model: selected student, a very specific goal (talking "genteel" enough to be a lady in a flower shop), and an ingenious educational program involving verbal drills and occasional exposure to the speech of real ladies. The test by which its success is judged is Eliza's triumphant performance at the ball. And yet, immediately after the ball, Eliza cries in despair, "What am I fit for? What have you left me fit for? Where am I to go? What am I to do? What's to become of me?"

What has gone wrong? The aims of both Eliza and Higgins have apparently been met: She speaks like a lady in a flower shop and he has won his bet. But neither anticipated the effects of variables in and

2. Alan Jay Lerner and Frederick Loewe, *My Fair Lady* (New York: Coward McCann, 1956).

beyond the program. Pickering is one. He is not part of the program. Instead he is an uncontrollable element in the setting. It is his constantly treating Eliza like a lady and not like a flower girl that, she says, makes her think like a lady. And since she thinks like a lady, she can no longer think like a flower seller. She is the beneficiary (or victim) of liberal education by her adoption of the values she was exposed to in the course of her instruction.

Most of the issues America faces in providing higher education for everybody are illustrated in Eliza's experience. Higgins as an educational planner exhibits a fairly common combination of expertise in manipulating some of the variables and total ignorance of the probable consequences of others ("Why can't a woman be more like a man?"). Mr. Shaw gets Eliza and Higgins satisfactorily out of their dilemmas. Can today's educational planners, with care and "a little bit of luck," be as successful?

Planned Programs

JOSEPH J. SCHWAB

The terms of analysis provided by Mr. Furniss seem adequate as well as apropos. I shall therefore apply them in the light of certain other matters.

The weight of evidence persuades me that the United States and Western Europe will continue for a substantial time to be a high GNP culture and that our educational institutions will remain substantially in the service of such a culture.

To say that the United States will remain a high GNP culture is to say that we shall continue to demand material goods and comforts—air conditioning and central heating, rapid communication and mobility, plentiful food and drink—professional entertainment, frequent alternation of pleasurable stimuli, decoration, and adornment, and, increasingly, differentiations of life styles based mainly on decoration, adornment, and choice of entertaining stimuli. It is also to say that we shall continue to demand, or at least admit the prudent need of, continued, accelerating distribution of these goods throughout our population. I remind you, however, that this second characteristic of a high GNP culture—distribution—takes two forms relevant to educational policy. There is, on the one hand, the distribution to demanding clients who are white and of Eastern or Western European derivation, a distribution that began about 1940 with the GI bill and is now so large, so old, and superficially so successful that it is overlooked by many of us. On the other hand, distribution to blacks, Mexicans, Amerindians, Puerto Ricans (and perhaps women) has barely begun and is, therefore, dramatically visible.

To say that systems of higher education will remain in the service of such a culture is to say that the new demands concerned with universal higher education are not demands that we prepare students for return to Walden Pond, to austere and simple lives, for graceful and loving non-achievement, for revolution, or for merely violent demands for change which the demanders are left unequipped to help bring about. It is to say, rather, that our various educational institutions, behind our traditional pink cloud of professed egalitarianism, will continue to afford to differing clienteles differing expanded options concerned with earning, enjoying, and controlling the goods of such a culture. Each cluster of expanded options will be characterized by definite and often well-disguised ceilings. Some of these ceilings will be imposed by self-interested conspiracies to set upper limits to aspiration. Others, however, will be set in the interest of students and in the light of factors involved in the dynamics of aspiration.

Some of these factors are obvious. A program that demands learning competences which are inaccessible to its students must merely fail. A program that proposes to repair shortcomings of this kind in the summer or an extra year is innocent or cynical, for many are matters not of learning merely but of habit, and some are habits that have been constrained from the cradle. A program that seats a handicapped minority of students amid capable ones virtually assures frustration and injury of the minority and their long-lived hatred of those who injured them. Some of the factors are less obvious. There is a limit, for example, to the bearable span between parents' achievement and scion's aspiration; retreat, withdrawal, even severe characteral breakdown can ensue on enticement or pressure beyond that limit. A second example: for most mobiles, the parental acts that initiate aspiration and the processes of detecting and satisfying expectations that are demanded by most of our public schools and by those whom the aspirer would join lead to a trained incapacity for risk and uncertainty. For such students, clear educational objectives, definite assignments, and literal masteries constitute the essence of education; a curriculum that, from the start, poses problems without unique solutions and invites inquiry or critical judgment will rouse massive anxiety, not be believed, and merely not be comprehended.

In sum, I suggest that the hope of universal higher education will not be well served by a universal mix in which all institutions try to be all things to all students. Neither will it be well served by ad hoc models. For without an anchor in deliberation and choice about the fitness of educational means and purposes to the futures as well as the present of those to be educated, collegiate operations are not likely to speak to "today's issues and needs" but to the noisiest opinions about them, as exemplified in the doctrines of the most threatening party of students or in the seductively "in" platitudes of the *New York Times* weekday book reviews. And if by chance a four-year college does serve today's issues and needs, tomorrow's graduates will curse it for its lack of foresight and courage.

The hope of universal higher education will be better served by an *intelligent* expansion and radical revision of the *diversity* of production model programs which have characterized American higher education since 1940.

I do *not* suggest that these production model programs are intelligently planned or, in fact, successful. On the contrary, the patent inaccessibility for many of our students of the ways and circumstances in which we teach, and their revulsion against many of the aims and much of the substance of our teaching are ample evidence to the contrary.

I suggest that our most massive mistakes or venalities lie in three areas.

1.   The insane numbers to be dealt with and the consequent anonymities and bureaucratic-functionary tyrannies which now characterize many institutions.

2.   The complacent ignoring of the complexities of human beings involved in our selection of students. We have acted as if position on the scale of a single variable—scholastic aptitude—were all that determined the appropriateness of students to a program. It is in relation to this error that I have referred to such factors as aspiration span and tolerance of uncertainty.

3.   The third massive failure derives from the apparent bankruptcy of faculties with respect to the aims, methods, and materials of education. On the whole, only two alternatives are commonly entertained: (*a*) different degrees of dilution and dosage spacing of standard departmental medicine; (*b*) surrender—wishfully or in desperation—to the moment's most popular whim. What is conspicuously missing is treatment of accumulated skills and knowledge as *resources for* instead of *defining principles of* education; that is, skillful, inventive, and sensitive selection of accumulated skills and knowledge and their adaptation to the problems of the supposed wants, real needs, and accessibilities of students,.

Programs: Industry's Role

DOUGLAS M. KNIGHT

AMONG THE CONCERNS about *programs* for a vastly expanded clientele for postsecondary education, my concern here is to suggest some programs alternative or complementary to those of the established educational system—or pseudosystem. (As Mr. Furniss points out, our "system" is not so much a system as an astonishing number of institutions that *look* like members of systems as we group them by type, size, and educational mandate.)

If the consideration of programs is to mean anything more than a game, we certainly should look at the alternates to our present routine. Neither the public nor the colleges can support universal post-high-school education of the conventional sort; at least we cannot do so until we solve the chronic financial and intellectual puzzles of the institutions already overgrown and yet so precariously alive at the moment.

The need for some kind of education beyond our present pattern and volume is clear. If we are anxious about the quality of human life and the rapid obsolescence of human effectiveness, we already have two excellent reasons to devise programs to meet such a demand. I feel certain, however, that none of our current formal structures is adequate or appropriate for the whole job. I should like first to display the range of needs, and then suggest a few of the resources that can help meet them.

Beyond the high school we face diverse needs: the need to remedy education that failed fully or partly in the normal high school years; the need to augment a high school curriculum with more specific or advanced vocational training; the need to retrain those who have been away from school for some years, and must catch up on an old career or start a new one; the need to open new ranges of experience for those with time and interest but no knowledge; the need for knowledge and guidance in attacking our major individual and social problems. These needs (and therefore the necessary programs) are diverse; they speak to many age groups and many educational levels. This very diversity of purposes calls for a diversity of resources, and the word *resources* in itself implies a further diversity. Financial, intellectual, and institutional resources must all come to bear on the needs.

We have in this country several "secondary systems" of resources. The churches and the community centers are making an honest though fragmented effort; public television and some local commercial television and radio stations are involved; the libraries are a major resource once an individual knows the beginning, at least, of his own need. Far and away the greatest potential capability, however, lies in the industrial training facilities of the country, which are already meeting many of the major needs for post-high-school education. They offer in addition a capability for shaping and producing programs that can be adapted to many new purposes.

Major reasons exist for this use of industrial talent, quite beyond the fact that it is there. Most important is that many of the problems and areas of interest which now call for national educational attention also demand attention from industry, for it has, along with all its other productive commitments, a major interest in the health of society and the enrichment of the lives of its employees. In other words, even if there were not a recognized national need for many additional kinds of postsecondary education, the need would still be present in industry. But no line divides the national and the corporate need, and we are just beginning to see what could be accomplished by a real wedding of diverse competences for some common and urgent purposes.

What programs is industry most competent to develop? The range is as great as the problem. Obviously, formal training in the traditional disciplines is not industry's forte, but some new approaches to mathematics may be; formal exposure to social theory is probably not industry's business, but encounter with major social issues certainly is; the history of chinamaking belongs in a museum, but the crafts of pottery may belong in an industrial training center. The talent and experience of industry lies in the solution of specific problems through the imaginative use of generalized or abstract knowledge; and that thrust, that direction defines both its training programs and its educational promise. Industry can be a valuable ally where there are specific skills to learn or purposes to realize, wherever there should be economy in time or investment, and often, I believe, where a new educational idea must be given some rigorous test. Industry has no magic to offer, but it does offer a good deal of expertise at solving the problems of diversity, numbers, and financing in postsecondary education.

California's Master Plan:
Some Kind of Education for Nearly Everybody

CHARLES J. HITCH

HIGHER EDUCATION has traditionally been expected to play a major role in providing opportunities for self-improvement and advancement; for part of our society it has performed this function well. There are, however, many additional groups who have specialized educational needs to which higher education has not yet adapted itself. One of higher education's major challenges is to find ways to develop the initiative and flexibility to serve a larger proportion of society.

The state of California has a Master Plan for Higher Education which constitutes a working model of a system to provide a high degree of access to potential students of college age. In the state are three segments of public higher education and a diverse group of private colleges and universities. The public institutions include 92 community colleges, which account for 49 percent of the full-time undergraduate enrollment of 532,000. In addition, the community colleges have a total of 344,000 part-time students, who represent a substantial variety of backgrounds and interests. Because these institutions are dispersed among many different communities, they are particularly well adapted to the task of teaching the technical skills needed by local employers. In addition, these institutions play an essential role in allowing individuals to study the traditional liberal arts fields without having to uproot themselves from their local communities. For those who are unsure of their ability and desire to pursue liberal arts studies, community colleges provide a foundation on which to decide whether to undertake the greater expense and larger academic risks of attending a four-year institution.

Our twenty state colleges and our eight general campuses of the University of California respectively account for 26 percent and 13 percent of full-time undergraduate enrollments in California and the private institutions account for the remaining 12 percent. According to the California Master Plan, our community colleges accept virtually all applicants, whereas our state colleges and the University of California have stringent admissions standards. In order to qualify for admission to a California state college, an applicant must be in the upper third of his high school graduating class, and to be admitted to the University of California, he must be in the upper 12.5 percent of the high school graduating class. In addition to providing undergraduate liberal arts education, our state colleges provide a wide variety of graduate programs leading to the master's degree and professional certificates such as teaching credentials. The University of California is responsible for providing graduate education leading to doctorates in most fields and professions.

I am not sure that the provisions of our Master Plan for Higher Education are precisely appropriate for the circumstances in our own state or in other states. But I strongly endorse its principle that the functions of higher education are sufficiently diverse that there should be separate institutions of higher education with responsibilities for serving specific groups of students, and the implication that the separate institutions should have different admissions standards. I believe that the diversity of our system of higher education is an important reason why approximately 80 per cent of California's high school seniors now go on to college—at least for some period of time.

Those critics who charge that it is elitist to have separate institutions of higher education with different admissions standards are, in my opinion, misdirected in their criticism. Any given type of education, out of the many types of higher education, will benefit students of particular interests and abilities more than others. The important consideration is to ensure that students have the opportunity to attend the institutions which are suited to their interests and abilities. An important corollary in ensuring that students choose institutions that are suited to their interests and abilities is to provide adequate financial aid. A needy student who has the desire and ability to attend a distant four-year institution may require substantial financial assistance.

Although financial aid is an important part of any policy intended to increase access to higher education, it is at least as important to reconsider how we manage our institutions Here are some comments on changes that might be considered.

At this time a substantial number of graduates who have been full-time students in California's community colleges go directly on to attend four-year institutions. If our community colleges and four-year institutions were to cooperate in providing more financial aid and, when necessary, remedial training either within the community colleges themselves or at four-year institutions, many more community college students with the requisite intellectual ability could be given a four-year college education. The community colleges should provide a genuine second chance for late starters and those from disadvantaged backgrounds who fail to qualify at the end of high school for admission to the four-year institutions.

In California, as in most other states, we have experienced high dropout rates in our four-year institutions. While many of these dropouts reappear at other four-year institutions, we are nevertheless not adequately serving our dropouts. One suspects that some of our dropouts come to four-year colleges more from social pressure or parental insistence than because of a real interest in obtaining a liberal arts education. The high schools and community colleges should provide better information on opportunities for vocational and technical training to help ensure wise initial college choices. Our four-year institutions should make this information available, along with adequate psychological and vocational counseling, to students who are considering dropping out.

I believe that many of our dropouts are sincerely interested in receiving a liberal arts education but on a part-time basis. Currently California's four-year institutions—particularly the university—do not provide adequate opportunities for part-time work toward undergraduate and graduate degrees. By developing part-time degree programs, we would be better able to serve many of those who would otherwise be dropouts. We would also be able to serve qualified individuals who cannot afford to attend college on a full-time basis.

Perhaps the most important benefit of developing part-time undergraduate and graduate degree programs is that we would be better able to serve the educational needs of the vast number of academically qualified individuals who develop an interest in receiving an academic education after they have been working for a number of years, and of those individuals already college-educated who would like to undertake further study in order to advance in their field or to enter an entirely new field.

We should experiment with some of the possibilities that I have discussed, especially the development of part-time degree programs. This undertaking would require us to determine the specific educational needs of the groups that would benefit most from part-time degree programs. It will also require us to find how best to coordinate part-time and full-time programs within our institutions. I believe that if we do some careful planning we can develop programs which will very substantially increase the proportion of the population that higher education serves and thus increase the service of higher education to society.

MARTIN TROW

Admissions and the Crisis in American Higher Education

FOR TWENTY YEARS ALMOST ALL THINKING ABOUT THE FUTURE OF AMERican higher education has assumed a rapid and continuous growth of enrollments within institutions much like those we know. Our natural propensity to think about the future in the categories of the past was strongly reinforced by the impressive continuity of the growth of higher education over the past eighty to ninety years. As Eric Ashby has shown, if enrollments in American colleges and universities since 1890 are plotted on logarithmic paper, the result is a straight line.[1] Looked at another way, if undergraduate enrollments are plotted as a proportion of the population aged eighteen to twenty-one, we find a steady growth since World War II of a little more than 1 percent a year. Graduate enrollments have increased even more rapidly. Moreover, as society moved toward universal postsecondary education, these growth rates could be expected to continue and the forces making for this movement could also be expected to continue equally strongly. There is the rising "educational standard of living" of the American population, which for nearly a century has viewed formal education with almost religious faith as the chief vehicle of social mobility. In addition, there are the rising educational requirements for many occupations and the parallel growth of occupations requiring higher education. As I wrote a few years ago:

> The American commitment to a rapid and apparently indefinite expansion of opportunities for higher education appears to be beyond serious challenge: discussions about higher education take the form of arguments over the organization and financing of the expansion—that is, questions of *how* rather than of *whether* it should occur. This is true in part for reasons that underlie the growth of the system itself. As I have suggested, the values of the society, the transformation of the economy, and the increased and highly visible role of education in social placement, underlie the widespread popular sentiment in favor of higher education. And the traditions of the heterogeneous, popularly (often publicly) controlled

1. In "Any Person, Any Study," a paper prepared for the Carnegie Commission on Higher Education, Summer 1970.

and financed scatter of independent colleges and universities help to convert these popular sentiments into institutional growth.[2]

With over 7 million undergraduate and graduate students in our colleges in 1970, we look forward to over 10 million by 1978 when, by these projections, there would be almost as many graduate students enrolled as there were undergraduates just before World War II. Moreover, until very recently we had every reason to believe that the broad and heterogeneous "system" of American higher education was well adapted to this rapid and continuous growth. Our state universities appeared to be capable of almost indefinite expansion, either on their home campuses or through a network of satellites. Institutions of 25,000, 30,000, or even 40,000 students became a familiar part of the American scene. The junior college has, over the past two decades, begun to show itself as a major instrument for mass higher education (while undergraduate enrollments in four-year institutions were growing by about two and one half times between 1955 and 1970, enrollments in junior colleges were growing by a factor of nearly five). And in California and elsewhere, state-wide master planning seemed to have answered the nagging problem of how access to the system could be ensured at the same time that the unique characteristics and higher standards of universities and graduate and research centers were preserved. Not long ago the multiversity and the junior college seemed the twin expressions of the American genius that had created, first, the common school, then universal secondary education through the comprehensive high school, and now mass higher education moving inexorably toward a universal exposure to postsecondary schooling. During those years our analyses and projections were made with great confidence and indeed with something like euphoria. And if we had any doubts about the superiority of American forms of higher education, they were dispelled by the widespread evidence that American institutions were the model for educational reformers all over the world.

These projections and predictions may have been well founded when they were made; we were confirmed in our wisdom by every new set of opening enrollment figures. If we assume that enrollments will continue to expand within the colleges and universities with which we are familiar, then it is reasonable to reexamine the criteria by which we admit students to segments of the system and to specific institutions, to examine the biases in the criteria and the consequences of modifying them, to raise questions about whether the quality of intellectual life in an institution is threatened or enhanced by "open enrollment" and how enrollments

2. Martin Trow, "The Democratization of Higher Education in America," *European Journal of Sociology*, 3 (1962), No. 2.

in individual institutions are to be controlled if existing criteria for admission are modified or discarded.

I would like in this paper, however, to question the underlying assumption about the development of American higher education itself. Despite the shocks of the past several years, most of our thinking continues to be predicated on the growth of the system toward universal higher education in our familiar institutions by the turn of the twenty-first century. If that does not occur, if indeed the direction of development of higher education changes, then the problems of admissions, along with much else, will change as well. I would like in this paper at least to speculate in that direction. For I believe that the signs are growing that the future of higher education will not be an extrapolation of the past. I believe that it is possible, and indeed even probable, that the current crisis in our colleges and universities will lead within the next decade to very large changes in the character of higher education in this country.

It is, of course, more common to see the present turmoil as resulting in a series of reforms and changes which leave the essential character of higher education in America unchanged: such changes as a movement toward more "open" admissions; larger student representation in university governance; fewer or more flexible curriculum requirements; the growth of smaller colleges or cluster colleges within larger universities or as consortia. And the observer can point to other trends of reform. But it may be useful at least to consider the possibility of much more radical changes in the existing system—especially in the big universities that dominate it—which in their character and effects go far beyond the kind of reforms I have enumerated. This exercise, even if it fails as a prediction, may have value in helping to identify the points of weakness and strain in the university and its component parts, and in alerting us to the processes to which these weaknesses and strains give rise. But if in fact we do not continue to move toward universal formal postsecondary education directly after high school, and moreover if the multiversity begins to break up into smaller, highly autonomous units with quite diverse functions, then the whole nature of admissions may change drastically. And if I am correct in this prediction, then we cannot even speculate on what those emerging patterns of "admissions" will be unless we can imagine the new patterns of higher education that will emerge out of the turmoil and confusion of the present. And that in turn depends on our assessment of the current crisis, to which future developments and institutions will be a response.

Alternate "Scenarios"

Let's consider first some of the signs that the university is functioning less and less well, and then consider some of the more basic sources of the breakdown. In this way we may be able to make some guesses about how far the breakdown will proceed; the extent to which it is affected by the immediate, larger political crisis arising out of the Vietnam war; and the extent to which it reflects more persistent tendencies in the society at large.

There are broadly three alternative prognoses: The first is that American higher education is going through certain difficulties at the moment tied to the crisis in the larger society and that when this crisis is resolved the universities will recover and proceed with the orderly development we have seen since World War II—toward the provision of postsecondary education for nearly everybody in the society, and in institutions much like those with which we are already familiar. The second prognosis suggests that the big universities have begun a slow decline, largely as a result of their responsiveness to popular forces that tend to weaken their elite functions, and partly because of their growth in size and cumbersomeness. Nevertheless over the next few decades the system should be able to carry the bulk of mass higher education in these big institutions while some of the most vulnerable functions of the universities—the training of elite graduate students and certain kinds of basic research—would probably come to be housed in more protected environments, perhaps outside the university. The third prognosis (or scenario)—which is closer to the position I am taking in this paper—is that, as a result of a number of forces both internal and external to the university, there will be over the next few years very marked discontinuities in the development of these institutions, and that the form the American system of mass higher education for increasing numbers and proportions of the group aged eighteen to twenty-two or twenty-four will take becomes more problematic.

If, as I anticipate, the leading universities, both public and private, will face grave crises within the next few years, the underlying reasons are to be found in the breakdown of consensus among the faculty and students about the basic nature and functions of the institution. In addition, the breakdown will reflect the growth of involuntary attendance in these universities, and a rebellion against them by large numbers of students who will no longer accept the constraints that formal academic programs represent to them.

The breakdown of consensus

Universities have generally been able to assume a broad acceptance by all the participants of certain norms and values which reflect a common conception of the basic nature of the institution and of its functions. The importance of this broad consensus about the nature of the institution has been obscured in the past in part because when the consensus is operating no one notices it; it operates as a set of unquestioned assumptions and comes into question only in a crisis like the present one, when the consensus no longer can be assumed. But in addition, it has not been clear that there has been a consensus underlying the operations of the big universities because the broad conception of the university allows for such variation, for so many different specific conceptions of mission and function.

The multiversity could not be identified with the traditional liberal arts college exclusively, or with the graduate school committed to basic research, or with any single definition of the academic role. Rather it encompassed all of them. The underlying consensus was not around any specific set of academic values but rather around a set of values that justify the coexistence of quite diverse educational enterprises. These were the distinguishing values of the multiversity: a basic tolerance for the broadest range of functions and services and a very flexible set of governmental arrangements which were (or were thought to be) educationally neutral, did not interfere with any educational programs, and preserved a high measure of autonomy for organizational subunits, chiefly the departments but also including research centers, schools, colleges, and the like. The multiversity was tied together by a complex set of procedures both collegial and bureaucratic which managed to effect the necessary degree of coordination of a very wide range of diverse activities and people, maintained necessary control over expenditures and personnel records, and provided the degree of accountability necessary for any public agency, while preserving for the teaching and research units a very high degree of freedom and autonomy. These procedures, while often irritating and cumbersome and slow and faulty in other respects, nevertheless gained acquiescence from most of the participants in the institution; and indeed the basic assumption was that the procedures themselves could be modified through other regular procedures.

Thus the university has rested on certain broadly shared norms and values, some of them procedural (institutionalized in the university), some of them substantive (institutionalized in the department), and focused on the central characteristics of the academic role. This consensus has broken down, both within the faculty and among the students. Our relations with our colleagues and our students no longer can be built on a broad set of shared assumptions, but are increasingly uncertain and a source of continual strain and conflict. The breakdown of consensus takes many forms.

First, there is the increasing politization of the university and the classroom. Growing numbers of faculty, especially younger faculty, do not accept the proposition that the freedom and autonomy of the university is built on the assumption that it will not engage in political activity and that the classroom will not be the locus for partisan recruitment or persuasion. Political loyalties and commitments in the larger society show themselves increasingly in the curriculum, in debate within academic senates, in positions men take on the organization and structure of the university, and finally in the recruitment and promotion of colleagues. This tendency has extremely corrosive effects of various kinds on the climate of the university. (1) It encourages direct political acts by students, including pressure and coercion on "noncooperating" faculty to be more accommodating to the political demands of activist students. If activist faculty can introduce their political preferences into the academic realm, then so can students, and with less restraint. (2) Political criteria, like any other nonacademic criteria, inevitably work to reduce the quality of men recruited and retained in the system and thus lower the intellectual level of analysis and discourse. Partisan positions on intellectual questions run directly contrary to the commitment of the academic man to the objective, skeptical examination of all questions and to the primacy of evidence (and, above all, of negative evidence) over received "truths." (3) The use of the protected resources of the university for partisan political activity inevitably engenders counterpressure from politically interested parties outside the university. The autonomy that the university claims as necessary to its disinterested inquiry is undermined by the surrender by some of its participants of a disinterested posture. Commitment is appropriately met by countercommitment. If academic men use the resources of the institution—its name, their access and special relationship to students, and their own time and that of their assistants —for political activity, they are then legitimately attacked as exploiting a special and privileged position. But for various reasons (to which we will return), it is extremely difficult, perhaps impossible, for external authorities to identify individual faculty members who exploit their privileged positions. The sanctions, when they are imposed, inevitably are directed against the whole institution that is unable to control its own members who violate its own principles and values. This process will be one of the major forces undermining the university and threatening its survival.

The politization of the university is surely the greater threat, but the conflicts over the governance of the university are a clearer symptom of the breakdown of consensus. The symptom, of course, is not the arguments for one form or another of governing arrangements but rather the high and increasing prominence of governance as an issue. Over the past several years the widespread discussion of forms of university governance has largely assumed that changes in the governing structure to include hitherto unrepresented groups would solve the crisis of government and reduce the level of intensity of attacks on the legitimacy of the presently constituted university authorities. My own view is that the discussion of student representation on governing agencies and committees has largely concealed the real issues by preserving the fiction that the students who would sit on these committees would substantially share the academic values of those faculty already sitting on them, yet would bring to them a somewhat different perspective, new ideas, and special concerns and considerations that academic men are likely to underemphasize.

In fact, the students who have been pressing most vigorously for a place on these governing boards have done so in the name of student power, and have called for a much more fundamental reconstitution of the university and more radical changes in its character and its role in the larger society. And indeed very often when students do come to sit on committees or in departmental meetings, they come to play a role quite different from that of the academic men already sitting in these governing bodies. Their primary loyalties are often to the Movement—its values and purposes—rather than to the bodies on which they sit and the values and purposes of the old consensus. Indeed it is precisely that consensus which they are most firmly committed to breaking up. The presence of students in increasing numbers on the governing bodies of universities makes of committees and departments a battleground for fundamentally opposed conceptions of the university: on the one hand, a traditional view of the liberal university committed to teaching and learning and with sharp limits on its permissible intervention into the political life of the environing society; on the other, a profound hostility to that society and a deep and passionate belief that the university is and ought to be a major weapon for its reform and transformation.

These different conceptions of the purpose of a university have implications for every action, every decision of the university. And since the stakes are high, the tactics and forms of controversy are increasingly intense.

Large parts of the university are still insulated from the sharpest experience of these conflicts, and in some of the professional schools and most of the old science departments, in engineering and in business administration, the old assumptions still obtain, and reports of breakdown in the social sciences and in some of the humanities departments are greeted with skepticism and a faint air of moral superiority. But every month more academic men experience at firsthand the corrosive forms of ideological controversy, and begin to see how these make their work increasingly difficult, and finally impossible. That kind of controversy, unlike the old and familiar forms of academic politics, makes collegial relations difficult; it demands unlimited commitments of time and energy; it makes the ordinary compromises of organizational administration impermissible as unprincipled and corrupt; and worst of all it is charged with a kind of moral passion that makes any tactics seem to be justified by the virtuous end.

It is only in the collapse of consensus that we discover how important it was for a climate in which we could carry on our work. The new climate makes demands on our time and energy and emotional equilibrium which are incompatible with the pursuit of our subjects and work with students that are or ought to be the main business of academic men.

"Reconstitution"

The fragility of academic norms and commitments among faculty members in even the leading colleges and universities became dramatically clear in the responses to the Cambodian invasion of May 1970. In many institutions faculty members eagerly set aside their course material and syllabi and entered on a cooperative "reconstitution" of their courses with the politically active and involved fraction of their students. Sometimes faculty members made provision for those students who wished to pursue their regular course of studies and also carry on political work outside. In other cases, faculty members simply modified their courses and brought them around to the discussion of the then current events, and in many cases these issues were wholly outside the professional competence of the instructors. In still other cases faculty members ceased to meet their classes altogether and pursued political work more or less full time. And in still other cases faculty members gave credit for instant ad hoc courses whose content was largely political activism, leafleting, and the like. It is very hard to establish the numbers in each of these categories, which in any event are fuzzy.

What is undeniable is that enough faculty members wanted these freedoms so that the administrative officers and deans and department chairmen in every leading university in the country had to make some gesture toward relaxing the ordinary procedures to allow these extracurricular activities to go on within the curricular framework. It is surely true that the invasion of Cambodia set off a wave of indignation and anger throughout the colleges and universities and created pressures against the continuation of normal academic life. What I think was significant in May 1970 was, first, the alacrity with which the academic program was modified, and in some cases abandoned, by significant numbers of faculty members; second, the degree to which administrative officers felt obliged to accept and legitimate these very considerable modifications of the academic program; third, the tendency to institutionalize these new arrangements in ways that would surely have continuing effect on the academic program in the coming years; fourth, the readiness of many to blink at the open use of the classroom and university facilities for partisan and political agitation and activity.

In my own view these events have very substantially eroded the claim of the universities and of their faculties to autonomy and self-government. The encroachments on university autonomy may be slow in coming but, I believe, are likely to be sure. They, in turn, will engender defensive re-actions by faculty and students, manifested through faculty strikes, open noncooperation, the refusal to carry out administrative duties, and further direct use of university facilities for partisan political purposes. This in turn will, in a familiar escalating cycle, lead to further efforts at repression, further angry defiance, and in—I think—a relatively short time to a break-down, a physical closure of at least some institutions.

The undergraduate curriculum

Another symptom of the breakdown of higher education is the col-lapse of the undergraduate curriculum. Debates over the curriculum—what should be studied, what combination of subjects, taught by whom, how organized—are evidence of the involvement of academic men in this central function of the college or university. Many teachers have observed that faculties are always tinkering with the curriculum, modifying these requirements, introducing those, changing the sequence of courses and the required or recommended mix of subjects and areas. And this process goes on continually because it is very hard to demonstrate the clear superiority of one set of arrangements over another and also because men differ in their views and change their minds.

But common to all of the positions was that those who pressed cur-riculum changes and argued for them and carried them through the course committees and curriculum committees and so forth had some coherent idea of what an undergraduate education should be like. The debates and discussions required them to justify their positions, to think into their assumptions, and to compromise or adopt alternative positions. Above all, they were required to communicate with their fellow teachers about this shared enterprise. Arguments about the curriculum, whether in an undergraduate college or in a department, are the major centripetal force in the academic community, and tend to counter the centrifugal privatizing force of men's own individual specialties and research interests.

I think it can be demonstrated that in recent years a great deal of the interest and conviction that formerly went into these curriculum discus-sions has drained away. Very few people are interested in arguing *any* position on the curriculum or discussing it with their fellows. There is less and less conviction that any curriculum, any set of courses, sequences, mixes can be defended against any other. The only positive force is that of the students who press more and more strongly for fewer and fewer requirements, fewer and fewer rules regarding sequences, fewer and fewer constraints on their freedom to put together their own course combinations as they see fit. For these students, who reflect widespread feelings in this generation of students, all disciplines are seen as restraints and all restraints as tyrannies and therefore as intolerable. Under those strong pressures curriculum plans collapse. Any efforts to develop some coherent program of general education is dismissed; even the breadth and depth requirements, which were its weak and expediential successor, are undermined, and undergraduate programs move toward the limiting conditions of a period in residence and a set number of units to be completed for graduation. These survive, I suspect, chiefly because they provide the minimal grounds for claiming that there is any substance behind the certificate of graduation.

But as these claims come to be eroded and the certification function weakened, it will be harder and harder to "impose" what will increasingly be felt to be an intolerable residential or credit unit requirement for graduation.

Student Rebellion and the Breakdown of the Universities

When we speak of student rebellion we ordinarily think of demonstrations, sit-ins, the visible and dramatic disturbances of one kind or another that have dominated the news about higher education since the Free Speech Movement at Berkeley. That kind of rebellion, as it affects the climate for teaching and learning in the university, certainly will contribute to the breakdown of the system.

But there is another kind of rebellion that may be even more important in its long-range implications, and that is the rebellion of large numbers of students against the universities and their forms of instruction: against the constraints of the formal academic programs and curriculum, the requirements and the lectures, the seminars and the papers, the reading lists and the laboratory assignments. Behind this rebellion, which is rapidly undermining all the assumptions about the relations of students and teachers, lies the issue of involuntary attendance in colleges and universities that is a concomitant of the movement beyond mass toward universal higher education.[3] As I have suggested elsewhere, the expansion

3. This section draws on my paper, "Reflections on the Transition from Mass to Universal Higher Education," *Daedalus*, Winter 1970, pp. 24–27.

of American higher education, in numbers and functions, is transforming it from a system of mass higher education into one that will bear responsibility for nearly all of the college-age population—that is, into a system of universal higher education. That development, clear in trends and projections, is obscured by the fact that currently only about half of all high school graduates across the country go directly from high school to some form of higher education. But in the upper-middle classes and in states like California, the proportion of youth going on to some form of postsecondary education is already over 80 percent. For young people in those places and strata, universal higher education is here: nearly everybody they know goes on to college. And those strata and areas are growing inexorably. Many of the difficulties now being experienced by American colleges and universities reflect the strains of this transformation from mass to universal higher education.

Involuntary attendance

In the recent past, attendance in our system of mass higher education was voluntary—a privilege that had in some places become a right, but not yet for many an obligation. Whether seen as a privilege (as in certain selective, mostly private, institutions) or as a right (in unselective, mostly public, institutions), voluntary attendance carried with it an implicit acceptance of the character and purposes of the institution as defined by "the authorities." The authority of trustees or administrators or faculty to define the nature of the education and its requirements could be evaded, but was rarely challenged by students. With few exceptions students played little or no role in the government of the institution.

The growth of enrollments and the movement toward universal higher education has made enrollment in college increasingly obligatory for many students, and their presence there has become increasingly "involuntary." In this respect, in some strata and places, colleges begin to resemble elementary and secondary schools, where compulsory attendance has long been recognized as increasing problems of student motivation, boredom, and the maintenance of order. The coercions on college students take several forms. The most visible in recent years has been the draft, which has locked many young men into college who might otherwise be doing something else. But other pressures will outlive the reform or abolition of the draft: the unquestioned expectations of family and friends and the consequent sense of shame in not meeting those expectations; the scarcity of attractive alternatives for youngsters of eighteen and nineteen without college experience; the strong and largely realistic anticipation that without some college credits they will be disqualified from most of the attractive and rewarding jobs in the society of adults. As more and more college-age youth go on to college, not to be or to have been a college student becomes increasingly a lasting stigma, a mark of some special failing of mind or character, and a grave handicap in all the activities and pursuits of adult life.

The net effect of these forces and conditions is to make college attendance for many students nearly involuntary, as a result of external pressures and constraints, some of which do not even have the legitimacy of parental authority behind them. The result is that we are finding in our classrooms large numbers of students who really do not want to be in college, have not entered into willing contract with it, and do not accept the values or legitimacy of the institution.

In the past, the relative accessibility of higher education brought large numbers of students to American colleges and universities who had little interest in learning for its own sake, but who had strong ambitions to rise in the world and wanted the degree and sometimes the skills that would help them better their status. We are now seeing large numbers from more affluent homes who similarly enter colleges without much interest in bookish study, but who also are less interested in vocational preparation or social mobility—who either have little ambition for a middle-class career, or else take it completely for granted, or, as in many cases, both. These students also differ from the members of the old "collegiate culture" who took refuge from the higher learning in the "gentleman's C" and the distractions of college sport and social life. But these students, already securely lodged in the middle and upper-middle classes, were not inclined to challenge any authority, especially when the institution made its own relaxed compromises with their styles and evasions. For the members of the old collegiate culture, as for the vocationally oriented and the serious students with an interest in academic work, a willing contract with the college of their choice was implicit and, for the most part, honored.

The entry of large numbers of "involuntary" students introduces into the university considerable resentment and hostility directed to, among other things, its conceptions of achievement and ambition. There have always been large numbers of people, in this as in other societies, whose ambitions were modest or who felt that the human price of striving and ambition was not worth the uncertain gain. But these views are represented more strongly in the university today, where they assert their legitimacy in ways the institution seems peculiarly unable to counter. Part of the attack is on the ends of ambition and takes the form of the rejection of academic institutions and programs that threaten to fit people for jobs and careers in a "sick society." Part of the complaint is that academic or intellectual work is intrinsically dehumanizing, separating people from one another, destroying their human qualities, authenticity, and so forth. This sentiment sometimes takes the form: "Look, stop trying to put us on your treadmill; your own lives are spent running around doing pointless things. We just want to look at the flowers and love one another." This point of view, in its pure form, is clearly incompatible with any kind of consistent goal-directed effort. But many students, under the constraints to be enrolled in college, hold views close to this while continuing to attend classes and earn credits. Such students pose a special problem for the university. They are not only bored and resentful at having to be in college, but they are also quite vulnerable to the antirational or politically radical doctrines currently available in the university—and especially to those that explain and justify their distaste for formal academic work and their reluctance to get caught up in the patterns of striving and achievement.

Reconstitution: the attack on academic routines

Before Cambodia and Kent State, one could see the growth in the numbers of involuntary students as having a marked but gradual effect on the character of American higher education. I anticipated that their hostility would express itself chiefly through the already familiar forms of campus discontent with targets like the war and ROTC; I also expected that these students would continue to exert pressures within the university against formal requirements and toward greater "flexibility" in the curriculum and for more "relevance" in the curriculum, which often conceals the demand for less dependence on books and reading and more on field work and contemporary experience. But I must confess that I saw these pressures and tendencies as having a gradual effect on the character of our leading colleges and universities. I counted not so much on principled resistance or on a rebirth of interest in a coherent undergraduate curriculum as I did on the sheer inertia of academic committees and the conservatism of collegial procedures and the endless discussions that mark academic decision making.

Viewed in that way the changes that were slowly coming about in American colleges could be seen as a mixture of gains and losses. The decline in the self-confidence and authority of academic men and in their conceptions of liberal education had led to the collapse of general education and its replacement by the intellectually much feebler structure of breadth and depth requirements. On the other hand, student pressures for greater flexibility were beginning to lead men to question the necessity for conventional forms of instruction that had outlived their usefulness. The sheer necessity to rethink the forms of instruction was a gain, and perhaps worth the losses in standards of performance that accompany them. There is a very clear parallel between what was happening to the curriculum in our colleges and universities and the transformation of the secondary school curriculum in the first two or three decades of this century. As I have written elsewhere about that transformation of secondary education in this country:

> With schools full of children for whom the traditional content and purpose of the secondary school curriculum were irrelevant, educators needed some rationale and justification for what they were doing. And what they were doing was trying to teach something that promised to be of some use for these . . . students in ways that would hold, at least fleetingly, the interest of indifferent students whose basic interests lay outside the classroom. It was precisely the interest and motivation that one could no longer assume in the student, but had to engender in the school, that lay at the heart of W. H. Kilpatrick's influential *The Project Method*, and before that underlay the importance of motivation in Dewey's writings.[4]

In colleges and universities, as in the secondary schools before them, the growth of involuntary attendance is forcing changes in the curriculum, away from the intrinsic logic of the academic disciplines, and toward the interests that students bring with them to the classroom. The necessity to motivate, rather than being able to assume motivation, means that the instructor has increasingly to ask how the material can be approached in ways that will "turn the student on." This might mean changes in the form of instruction; it might mean changes in the emphasis given to different aspects of the subject; it might mean efforts to involve the students more directly in the definition of the course content.[5] And in recent years all of these tendencies were to be observed in the colleges and universities as new committees were created to bring student views more directly into the structure of curriculum formation and decision making. Berkeley's own Board of Educational Development was a case in point: it was set up explicitly to provide a means of introducing courses directly responsive to student interests that might not otherwise have been approved by a more traditional Committee on Courses, and the board has been more and more influenced by student initiatives in course creation.

But until recently all of these tendencies were relatively slow or were peripheral to the main work of the institutions, which, by and large, continued to reflect the more traditional form and content of the

4. "The Second Transformation of American Secondary Education," *International Journal of Comparative Sociology*, September 1961.
5. Of course all of this is much more pronounced in the social sciences and humanities than in the natural sciences and professions.

academic curriculum. It has been the shock of the Cambodian invasion
and the academic response to that event which has led me to believe
that these processes are likely to be much faster than I had assumed. In
a sense, the events of spring 1970 have greatly accelerated the transformation of our colleges and universities and have shifted the pattern
of slow decline that formed the second scenario that I discussed earlier
toward the pattern of institutional breakdown that is my third prognosis.

The response to Cambodia has had its effect not so much by changing
the attitudes and values of academic men or students, as by revealing
more sharply than would otherwise have happened how thin and fragile
is the normative structure of assumptions on which the university is
based. It has accelerated all of the tendencies that were at work by
destroying the unawareness and inertia within the academic community
that has allowed the increasingly empty academic routines to continue
to carry the older academic values. The academic values of patient
inquiry, the sequential development of ideas, the emphasis on reasoned
discussion and criticism, the continual reference to evidence, and the
special attention to negative evidence—all of these values are institutionalized in the academic routines. The attack on those routines arose in
part because they had become in some cases unreflective and stultifying;
but the attacks drew their strength much more from the fact that those
routines no longer appealed to students who had little taste for that
kind of traditional academic study. Nevertheless so long as those routines,
embodied in the regular classes and lectures and seminars, went on, the
values themselves had a place and were in formal and symbolic ways
reaffirmed by being lived out. The reconstitution of the curriculum that
followed from the Cambodian invasion first of all took the form of an
attack on "business as usual"; that is to say, an attack precisely on these
academic routines and inevitably on the academic values which they
institutionalized.

What is most significant in the events that followed the invasion of
Cambodia is not that radical students attacked the university, its "com-
plicity in the war," its "institutional racism," etc., etc., and demanded
that it be shut down. On the contrary, what is perhaps most astonishing
is how little influence the most radical and violence-prone students have
had since larger numbers of students have been drawn into political
activity. It is the latter, more moderate students who have dominated
the climate of most of the leading campuses, certainly as compared with
the awful "trashing" and turbulence of the preceding few years. But what
is most impressive is how eagerly large numbers of students turned away
from the normal routines of their course work and toward a fundamentally different kind of activity in and around the university.

The "reconstitution" of the university was seen by large numbers of involuntary students to be a kind of liberation; and in the universities we have seen the euphoria that is associated with this liberation from the hated books and course work. The atmosphere on the campuses has been extraordinarily warm and positive. Students who had been sullenly submitting to the "tyranny" of the curriculum have suddenly discovered in large numbers that they don't have to go to those classes any more and, through the various arrangements that have been made for them, can continue to get credit and "proceed" toward their degrees. The appeal of reconstitution is very largely the appeal of liberation from the dull and uninteresting academic work that they had been engaged in. I do not mean to suggest that the courses from which they have been liberated are intrinsically dull, but only that they are dull and coercive and oppressive to the large number of students who do not bring to those courses any genuine interest in their content.

Cambodia and the reconstruction of the curriculum that has followed it in varying degrees in different subjects has greatly accelerated the shift in the curriculum toward the interests of the students. It has shifted the work of the students (1) away from books and toward action, (2) away from analysis and criticism and toward affirmations and commitment, (3) away from solitary work toward collective enterprises and the pleasures of cooperative sociability, (4) away from the competitive pursuit of grades toward collective "grades" and other evidences of warm approval that attest to their right feelings and moral commitments, (5) away from what they take to be an arid objectivity and a search for negative evidence, toward the enormous rewards of the suspension of disbelief, of a commitment to a movement larger than they and the social confirmation of one's moral rightness and the adequacy of one's understanding. Perhaps most important, the political enterprises that many students have begun to engage in provide a meaning to their lives that their work in the classrooms and in the formal curriculum was not providing.

Adult roles: inside or outside the academy

The rebellion of large numbers of students is associated with the enforced attendance that I have already spoken about and with the concomitant prolonged adolescence and the denial of full adult roles and responsibility that such perceptive observers as Bennett Berger, Bruno Bettelheim, and Erik Erikson have spoken of. Bettelheim, in his recent essay on "Obsolete Youth," has observed that

> Campus rebellion seems to offer youth a chance to short cut the time of empty waiting and to prove themselves real adults.

And he speaks also of the

> need of late adolescents to feel that their labours make a difference in the
> world, and the depressing conviction that they do not. For it is hard to
> see how the average social science student or the student of humanities
> can get a sense of importance of his studies until such time as he is deeply
> immersed in them: and this takes effort and concentration. Even then,
> the feeling may be somewhat esoteric. But what swifter and surer way to
> feel active than to become an activist?

And Bettelheim agrees that

> our institutions of higher learning have expanded too fast. Under public
> pressure for more education for all, they have steadily increased enrolment
> without the means to make parallel adjustments in the learning situa-
> tion. One result is far too large classes; another is the anonymity, the
> impersonal nature of student-faculty contacts against which students
> rightly complain. Too many classes in our large universities are taught
> by teaching assistants (some of whom share the same dilemma as the
> students, and hence tend to side with rebellions).[6]

And indeed, as I have suggested elsewhere, the teaching assistants in
our large universities may be a special problem as they organize counter-
courses and counterpressures at the very heart of the undergraduate
liberal arts college.

Although one may identify many specific elements in the present
situation in colleges and universities, the central issue seems to me to
be the paradox that has been thrown into bold relief by the Cambodian
affair and what has followed: the hatred and sullenness and disaffection
of our students and of sections of our faculty are much wider and deeper
than we have realized; and the direct political attacks on the university,
serious as they have been, are only the visible tip of the iceberg. And
when an occasion arises that allows the routines of academic life to be
broken, large numbers have seized the opportunity to create a new set of
activities and relationships that are more rewarding to them, that call
out more spontaneous energies and motivations than most of us can
evoke through the ordinary routines.

The paradox arises because the activities that reach these students in
ways that the academic work cannot are often activities which are profoundly inimical to the welfare of the university as a place for teaching
and learning governed by the canons of inquiry and the rules of evidence
and of logic. Moreover, these activities violate the implicit contracts between the universities and their supporting environment and the larger
society and thus throw into question the continuation of the autonomy

6. In *Commentary*, September 1969, pp. 33, 34.

of the university that is a prerequisite for free inquiry and scholarship. What is most troubling in the present situation is that the destruction of the academic programs is so rewarding and so widely applauded within the academy. It is hard to imagine that anything like the situation before Cambodia can be restored. If it is not, if there is continued "reconstitution" of the curriculum, which inevitably will mean its continued mobilization at the service of specific political ends, then the cycle of attack and counterattack that I spoke of earlier seems to me to be inevitable. And the question then arises: What will be the probable actual course of events, both in the medium and long run?

I have said nothing thus far about what is more widely perceived as the central danger to the university from within; that is, the direct attack on academic freedom from radical activists, the disruption of classes, the pressure and intimidation that has begun to be experienced by faculty members who resist the politization of their classrooms and of the academic community. These coupled with the outright rioting and invasions of research centers and the like are indeed a very important source of difficulty. If they become more widespread, or continue even at their present level, it will be hard to maintain the university, and especially its most vulnerable activities in the social sciences.

But I think it can be shown that these kinds of activities are organized and carried on by a definable group of political activists and ideologues who represent on large campuses substantial numbers of people but relatively small proportions. Furthermore, their very excesses tend to alienate them from larger groups of people, as, for example, when their spokesmen tell the students that they must be prepared to kill their parents if they are to be true revolutionaries. Such activists and their allies among the street people and nonstudents in the area may continue to constitute a serious threat to academic freedom and to the universities. But taken by themselves I think that threat could be met. I think people in these movements are likely to destroy their own mass following; the groups themselves have a perennial tendency to split and quarrel among themselves; and finally, I think it is possible slowly to learn to manage the direct physical violence through the intelligent use of police force. Moreover, universities, their administrators, faculty members, and large sections of their student bodies do in fact learn over time about the nature of the most activist groups, begin to see through their rhetoric, and learn to unmask their moral pretentions and their cries of outraged innocence. There is a kind of inoculation effect, so that over time the same tactics will not work in the same institution as successfully as they did earlier.

I have stressed in these notes what, to me, is the much more serious evidence of a general rebellion—or if not general, at least a much more widespread rebellion against the academic enterprise by large numbers of students who are in no sense radical activists or militant leaders. I believe we are seeing the consequences of the profound error of prescribing for half, and in some strata for 70–80 percent, of the age-grade a form and content of education that closely resemble the bookish, traditional, academic education that was designed for 5–10–15 percent of the age-grade. We are seeing now most dramatically that a serious interest in bookish studies is not present in the whole of the youthful population, nor is it synonymous with intelligence or verbal skills and the capacity for abstract reasoning. We see in our colleges and universities young men and women of great talent and intelligence who recoil from the courses of study we prescribe for them.

Thus, in our rapid move through mass toward universal higher education, we have brought into the colleges and universities large numbers of students who are weakly motivated for the standard academic roles. These developments, coupled with an event that allowed them to become general knowledge, coupled with other parallel processes within the academic community itself—changes in the recruitment to college and university teaching, a weakening of faculty authority and of confidence in their special expertise, and deep confusion and conflicts about the central characteristics of the institutions themselves—these things taken together are making our leading colleges and universities unworkable.

Alternatives to universal higher education

It seems to me there are two questions then before us. First, what may be the ways in which this breakdown occurs? Some forms of breakdown may be far more destructive than others to the inevitable revival of some kinds of higher education of high quality. It may be that we can, if not prevent the breakdown of the system, at least influence the process by which it ceases to function in its present form, and then influence the nature of the institutions that arise in its place. Second, in the slightly longer run we might ask whether we can envision something quite different from mass and universal higher education, now confined largely to the age-grade eighteen to twenty, focusing so much around bookish studies. We may turn to that question by asking what are the central functions that these institutions have been performing, how will the functions be distributed, and through what mechanisms will they be performed if the present institutions no longer are performing those tasks in the same ways as they have been.

It is possible that we are facing a very great disaster: it is arguable that the liberal colleges and universities in the United States are central bulwarks of the liberal political order, and that the decline or even the collapse of these institutions of higher education will gravely weaken our liberal society and its political institutions. There is a slightly more hopeful way of looking at these events: Let us say that the institutions of mass higher education as they have evolved in the United States have many admirable qualities, but that in some fundamental respects they were stifling and inhibiting the creative energies of both faculty members and students. In those respects the institutions were making much less than their potential contribution to the life of this society. We can perhaps only at this moment of grave crisis invent alternative institutions that would not rest so heavily on forms of coerced attendance and that could engender around their activities the kinds of energies and enthusiasms that we have witnessed recently but that would be exercised in ways that do not threaten the scholarly values and intellectual processes that are now institutionalized in the colleges and universities. The kinds of enthusiasms we are seeing, although they may be incompatible with bookish and scholarly studies, are not incompatible with other kinds of creative and fruitful activities that might be organized outside and parallel to the academic programs of colleges and universities.

Before we are confronted with a worsening of the problem, it would be of some use to think about what might be done with large numbers of young men and women who have completed secondary school; who have great talent and intelligence and energy; who are ready for larger, more adult responsibilities and tasks than we allow them in the colleges and universities; who are not nearly so hostile to the society as their spokesmen claim; but who want more than anything else to put their energies at the service of the poor and the despised and toward a better and more just society. Insofar as our colleges and universities have ignored those strong and generous impulses and those healthy strivings for adult status, then they have been guilty of a grievous error. There is a fraction of youth that can achieve its adult roles and intrinsic satisfactions through serious prolonged formal study. That proportion may be 10, 15, or even 20 percent of the age-grade. But I am sure it is not 50 or 60 or 70 percent of the age-grade. That reason is enough to believe that the future of higher education cannot be an extrapolation of past tendencies.

The current grave social and political crises only shorten the time we have for inventing viable alternatives to college attendance for all immediately upon graduation from high school.

Some Possible Developments and Their Implications for Admissions

I can anticipate a number of developments growing out of the crisis at the multiversity and the wider turmoil within higher education. These developments are not mutually exclusive and may indeed emerge simultaneously and in different parts of the country and the system. They will in fact constitute different responses to the difficulties that I have been sketching.

1. There will be efforts to suppress expressions of dissent on campus through increasingly coercive pressures on students (and faculty) to accept the authority of the institution and its administrative leadership.
2. There will also be efforts to postpone the formal education of a growing number of high school graduates, and to divert many young men and women to other kinds of work and informal learning off campus.
3. There may be an increased readiness to admit larger numbers of adults with broken or interrupted educational careers to the central university programs, rather than confining them to summer school and extension programs.
4. Simultaneously, I think the universities will undergo further internal differentiation, while incorporating activities that in the past have not been seen as a legitimate part of formal higher education.

Each of these responses will have different consequences for the pattern of admissions, both to the system as a whole and to the individual institutions.

Suppression

There will be widespread efforts to suppress the high levels of dissent and the more turbulent expressions of discontent on campuses. We may see—indeed are seeing—governing boards and legislatures intervene directly into the selection and promotion of faculty, into the procedures for admissions, and into the curriculum and the classroom itself. Substantial interventions from outside the university of course reduce the autonomy of the institution and its freedom to define its mission and character. Essentially the result must be to undermine the freedom necessary for genuine higher education and to move colleges toward the norms and practices of the public high schools. Where this process develops, there will be a parallel tendency for college admissions to be governed wholly by broad social and political considerations.

The loss of autonomy over admissions substantially weakens an institution's capacity to determine its own character, and makes it much more responsive to social and political pressures that arise outside the institution. I would anticipate that the model of the comprehensive high school and open-door junior college will be increasingly applied to four-year colleges, especially in the present context of pressures for open enrollments.

But this effort to convert college into grades thirteen through sixteen presupposes a body of immature and docile young men and women prepared to accept the continuation of their high school experience. However attractive that may be to some conservative governors and legislators, I think it cannot be widely successful as a policy. But we should not underestimate the extent or depth of the anger in the general population toward the colleges and universities. Politicians who are experts in the management of discontent will surely appeal to these feelings through repressive policies directed at the colleges and universities.

But despite the strong political pressures behind it, I do not think repression can be widely successful. It fails to meet the growing restlessness of youth (who are even becoming increasingly rebellious in high school); and it will encounter the intrenched opposition of most college teachers and administrators, who will strenuously defend the privileges and prerogatives of higher education for good reasons and bad. Existing colleges and universities can be gravely damaged by repressive policies (which include budgetary starvation as well as direct interference in educational policy). But I do not believe a large section of higher education can be effectively governed through the structures and values of the public high schools.

Postponement and diversion

I believe that the current crisis will also strengthen the growing tendency to encourage or even require students to delay their entry into college until they have spent a year or two or longer in the larger society. Students who return to college after a period in military service, national service, or some other kind of work or study at home or abroad, are making a much clearer personal and voluntary decision; many have a clearer idea of what they want to do with their lives and show a greater tendency to see college as a resource rather than as a place of involuntary confinement. And as our continuing experience with veterans has shown, students who do not enter college directly from high school have an emotional maturity, a sense of personal identity, and a fund of direct experience in the world that makes their college studies much more relevant and meaningful to them. Young people who apply for admissions after a period of work in the larger society can offer a great deal more than their high school grades or college board scores to an admissions office. They are able to offer direct evidence of their capacity to choose and to fill adult roles, and to deal with tasks and ideas and people, evidence that surely will weigh heavily with any admissions office, whatever criteria, rules, or standards it may be applying.

The patterns of diversion and postponement that I have been discussing can be adopted by any single institution; or it may become a more accepted policy for state systems or for the national system of higher education. In the latter case, it will be effective only if a good deal more thought and resources are directed to the question of what alternative activities young men and women out of high school can enter apart from formal higher education. Little thought has been given to this question so far. The occasional references to "national service" have distinct involuntary overtones: they seem too close in concept to the military service to which they are often seen as an alternative. And indeed it is difficult to imagine who would administer a really large program of work and informal learning for youth of post-high-school age. The only institutions that have any experience with large numbers of young adults are the military and higher education. It may indeed be that higher education does "own" the years between ages eighteen and twenty-two of the whole population and will have to accept the responsibility for organizing the lives and learning of much of that age cohort even when it is away from the university and off campus. But to do that may well change the character of the university itself.

The pattern of postponed education and the diversion of young adults to other kinds of experience is an effort to affect the numbers and kinds of students who enter the colleges and universities so that those who do come are in fact making a voluntary choice and entering into a contract with the institution. But we can also imagine changes in the character of the institution itself which has the same ends. I suspect that we will see in the near future a greater differentiation within the multiversity, and the incorporation within it of a great many activities which are not now thought to be appropriate to a college or university.

Differentiation and incorporation

The progressive internal differentiation—some would call it the fragmentation—of the multiversities is, I think, already well under way. In the present circumstances of profound "dissensus" on social, political, and intellectual matters it is clearly impossible to design a common curriculum or to arrive at any basic educational agreement in a college of letters and science of ten- to fifteen-thousand students and eight- to nine-hundred faculty.

Many institutions are creating smaller "experimental" colleges, and I believe that this tendency will go much further as the weaknesses of the enormous "paper" arts and science colleges become clearer—colleges which can offer neither a coherent educational philosophy, nor a close and continuing association with a group of teachers, nor anything else but the chill indifference of permissiveness and a thick catalog. I have suggested a number of times that the chief failings of the present educational structures are the high degree of involuntarism in their membership and the lack of consensus in the conceptions of the nature of the enterprise among those who direct it. I suggest that the successors to the present multiversities will be a congeries of much smaller units marked by a high degree of voluntarism in their membership and a higher degree of agreement on what they are about. The size of these units—they may be called "colleges" or "departments of interdisciplinary studies" or "field majors" or whatever—will be governed by the number of people, teachers and students, who can come together around a common notion of how to organize their time, energies, and other resources in ways that serve their common interests and purposes.

When there was wider agreement about the nature and qualities of an educated man and about the characteristics of a liberal education, such a "consent unit" may have been relatively large, though the liberal arts colleges which have most closely approximated this kind of consent unit have rarely exceeded two- to three-thousand undergraduates. Today, in a period of much greater dissensus, my guess is that these "consent units" will be much smaller, perhaps averaging no more than two- to three-hundred students and ten to twenty faculty members. These will be the building blocks of any larger educational enterprise, much as the graduate departments are of a graduate school today.

But if in fact these units, which will organize what is now seen as "undergraduate education" (and perhaps a good deal more than that), ought to be genuine "consent units" and not merely small fragments of a larger structure of involuntariness and constraint, then the question of admissions to each unit must be a question to be decided by that unit for itself. The essence of the matter is that students or faculty who join such a unit must be able to affirm their desire to engage in its work, and thereby accept an implicit or explicit contract to be governed by its rules and to cooperate in its activities. The commitment thus made may be tentative and subject to withdrawal on short notice. It need not be enthusiastic, but it must be positive. As a result, the members of these educational units will show a much higher degree of homogeneity in their central educational values and purposes and in what they want to be doing at this moment in their lives.

This pattern, which I think is already emerging, is a way of coping with the basic difficulties which the present system is not able successfully to deal with. At the heart of these difficulties lies, first, the breakdown in the working consensus about the nature, functions, and character of the university among the faculty, and, second, the increasing, conscious rejection of the university by a large proportion of the students. The cumulative effect of these developments means that the colleges and universities no longer gain the willing assent of their participants for their routine activities—in the jargon of the times, they are increasingly less legitimate, and their authority is increasingly seen as repressive and tyrannical.

Higher education, I think we are now beginning to recognize, cannot flourish in an atmosphere of constraint and of illegitimate authority. As Eric Ashby and Mary Anderson have observed, "The teacher-student relationship requires at the minimum a voluntary consensus about the purpose of the institution they have voluntarily entered."[7]

Consent units

The most effective, perhaps the only effective, organization of learning is a consent unit—a group of students and teachers who come together freely to teach and learn some skills or to explore some problems or issues or ideas. This consent does not have to be expressed in strong enthusiasm or a deep commitment to learning. Indeed in the past it most commonly took the form of a relatively passive acceptance of the rules of the game as defined by the faculty and college authorities, by students who were primarily interested in earning a degree and acquiring skills for vocational use later on. But what was acceptable to the vocational or "collegiate" student of a decade or two ago is not acceptable to the involuntary and politicized student of today. What for the former was a reasonable constraint on his freedom in the service of his desire to earn a certificate or learn some skills or take part in the pleasures of the collegiate subculture is today seen as an illegitimate constraint on his freedom and the expression of his own impulses, and is therefore tyrannical and intolerable.

I think we are currently admitting very large numbers of students who feel this strong antipathy toward the present forms of education. As a result, the big educational structures which now administer the admissions procedures are less and less viable. They are admitting people to institutions without gaining a positive affirmation from those people they want to belong to those institutions—at least as they are presently constituted. The educational units that will replace these large undergraduate colleges will be much smaller, closer in size to the graduate departments. These units, I think, will govern their own admissions as they will govern their own educational activities. The criteria for admission to any of them will differ as much as their basic missions and conceptions of themselves. Some of them will be committed to traditional scholarly work, and require evidence of interest in pursuing that kind

7. Ashby and Anderson, *The Rise of the Student Estate in Britain* (London: Macmillan, 1970), p. 143.

of bookish studies. Other units may center on providing vocational training for more or less specific occupations, with the requirement that there be some expression of interest in preparing for those occupations. Still others may organize some kind of service to the larger community, and quite different criteria may be applied to candidates for such units.

The increasing differentiation of the university will facilitate the tendency to incorporate other activities which are now not thought of as part of formal higher education. For if, in fact, we begin to provide an educational experience for most young men and women of college age, then the activities they will be engaging in must be nearly as wide as the range of talents and interests that one finds in a whole generation of youth. And *pari passu*, the criteria by which students select themselves and are admitted to the units of their choice will be equally varied and will reflect the enormous range of activities that will in some way be organized under the rubric "higher education." Among all of these activities, what we now know as a college education—largely confined to formal bookish liberal and vocational studies—will persist, but only as a fraction of the total number of educational activities that the "university" will be engaged in.

It may be that when motivation becomes highly uncertain, as it has in contemporary American colleges and universities, then the small undergraduate "colleges" or consent units that I have been describing will tend to admit candidates primarily on the basis of evidence of their interest and motivation in the work of the unit rather than on evidence of academic ability or other traditional measures of talent or potential. Perhaps institutions can apply severe tests of ability only when they can take motivation for granted. But whatever criteria are applied, I think it important that the educational unit be able to control its own admissions policies. These consent units must have the highest degree of autonomy, of the order now enjoyed by graduate departments in major universities, and must be able to define their own work and select their own members. To impose a general pattern of admissions on them or to dictate the criteria that they employ would be to undermine the very qualities of voluntarism and consensus that will enable them to perform their educational functions. It must be recognized, and I believe that events are forcing this recognition, that there is no longer a consensus about the nature of the university, nor can we assume that students accept an implicit contract on admission to the university. These contracts must be more varied in character and more explicit in their expression, and thus tied closely to the smaller units that will be the functioning educational enterprises of the emerging university.

There remains of course a very large question—at its heart a political question: What kinds of activities will be given a home in the university and, thus, a claim on its resources and its protection? The larger society will have to answer that question for the university of tomorrow, just as it does for the multiversity of today. We may or may not like the answers then, depending on our own values and the political complexion of the larger society. I suspect that the fate of liberal education—whatever its organizational form—is and will continue to be profoundly dependent on the fate of liberal democratic values in the environing society.

A Plague on One House Only

TIMOTHY S. HEALY

TOWARD THE END OF Shakespeare's *Troilus and Cressida*, Paris of Troy asks the blunt and good-humored Greek Diomede,

> Who . . . merits fair Helen most
> Myself or Menelaus?

Diomede answers savagely and concludes by saying,

> Both merits poised each weighs nor less nor more;
> But he as he, the heavier for a whore.

There is a sense in which crying "a plague on both your houses" makes a grave man, but I am afraid that Professor Trow has broken the rules seriously. He is, in reality, under all those words calling down plagues on only one house, the house of youth. Being young these days may indeed, and alas, be something of a disease, but it ought to be still the part of rational elders to object to it being declared a crime.

Throughout his long and able analysis of our troubles, Professor Trow seems to me to be standing on a fixed and immovable supposition, which, for the sake of this brief comment, I will have to simplify. It is our absolute duty to preserve at all costs the "standard academic roles," the "autonomy of the university," and to some extent the "old and familiar forms of academic politics." So Professor Trow is playing Diomede without Diomede's detachment.

The major forces for either disruption or for change within the university are the faculty and the students. Calling on only one party to change its ways is simply not helpful. If every faculty privilege, every faculty prejudice, every faculty device for the perpetuation of incompetence is to remain unchanged, then indeed we are bound for some sort of Armageddon; and all Professor Trow's insightful suggestions are not going to slow the pace.

The Trow paper takes two stances that I should like to call in question, and I do so very hesitantly since I agree with so much in it.

Let me take first the most obvious premise, that most, if not all, of our troubles come from the presence on campus of unwashed hordes of dragooned students who refuse to share our "consensus" because they don't want to be there in the first place and are present thanks only to unnamed but sinister "popular forces." Their restlessness and resentment thus upsets the good hard work we, as faculty members, can do with the well-scrubbed elite who share our values and partake in our consensus. That analysis simply won't wash. It's precisely our well-scrubbed and superbly prepared elite who are in revolt, and were, long before the mass of students got anywhere near the action. And the popular forces that are currently bearing down on the university are essentially conservative; therein lies the precise danger they present to us.

It may be illuminating to realize that the steady decline of admiration for our curricula does not occur in the hard sciences, in mathematics, in medicine, engineering, or even in business. What seems to be operative here is that where the curriculum makes sense, there really is very little student resistance to it. In the humanities, however, where the curriculum has not made sense for well over a hundred years, and in the social sciences where the curriculum seems never to have made sense and perhaps never will, this erosion of admiration for the curriculum is most noted. Perhaps we humanists and social scientists should go to school to our scientists and find out how and why they are able to present a coherent picture of reality, or even of a very small piece of reality, that can capture and hold the imagination of the young, while we who claim to do so much more actually do so much less.

The impact of saying that "we have . . . large numbers of students who are weakly motivated for the standard academic roles" is considerably softened when we take no time at all to ask whether the real rot lies precisely in those standard academic roles. Professor Trow is not far from former President Perkins' suggestion several years ago that, if the undergraduates do not fit our conception of their roles, they should simply be shut out.[1] The logic is flawless provided we can swallow the premise that our conception of the role they ought to play is itself a law of nature. Diomede, for all his posture of detachment, remains very much a Greek.

That leads me on to the second premise of this paper: that the other half of our formula for trouble, the faculty, enjoys right, justice, and sweet

1. James A. Perkins, *The University in Transition* (Princeton, N.J.: Princeton University Press, 1966), p. 45.

reasonableness on its side. Again I must beg to differ. It is, after all, initially to the faculties that we owe (perhaps to our profit) the steady erosion of any visible or accountable authority in our universities. Compared to what the heavy guns of the faculty have done to the authority of deans and presidents, the assaults of the students resemble nothing so much as an attack on a tank with a Flit gun. To go on from that and claim that there is any innate sanctity of either vision or process in "the old and familiar forms of academic politics" is to fly in the face of much evidence. The Mandarin exquisitries of most faculty senates are surely familiar enough to all of us. Nor do I feel that the mere introduction of students onto such bodies will work much magic or mayhem. It is true, as Professor Trow says, that students' primary loyalties will not be to the bodies on which they sit. I choose to read this as a sign of the innate intelligence of students, since the same lack of loyalty can be found most fully among the faculty themselves. Faculties add one notable qualification, since they claim that the higher loyalty to trade or discipline should, of rights, take precedence over any loyalty possible to the institution or to the students whom they are, in general, paid to teach. At their best, academic representative bodies will serve well some discipline, or at least the current fashion in a discipline. At their worst, most of them are devices whereby unearned privilege is perpetuated by the incompetent in the long-term interest of others equally or more incompetent than themselves. The students may not buy this. If they don't, we all have the consolation of knowing that nothing we ever taught them has aided their refusal.

I should like to finish with my deepest agreement with Professor Trow. The real danger is still, as perhaps it always is in America, from the right. The leaders and the shock troops are out: the Vice-President attacking most ably on a wide front, Governor Reagan in the West sheltering behind the iron Pyrenees of law and order, and, of late, in the South, Chairman Erwin moving in for a quiet regental kill. It may well be that the occasion of this confrontation is what we call "disruption." But it is almost sure that one of the major causes of the disruption itself is that we, the faculty, have not lost but radically violated the academic consensus we inherited. We now have it made, in spades. We have an armory of sacred symbols—"academic freedom," "tenure," "the autonomy of the university"—with which to belabor anyone trying to remind us that we draw on the public till in payment of a public service we have long ceased to render. And we stand ready to use any technique, including labor unions, to make sure that our safe, comfortable, and almost laborless enclave is protected.

I think American universities are a long way from Armageddon. But when it comes, let me prophesy that the opposed numbers will include both our students and the taxpayers. Against them we, the faculty, will be a very small and very lonely crowd. Ultimately the Republic itself will pass its judgment on both of us, the self-serving elders, and the disruptive young. If it had to pass its judgment now, it would have to play Diomede for real and say "Both merits poised, each weighs nor less nor more."

A Matter of Perspective and Priorities

MICHAEL CLEAR

SOME OF HIS READERS will accept Professor Trow's dark vision with less regret than he appears to be expressing. The rationale for this different reaction to the same set of facts is a matter of which side of the "discon-sensus" you are gazing from. If you do indeed disagree with many of the basic tenets of liberal higher education, you will not greatly mourn their demise. If you believe that what has passed for "objective" analysis has all too often been abject and fawning glorification of liberal values, you will not greatly mind the explicit introduction of values guiding the analysis—values that were no less present and dominant but were simply ignored. And, finally, if you believe that the procedural and substantive glue which seems to have bound academia together—that liberal consen-sus—was rather a subtle form of propagandizing, and that the liberal university thus has been the instrument in propagating and continuing "liberal" policies which simply maintain the existing political order and its distribution of wealth and power, then you accept the changes he predicts, not as distressful, but rather as a breath of fresh air.

Specifically, his suggestion that the university might be forced to split up into smaller divisions can be viewed less as a disintegration into feudal baronies and duchies than as a mature and realistic attempt to make meaning and sense out of the jumble of departmentalization and paro-chialization which has plagued higher education. A case in point might be the Michigan State residence colleges which attempt to handle policy questions in specific areas. In this context, the restrictions relating to cross-disciplinary interests and experiences are at an end and the curricu-lum is limited only by the imaginations of the student and his advisers. As the problems we face become increasingly complex, often the most meaningful approach to issues (given the tools of analysis Professor Trow subscribes to) will be to use each discipline to learn whatever is relevant to the problem. Problem solving rather than analysis for its own sake might be on the horizon and be accompanied by a strengthening of curricula rather than academic disrepair.

Once accepting these tentative conclusions, however, one is forced to make some qualifications to the analysis on which they are based. There are two major areas of concern I have about Trow's thesis: his approach to discussing consensus, and his approach to the "involuntary" student.

The liberal dream has always been procedural and substantive consensus. No rational individual can reject the thesis that the American political experience is solidly based on these consensual elements. Nor can one be ignorant that a rejection of liberal consensus requires a redefinition of political norms and standards. However, the experience of the European educational system indicates that the future of a political university may not be as dark as many predict.[1]

Regarding the important role the Cambodian incursion plays in Professor Trow's analysis, my initial and strongest objection must be that the Cambodian disgrace was neither a simple, isolated incident nor merely a facilitator of academic change. It was as significant a political act as had occurred in a decade. This act, coupled with the Kent State and Jackson State murders, made the total collapse of the American political system seem imminent. It appeared then that the forces of reactionism were in the ascendancy and that all the values Professor Trow praises were on the line. In the set of priorities to which I subscribe, the attempt to change the trend in foreign policy and domestic relations was infinitely more important than the veneer of the educational establishment.

In short, in times of grave national emergency, extraordinary actions may be required. This is difficult to say now, for the peace offensive failed, as had so many before it; yet not to respond to national outrage and disgrace might continue the "liberal democratic system" and in the process leave little beyond the shell of procedures without any substantive merit. It was a question of priorities, and this issue of priorities is one which Professor Trow ignores. I would have liked to see him measure the relative merits of normal liberal academic work and its continuance against the desperate need to alter what seems to many and to myself a suicidal foreign policy. It is this policy that is not only wreaking complete destruction in Southeast Asia but also effecting even more substantive (if that is possible) damage to the fabric of our political society. This is not begging the issue; rather, it is an attempt to inquire into the nature of what the real issue is.

If one can accept the view that the facade of order may be less important than a meaningful attempt to alter intolerable conditions, then

---

1. I suggest either of Louis Hartz's books on the American liberal tradition and nation building: *The Liberal Tradition in America* (New York: Harcourt, Brace & World, 1955); *The Founding of New Societies* (New York: Harcourt, Brace & World, 1964).

one can view with much less chagrin and more understanding the data Professor Trow presents concerning professors and students deserting their books and classrooms en masse for the barricades of political activism.

Trow's analysis of student unrest and the correlates of involuntariness of attendance, the lack of interest in academic work, and the concurrent primeval urge to look at flowers and make love, I suggest represents a most incomplete way of looking at a cluttered and complex problem. I reject the idea that today's dissenters and "moderate" revolutionaries are merely the nonintellectual and the non-goal-oriented who feel that because they have to be in college anyway, they might as well raise a little hell while they're there. Keniston's impressions strike me as being more convincing. He emphasizes that the rebellious students are not the dullards and flower people; rather they are an intellectual and social elite in prestigious and elitist universities.[2] They are neither nonintellectual nor ignorant. Indeed, my experience has been that the person most dissatisfied with the educational establishment has usually been the individual who has mastered it. He knows how to beat the system, knows how to work within it, and generally finds it unsatisfying. His orientation may be different from that of the traditional student, his ideology more persistent and confessional than the loose "democratic values" strain in American political thought, but he need not necessarily be nonacademically oriented.

Keniston suggests that the pivotal consideration is one of morality. The liberal approach to intellectual work involves "value-free analysis" and "research for its own sake." The nonliberal, more radical approach to intellectual labors demands in addition that the work mean something, and be able to effect meaningful alterations in a decadent social order. Against this background, *procedural* consensus can substitute for *substantive* consensus, and the same methodology can be equally well applied to whatever end. The university itself need not be in turmoil if different researchers are working for different ends within it. The only real differences are that the liberal apologist simply might have more competition for the research money available and the paradigms of belief from which the analyses derive their meaning may be completely different and alien to each other.

Professor Trow appears to suppose that hell-raisers raise hell because they can't do anything else and are genuinely nonacademically oriented. Another interpretation would be that many of the leaders in the general revulsion against the traditional academic establishment (a moderate rev-

2. Kenneth Keniston, "Morality, Violence and Student Protest," *Yale Alumni Magazine*, November 1969, pp. 53–59.

olution which in the long run, Trow suggests and I certainly believe, will prove far more damaging to the traditional educational world than the blood-and-guts approach of SDS-Weathermen) have tried the liberal route and found it lacking. The "objective" illusion was discovered to be an ethical vacuum, and methodology cannot be its own justification. Analysis has to go somewhere, be something meaningful, and problem solving is intrinsically more functional and fulfilling than esoteric model building without the benefit of reality.

In sum, without really attempting to do justice to the many questions Professor Trow raises in his paper, I have tried to question two premises upon which his conclusions are built, and even go so far as to suggest that the gloom with which he approaches his subject matter might in different hands be glee.

Speculations, Facts, and the Future

A. J. JAFFE

THE IMPRESSIONISTIC CHARACTER of Dr. Trow's paper and the lack of definitive information about past trends in admissions provide no basis for projections for the future. Admittedly, few hard facts about past trends in admissions are available, yet those could have been used to improve the types of guesses in the paper. Furthermore, it is difficult to evaluate Dr. Trow's speculations because he treats American higher education as a monolith. Some of his observations appear plausible for some schools and student groups and not for others. If he had treated the college system as the heterogeneous mix it is, and then talked about specific types of colleges—their past, present, and possible future—it would be more feasible to comment on this paper. Dr. Trow seems to have taken as his model (consciously or unconsciously) the highly selective and prestigious college, and assumed that all schools are of this type and have the same histories and problems.

In anticipation of my final remarks I should state that the essential problem as I see it is *not* admissions, but rather dropouts and diploma granting.[1]

1. I recommend Joseph Froomkin, *Aspirations, Enrollments, and Resources: The Challenge to Higher Education in the Seventies,* which uses facts as a basis for extrapolating the future. It is a report of research done in the Office of Program Planning and Evaluation, U.S. Office of Education (Washington: Government Printing Office, 1970; 151 pp.).

Definitions of "enrollment"

There are at least two possible definitions: (1) the number of warm human bodies actually occupying seats on any given day of the academic year; and (2) the total number of different persons who pass through the college system during any given period of years and for whom the college system bears some responsibility. These two definitions, in turn, have different implications for the individual college as against the entire college system. The individual colleges vary with respect to full-time and part-time students and students who attend one year, drop out the next, subsequently return, and are carried on the books for an indefinite period. Furthermore, do you count as enrolled in college those correspondence students who are working under some form of "external degree" study?[2] The college system has large numbers of persons who transfer from one institution to another. In addition there are foreign students, some of whom will return to their native lands. The numbers obtained from each definition are different.

Finally, there is no uniquely correct definition of a college, so that we are not even sure of the precise number of institutions for which we wish to calculate "enrollment."

Since I have no new definition to provide, I shall merely emphasize that the answers to the "issues and implications" of higher education for everybody will vary with the definition used.

Some numbers

We shall better appreciate the possible magnitude of the college task facing us after we look at some figures. Let us assume that those in the age range seventeen to twenty-three approximate the college-age population; this number increased from over 16 million to over 25 million between 1960 and 1970. From 1970 to the year 2000 it is likely to increase to between 28 and 30 million. (See Tables 1 and 2. I consider the high estimate of 39 million shown in Table 1 as unlikely in light of the recent changes in the birth rate.) Clearly there will be comparatively little increase in this population over the next thirty years.

The numbers enrolled in college increased from about 3.5 million in 1960 to about 7.5 million in 1970. Between 1970 and 1985 the number is likely to approach 12 million. The ratio of college enrollment to population age seventeen to twenty-three is (or may be) about as follows: 1960, 22 percent; 1970, 29 percent; 1985, over 40 percent.

2. For example, the New York State University College at Brockport is offering a program in liberal studies that permits persons over age twenty-two to earn a degree through a combination of means, including weekend seminars, independent study, tests, and applicable experience.

TABLE 1: *Population Aged 17–23, and Numbers Enrolled in College, Estimates for the United States to the Year 2000*

(in thousands)

Year	Population Aged 17–23 [a]			Estimated Number Enrolled in College [b]	
	High	Inter-mediate	Low	High	Low
1960 [c]	16,306	16,306	16,306	3,570	3,570
1970	25,535	25,535	25,535	7,424	7,424
1975	27,982	27,982	27,982	9,459	9,459
1980	29,606	29,606	29,606	11,181	11,181
1985	27,430	27,430	27,426	11,846	11,588
1990	27,112	25,241	24,729		
1995	33,281	27,361	22,549		
2000	39,073	30,268	28,265		

[a] U.S. Bureau of the Census, "Projections of the Population of the United States, by Age and Sex (Interim Revisions): 1970 to 2020," *Current Population Reports.* Series P-25, No. 448 (Washington: Government Printing Office, 1970).
[b] U.S. Bureau of the Census, "Summary of Demographic Projections," Series P-25, No. 388 (Washington: Government Printing Office, 1968), Table 7.
[c] Census count.

TABLE 2: *Percentage Change in Population Aged 17–23, 1960–2000*

Year	Estimated Percentage Change		
	High	Inter-mediate	Low
1960–70	57	57	57
1970–80	16	16	16
1980–90	−8	−15	−16
1990–2000	44	20	14
1970–2000	53	19	11

If in the year 2000 there should be the low population increase that I expect and something over 40 percent[3] of the age group enrolled, there may be about 13 million persons in college.

In short, college enrollment increased about 4 million in the ten years 1960 to 1970. In the next thirty years, 1970 to 2000, the increase will probably amount to about 5–6 million. Apparently the worst is over. The crucial importance of the population base in these projections can be seen from the fact that between 1960 and 1970, almost two-thirds of the increase in enrollment stemmed from the population increase; the remaining third is attributable to increased proportions graduating from

3. In theory the other 60 percent could be enrolled for external degree study. Do you wish to consider such students as "enrolled in college"?

high school and slight increases in the proportion of high school graduates going on to college.

These future numbers become important in understanding Dr. Trow's argument. He begins his paper by questioning the assumptions (held by some investigators) that there is a trend for more and more high school graduates to enter college, and for college enrollments to continue to rise spectacularly. His implication is that future increases will be much more moderate. He then argues that far more of the students in college today are not academically motivated, apparently as a result of the vast increases in total enrollments in recent years. This, then, leads to fragmentation of colleges into many small, independent baronies—the "consent units." Nowhere, however, does he consider the implications of a considerable slowdown in college enrollments. Remember, between 1960 and 1970 college enrollments increased over 8 percent per year. Over the next thirty years, however, the rate of increase may be less than 2 percent per year. How might this slower rate of growth affect the functioning of colleges and their possible "fragmentation"?

One effect might be that the colleges, no longer faced with the monumental problems associated with very swift expansion, would have the time, resources, and energies to develop more palatable academic fare, as well as more humanly acceptable environments, for their students—call this academic reform, if you will. Perhaps problems of administration could be given a lower priority than problems of the quality of the academic experience.

Crises, etc.

Dr. Trow's paper is replete with such phrases as: "some of the signs that the university is functioning less and less well"; "there will be over the next few years very marked discontinuities in the development of these institutions"; "the breakdown of consensus"; "increasing politization of the university"; "Another symptom of the breakdown of higher education is the collapse of the undergraduate curriculum," etc., etc.

All of the above (and other similar statements) imply the existence of verifiable historical facts from which trends can be deduced. Nowhere in Dr. Trow's paper are these facts and trends set forth, and I do not know of any other source where documentation can be obtained readily. Accordingly, I can only speculate, and at the risk of seeming to be egotistical let me aver that my speculations are as valid as those of anyone else.

Those of us who were college students in the middle and late 1930s will remember as much consternation, confusion, and rebellion then as there seems to be today, with the exception of physical violence against the university. (We were brighter than the present generation of college students in that we realized that the university administrators were completely incapable of righting any of the wrongs about which we complained, and accordingly we expressed our indignation directly to the professional politicians.) At that time we were worried about the economy and availability of jobs, about Hitler and the rise of fascism, the imminence and inevitability of World War II, and the Spanish Civil War. We were at least as disturbed as any of the college students are today. Did these exogenous factors produce crises and revolutions within the college system and completely alter the form and content of higher education? I do not think so, although this topic is one which is well worth investigating.

The same can be said about Cambodia and related events in the 1960s and 1970s. If Cambodia has as powerful an influence as Dr. Trow suggests and leads to a reorganization of the college system, what is to prevent some future new event from again changing the college picture? If and when peace arrives in Southeast Asia, will the colleges and universities which had been disintegrated into "consent units," according to Dr. Trow's projections, become integrated again? Clearly, we must look for long-run forces at work above and beyond any particular single news event.

Incidentally, we can consider one fundamental difference which may have existed in the college system of the 1930s as compared to today's. Available statistics suggest that there were proportionately far fewer college administrators in the 1930s and relatively many more teachers to whom the students had access. Might it be that the apparently tremendous growth in numbers and proportions of college and university administrators during the last couple of decades has contributed to the student unrest which we see today?

One long-run force and some of its consequences

Over the years the college system has been used as a means of achieving upward social mobility, particularly increased earnings. In the popular literature and mass media this point has been emphasized almost to the exclusion of other possible ways of obtaining increased income and status. The leaders of our nation have been hammering away at the younger generation that they must obtain a college education, or they are failures in life. In part this view arises from the mistaken belief held by many, including Dr. Trow, that "there are the rising educational requirements for many occupations and the parallel growth of occupations requiring higher education." Large numbers, accordingly, enrolled in college in order to get a "better" job. Many of these persons were not much interested in learning as such, and had academic backgrounds not particularly suitable for admission into the more prestigious institutions.

Accordingly they entered two-year colleges and those four-year colleges that traditionally admitted the less academically qualified students. Indeed, the available records on admission to the various types of colleges through much of the 1960s indicate that schools continued to admit more or less the same types of students as previously. Hence, we find the greatest increases in enrollment in the less selective schools. Whether this pattern is continuing into the 1970s can be determined only through further investigation.

Incidentally, insofar as each school continued to admit more or less the same type of student—just many more of them—the school's problems were probably more concerned with the administration of larger numbers rather than with the purely academic aspects. Of course, some colleges did change their student bodies by changing admission requirements, but they appear to be in a minority.

Having been admitted, many of these students (those who in past years probably would not have gone to college) either found it difficult to do satisfactory academic work, or simply decided that they really were not interested enough to continue. As a result the dropout rate is high. Indeed, open enrollment, or approximations thereto, seems to be a revolving door which leads persons out of college after only a temporary academic detour.[4]

We can hypothesize that the following is now happening: These dropouts and their next of kin—fellow students who just barely avoid becoming dropouts—are still imbued with the belief that a college degree is needed for the "good life." Their hopes for such a degree and its hedonistic aftermath were raised with admission to a college, and then dashed when dropout occurred. Accordingly, pressures are now being brought on the colleges to arrange matters so that everyone can obtain a degree.

The colleges can respond by granting diplomas by means of coin-operated machines, or they can introduce a smorgasbord of subjects so that everyone can find some area in which he can manage to obtain the coveted diploma. The "consent units" to which Dr. Trow refers simply constitute the smorgasbord.

The real questions

To what extent should colleges, or at least some of them, become diploma mills pure and simple? Any college that chooses to be one can

---

4. The dropout rate from four-year colleges appears to be higher in California and the West than in other parts of the country. Perhaps this dropout tendency may be attributed, at least in part, to the fact that 80 percent of California high school graduates enroll in college (noted by Dr. Trow) in comparison with only about 50 percent in the remainder of the country. The more who enroll, the more who drop out.

find a variety of ways of achieving its goal; I suspect that several different ways will be adopted for satisfying this "diploma hunger." Or should the open admissions policy be combated unto death? Are there other subjects suitable for inclusion in the college curriculum that are not now included, but that would satisfy this type of student and still supply him with a diploma?

In the next decade or so, if baccalaureate and higher degrees continue to be granted *ad nauseum*, the financial worth of a college diploma will decrease considerably. We may be already reaching the point where we will have more four-year college graduates than there will be jobs considered suitable for such an "elite." Even Ph.D.'s may have to take jobs teaching in high schools. If and when this occurs, will the colleges and universities be faced with a new set of problems such as the creation of a double Ph.D. degree in order to distinguish among different types of degree holders?

In summary, I think that the college system cannot refuse admission and diplomas to these new waves of students. It will have to work out some way of handling them and some way of maintaining the value of at least some college degrees. Fortunately, the waves of the future appear to be smaller than the waves of 1960–70.

In closing, I would like to return to an earlier comment. What colleges and universities is Dr. Trow talking about? Harvard, or MIT, or San Jose Junior College, or Tougaloo, or Pace College, or others, or all of these?

WILLIAM M. BIRENBAUM

Something for Everybody Is Not Enough

HOW SHOULD COLLEGES AND UNIVERSITIES RESPOND TO DEMANDS FOR higher education for everybody?

It is part of the psychology of the academic mind to recoil from rapid change, innovative uses of technology, or radical departures from time-tested traditions. Confronted with persuasive evidence that there is something deeply wrong with the practice of the scholarly professions, or that our academic institutions are teetering on the brink, shaken by bona fide crisis, we are inclined to appoint some new committees or—with great hesitancy and misgiving—to reach for the scotch tape.

Our country was prepared for today's campus disruptions in the period of 1776 to 1787. Although the mind of a Thomas Jefferson was anchored in Heidelberg, Oxford, Paris, Bologna, Rome, Greece, the early Christians, and the ancient Hebrews, minds like his transformed the old into something quite new, as in the case of his proposal for a university in Virginia. What was created then was not, of course, the latest thing. Nor was it necessarily the truth. But it was an adventure, a genuine new departure, unlike most of the institutions for learning we have created in this country since the Morrill Act—that is, most of our higher education establishment. A similar revolution is needed today to meet demands for appropriate educational opportunity for everyone.

The traditions of the university in the West (at least outside the Latin world) are anti- if not counter-revolutionary. Operating within these traditions the university has produced revolutionary knowledge, but, institutionally, the uses of the knowledge have been directed mainly toward the confirmation of the status quo, particularly the political and cultural status quo.

But in principle the main themes of our society run counter to this deployment of knowledge. In spite of Vietnam, poverty, racism, and the overbearing logic of our technology, the main themes of our country, in principle, were and still are revolutionary. The cutting edges of these themes are what people think, their thoughts as preludes to their conduct. They are reflected in such questions as these: Can the revolutionary knowledge developed in universities be used humanely, to confirm what Jefferson and his colleagues apparently meant? What does equality mean, and whatever it meant, can we still achieve a version of it consistent with this adventure? Are reason and democracy really consistent? Is war in behalf of peace, given what we know now, realistic? If the Negroes were property, can the blacks suddenly really be people? Are some genocides more decent than others, some cesspools more fragrant than others?

The themes of peace, integration, equality, freedom, and the humane use of knowledge are ones which, traditionally, fall beyond the purview of the university. The university tradition has been one of war between itself and the society which sustained it. The university has always been a primary instrument for segregating and honoring inequality among people. The university has championed freedom for some, but not for all. About the uses of knowledge, the university has claimed to be apolitical and above all that. Its success as a producer of revolutionary knowledge is based on traditions and needs which are not entirely or necessarily compatible with the traditions and needs of America's revolutionary main themes.

Furthermore, in dealing with these problems and tensions, the state of our knowledge does not operate with consummate neutrality. The knowledge tends to take sides—different sides—depending on what the issue is. The technology has a logic of its own, usually disrespectful of our partisan political biases. For black men and poor people, the science tends to repudiate what the Caucasians and the privileged have been telling them politically for a long time. Our learning institutions, the way they are organized and operate, do not always follow the logic of the revolutionary knowledge they themselves have produced. Our own success as knowledge-producers too often leads to unfriendly conclusions about our own prejudices, about time in terms of humans, about how people learn in those very institutions in which we have the greatest vested interest. Too often lately, if we really honored what we think, we would undercut our own status and privilege.

Counterposing the academic traditions against America's revolutionary main themes creates considerable tension. On the campuses, this tension is bound to get worse because the themes are reaching a unique period of maturity. It is a rare time, peculiarly rigged to repudiate everything 1776–87 meant, or to add a whole new dimension of proof in behalf of its meaning.

Quite often those who have the greatest power to produce change have the greatest reason to resist change. They often, it might also be added, are psychologically least prepared to endure the consequences of change, are most shocked by it. Yet, at this juncture in the country's course, a failure to change could be the most damaging to those most capable of producing it. This is the paradox those of us in charge of higher education in America now face. But we should work for change, because we have helped to produce the paradox notwithstanding our proclamations that our institutions (and we) are innocent victims of horrendous external forces for which we cannot be held responsible, that we are the nuts caught helplessly in the jaws of some giant abstract cracker.

If we are to succeed, we must understand the part our attitudes, and therefore our institutions, are playing in providing inadequate institutional models for a revolutionary society, in perpetuating class and racial divisions, in institutionalizing inappropriate segregation by age and place, and in fostering dependence rather than independence in our students. And we must learn to look in new ways at the uses of time in education, at the places where learning goes on, and at the nature of what is to be learned.

If this paper seems quixotic, it is not because it argues for a major overhaul of our institutions. It is because it assumes we can exert some control over our own attitudes, and that we will.

THE POLITICS OF AGE AND CHANGE

My three children are thirteen, sixteen, and eighteen years old. Like me, they are not very old. (But I may not be young enough.)

The GI bill paid for my "higher" education. My professional career began during the Age of McCarthy (Joseph) and the Korean War. I have worked almost everywhere in the university—teacher and administrator, board member and parent, from adult to graduate education, from the urban to the international field, in public and private institutions, large and small. Wherever I have worked, there have always been too many students and not enough money, threats to academic freedom and assaults upon faculty democracy, excessive teaching loads and inadequate parking space. In other words, each institution at which I have worked has been innovative, experimental, creative, and absolutely great.

There was a watershed in the state-of-our-greatness between the war against Hitler and the war to make Vietnam free. There was an abrupt change in what we know, what we are capable of knowing, and how we live. It was a mere second of history, but what a time—a time for wallowing in the mud and soaring into the sky, for the worst of all genocides and for walking on the moon. It was a watershed between not being very old and possibly not being young enough.

Between wars, human population reached a critical size and more than half of mankind moved into the cities. The machinery of our civilization changed. The computers changed irrevocably the life of our minds. The sun set on several empires, and the old colonialism died. Caucasians discovered that they were far less than half of the whole. A new art, a new music, and a literature appeared. A new power to understand ourselves emerged, shaking the foundations of all the understandings we had.

> *My friend, the professor on the Graduate Faculty at the New School for Social Research, said: "They disrespect history. They are not interested. The Greeks mean nothing to them, or Jefferson or Lincoln. They don't want to know." My friend in the Black Student Union said: "They say their history is a science. It is an art—their art. They are painting their own pictures. They made Western Civilization a required course, but even their electives are not true. They are free to teach untruths."*

> *The questions my children ask do not seem to give a proper weight to who I am and where I have been, to my rank, serial number, and possessions.*

These students at the college act as if they are the first generation to understand the impact of what has happened. There is so much they don't know. But their questions are embarrassing. Their questions disrupt what I mean. Our answers have disrupted their lives. We are disrupted, together—the traditions, the history. The continuity is broken. The campus community is built on the solid ground of the mutuality of our disruption.

> *They obtained the master-key to the campus and took over my office at seven in the morning. Eventually they gave my office back, and we've changed all the locks. Possession of it didn't help them. What they came for wasn't there. My office, on the second floor of the new building, is eight centuries old. It is always locked up by what I represent, so even though they took it over, they didn't get what they wanted.*

How do you occupy one hundred and twenty credit hours, tenured by the ranks, paid according to the AA schedule of the AAUP, divided into two thousand fifty-minute class periods, and entombed in a million books hidden away in guarded stacks? It's bigger than being black or being bombed. It's bigger than being educated.

> *They asked: If it's a Community of Scholars, where is the community? (Refer them to the schedule of office hours posted on the department chairman's door.)*
> *They asked: If it's Freedom and Democracy, where is the due proc-*

ess? (Issue them a copy of the union contract and ban them from the faculty meetings.)

They asked: *If it's Equal Access, how come the gates are locked? (Show them the range of their SAT performance, and hand them the press release announcing the expanded scholarship program for the culturally deprived.)*

They asked: *If it's Integrated, why is it all so segregated? (Give them an organizational chart of the departments, and explain the Scientific Method to them.)*

They asked: *If it's the City of the Mind, what are the walls for, and the gate? (We are locked in, we say, in order to be free. Academically free. The ghetto is free, but beyond the walls there is tyranny.)*

Inscribed over the gates to the stockade at Ft. Dix are the words: "Obedience to the Law Is Freedom." Over the gates to the campus, what shall we write? "We Know Better"? Meantime, whatever we write, everybody knows that there *is* a continuity and a tradition. It is in the Constitution, in the library, and in Vietnam, and if you can't find it in the final examination, the acid will show it to you.

We want to be left alone. The change we want the most is to be left alone. If we want to be left alone, we'd better talk the language of change. On the one hand, we are above and beyond the politics of this time. Above all else the university must not become politicalized. On the other hand we are captives of our ideology—the ideology of being left alone. In the pursuit of being left alone, we reveal that we have always been politicized, have always engaged in an internal struggle for power among ourselves and in a power contest between ourselves and the rest of the world—the basis for our privilege, what we profess, our profession. Called upon to defend ourselves now, our two hands thrash the air wildly. That is, we talk the language of change under duress.

Having been politicized for eight centuries or more, this is not the issue. Who shall get in is a *political* question, and who shall get out—"educated"—is too. The curriculum is a treaty between an oversupply of knowledge and an undersupply of time, a contract of value-laden choices, clauses *politically* charged. Getting the money and dividing it up, spending it is a *political* process. Teaching loads, being functions of the money supply and class sizes, are *political* conclusions. Black studies, two-year colleges, injunctions and the police, sit-ins and march-outs, the supply of heroin, Fourth of July speeches about due process and procedural democracy, ROTC and the defense contracts, honors programs and the conversion of the freshman year into a giant remediation department—all are planks in the platforms of our *political* parties.

The issue is whether an old politics is to be sustained or the university's campaign to be reframed comes within terms of a new politics. Reform means a redistribution of credit hours and of the budget, of who does what when. Reform means a redistribution of the decision-making power and of the rewards and punishments. The object of a structure is strength. Restructuring means dividing up strength differently.

Those who represent the status quo in American higher education draw a tenuous line between the possibility for reform and the promotion of revolution, of violence and disorder. There are students, some of the best, who cross this line often, back and forth, tentatively, exploring. Let us give credit where credit is due. Our lobbies in Washington and on the campuses are not completely without their purposes. Our students have found them out. Whatever else they may say about us, we have taught our pupils well. Above all else the teacher is a model of the older for the younger. Having already experimented with the strike, our students may soon discover their own unions. We meant them to be professionals all along, like us. Soon, we will get used to the idea that they've simply jumped the gun a bit. But, meantime, it is a bit awkward.

THE AGE OF JOBS AND POLITICS

If we are to continue to call these things "colleges," we must respect the distinction between training and education. To train them well, all we need do is dish the knowledge out to them more efficiently. Education is evaluative. It is the capacity to evaluate the knowledge, to evaluate having possession of it and the uses of it.

The most crucial educational problem in modern technical civilization is how to prevent the separation of technical power from moral responsibility. This is a problem of values, and it impregnates the most objective pursuit of truth, the purest of research endeavors.

> *He came to us from a high school serving Bedford Stuyvesant which somehow had neglected in all that time (during which he did not drop out) to teach him how to read and write or to handle numbers successfully. He arrived angry and afraid, knowing he was "deficient." And being part of the 10 percent with black skins, he was under the impression he was "different." Naturally we reassured him that we could fix him up—if he would but cooperate—in sixty credit hours, give or take; in two years, more or less; in twenty courses (plus the remedial preparation). After Electronics I, II, III, and IV, and Drafting, and Fundamentals Theory, after Machines Laboratory I, II, III, and IV, and Industrial Electronics Theory, and Selected Topics in Electrical Technology, after the required American history course and the freshman English sequence, I and II, he chose, for*

his one remaining elective, to take a course in sociology. And after we handed him his union card and offered to help him get his first job, he said: "Black is beautiful and this college is racist, and Vietnam, I, II, III, and IV is whitey's bag—not mine."

The assumption that the sciences and technologies are ever-changing and value free and that the humanities and social sciences are conceived in fixed, unchanging principles containing the absolute truths of our culture is as dangerous as the assumption that learning for vocation and learning for its own sake are mutually exclusive.

Academic prejudice notwithstanding, learning for its own sake and learning for vocation have coexisted in the university almost from the beginning. The more sophisticated and complex the work to be done, the more sophisticated and prolonged the preparatory education required. European countries have long recognized these relationships through tightly differentiated national educational systems. Many of these countries test their young at an early age, grouping them into various categories of potential talent and competence, channeling them into hierarchal institutional systems. In the service of national manpower projections, the educational systems in these countries predetermine the life-opportunities of the clientele, usually confirming class distinctions deeply embedded in their histories.

Academic elitism has always been tied to popular versions of what the classiest professions were and who was to be allowed access to them. This was true in the medieval university, which was devoted to job training for future governors, clergymen, physicians, and landed aristocrats. The Morrill Act was a uniquely American departure from this tradition, but in the twentieth century, though elitist Harvard itself came to reflect the impact of the land-grant legislation, the land-grant universities came to aspire more and more to elitist Harvard's image of what a European university ought to be in America.

The difficulty the sciences had getting into the prestigious European universities had nothing to do with status distinctions between pure and applied research. The pursuit of the sciences—pure and applied—required getting hands dirty, and this is what the elitist prejudice resisted. It was assumed that those who got into the university naturally would control the levers of power once they got out. This assumption encouraged the academic mystique that action could be reserved until later life. Learning, allegedly, was clean and perfumed, utterly contemplative, like an afternoon of a country squire. The wall around Oxford's superblock not only separated those who society thought "qualified" for the "higher learning" from those who apparently were not, but also separated the privilege of thinking (evaluating) from the responsibility for acting. This illiberal prejudice persists in contemporary liberal education and throughout the national educational structure. It is built into our admissions standards, into the class aspirations we have for those we have traditionally "educated," in contrast with those we have traditionally ignored. It is the difference between Oberlin and the New York City Community College, between Yale and South Dakota State University.

From the point of prestige and status—class—the segregation of learning for a vocation from learning for its own sake is always paralleled by a segregation of thinking from acting, of "scholarship" from activism. A *differentiated educational system tends to project the class prejudices of the society creating it into the educational institutions serving that society.*

> *"The 'natural aristocracy' pronouncements of Vice-President Agnew, together with President Nixon's emphasis, in his message on higher education of March 19, 1970, on vocational training at the expense of greater black participation in higher education strongly indicate that the administration views the community college as a ceiling for Black educational achievement. We strongly disagree with that view of our role in America's higher education." (Statement by black junior college leaders, six college presidents, and one provost, May 26, 1970.)*

The California version of a differentiated educational system has not only been widely copied throughout the country, but is also now being built into national policy. This version projects the problems of class into the nation's educational system. The adaptation of this model in Vice-President Agnew's home state illustrates what the projection of these problems into the higher educational system can mean. The University of Maryland is a giant into which the "most qualified" of the state's youth may be admitted. It has recently launched a new satellite four-year campus in white, middle-class suburbia. On its main campus black enrollment is 2.5 percent. Undergirding the university is a system of six state colleges, three of which are essentially all-black and three of which are almost all-white, that is, equal access. Beneath these are twelve public two-year schools, all but one of which cater to enrollments which in no way reflect the racial composition of the state. Throughout this system, categories of SAT scores are properly arranged according to the special mission of each part. (Of course, the values of the meritocracy allow for the most "talented" to escape from the lower echelons into the higher, even though denied direct access at the outset.)

Upon such differentiation the conservative and the liberal agree. The conservative says: maintain the standards. Keep the mission of the university pure. It is because our present notions of quality undergird the privileges of the status quo, that the conservative is for maintaining the standards. He is for putting a good part of American youth directly into jobs right after high school, or guiding them into vocationally or technology-oriented two-year colleges and calling it equal access. The liberal says: The new masses must be allowed in. What he means is: the politics and economics of the new urban America require a massive extension of the educational opportunity beyond the twelfth grade. He is for building hundreds of new two-year colleges, hoping to make the new masses employable—and calling it the democratization of the higher educational opportunity.

American society being what it is now, the projection of class is a projection of race into our higher educational system. To each his own, and something for everybody. The third proposition of the California-Maryland syllogism is: Something is better than nothing—a proposition that summarizes the progress of the blacks in America since the *Brown* case, and the progress of higher education since Berkeley.

Segregation According to Time and Place

The American educational system is divided increasingly into separate and distinct ghettos—elementary, junior, and secondary schools, junior and senior colleges, graduate and professional schools. We have dropped an iron curtain at the age of eighteen between the monopolistic jurisdictions of lower and higher education. Not only are the students more and more alienated from the educational systems through which they are processed, but the various bureaucratic parts of these systems are conducted more and more apart from each other. The age eighteen has no special significance in terms of the biological development of the human and his capacity to learn. For youth growing up in the contemporary city, reaching the age of eighteen has virtually no significance except artificially as a political boundary between the two institutionalized educational monopoly systems.

Each part of the educational system is based on a separate physical island, segregating levels of learners, students and faculties, the younger and older, teaching and research, learning and working, thinking and acting, from each other, constantly foreshortening the time in which any particular group of people may associate with each other in a common learning endeavor. Around each geographic and temporal educational ghetto, we repair and fortify those walls segregating campus from community, academic professional from nonacademic talent, and the acts of learning to think from the rich urban opportunities for thoughtful action.

At the collegiate level, during the period in which we have used the four academic years, each of nine months, paced relentlessly by the credit hour system, mankind has enjoyed his most phenomenal knowledge growth. What we now try to fit into this obsolete system just doesn't fit any longer. It can't be done—not in a time of the atom, the moon walk, TV, pot, the pill, the rise of non-Caucasians, and the fantastic growth of knowledge. We cannot keep Humpty-Dumpty together with bureaucratic panaceas which ignore the incredible gap between what we *may* know and the archaic institutional forms we have always used to help people know.

With the students coming into the higher system with high school diplomas that reflect their attaining the least success in a failing secondary system, the least prior education in the subjects vital to the conduct of free men—with these students we are doing the least. To these young Americans acutely concerned about social justice and being free, we respond with a narrow, uptight, incomplete, and ultimately dishonest version of the beauty of knowledge, the sanctity of the opportunity to learn, the intricacy and delicacy of probing the human mind and heart.

Finally, the educational ghettos are a tragic retreat from the idea of the college as a community at a time when one of the deepest longings in the hearts of the young is for a community. We move students around like pawns on a chess board, through bits and pieces of academic time and space, conceiving their learning-lives in the false and brittle terms of the bureaucratic conceptions of our educational institutions.

TIME AND PLACE ACCORDING TO STATUS

The idea of the campus as a *community* (of scholars or of anything else) has deteriorated; in some places, it is near collapse. Communities are governed. (Corporations are managed.) Some governmental functions require management, but the critical issues of government are different from those of management. They concern the qualifications for citizenship, the rights and duties of the citizens, and the processes regulating relationships among the citizens and between them and their government. Corporate managerial techniques are replacing principles of government on the campus. But university management is talked about as if it is government. The result is a confusion in structure and of purpose, the perpetuation of an old politics based on hierarchy and segregation, usually resulting in corrupt government unrelieved by efficient management.

Freedom remains one of the central themes about which the academic "community" talks. "Academic freedom" is the banner flown by those who teach. According to the myths, "being free" is essential to teaching but not to learning. Those who are taught *are being prepared* to be free, presumably at some later date. The discipline of freedom, like that of baseball, must at some time be practiced in order to be mastered. A part of the preparation for life in a free society is the mastery of the terms of freedom while one learns, in relationship to the acquisition of knowledge. In other words, the experience of freedom is essential for learning, both for those who teach *and* for those who are taught.

Within the frame of the academic corporation, new constitutions for government are being negotiated everywhere among teacher-employees, student-consumers, and the university managers. Each of these interest blocs brings a different political slogan to the negotiating table. The employees—often liberals in the political world, opposed to the Vietnam war, racism, and Spiro Agnew—are for faculty democracy. The consumers—even the moderate majority who basically want to do good without a disturbance of their routines for consumption—are for participatory democracy. Management—having generally forsaken the possibility of leading the corporation anywhere different from where it is—is for keeping the production going, keeping things cool. Under the tense circumstances of our time, making decisions tends to heat things up; no decision seems possible without alienating some substantial part of some constituency. Consequently, management generally avoids making fundamental decisions in order to keep things cool, or, when compelled to decide something, tries to decide in a manner not readily apparent to those most affected by the decisions, that is, undemocratically. Unfortunately, not making decisions has the tendency to heat things up now as much as making decisions does. Implicitly, among the three basic constituencies, quite in addition to the external relationships of the whole, there are genuine and far-reaching conflicts of interest.

The push for greater democracy (a political concept) within the framework of the academic corporation is increasingly harnessed to the pursuit of the conflicting self-interests (not always political) of the employees, the consumers, and the managers. This push is relatively new in contemporary academic life. And it is complicated because the pushers are also teachers, students, and administrative colleagues, maintaining that they are really citizens, associated in a community devoted to learning, eager to govern and to be governed justly. Labor-management relationships in America assume a hierarchal organization for production purposes and adopt confrontation politics for the resolution of conflicting interests. The high purposes of the university, on the other hand, assume a community organization in which freedom is honored, justice pursued, and reason cherished.

The thrust toward greater democracy on the campus, ignoring the deterioration of the "community" and its extensive transformation into the managerial-corporate format, encourages the resolution of freedom, justice, and reason problems through confrontation politics. What we have here is the extension of labor-management techniques to new realms of political and educational relationships and the substitution of these techniques for the principles of government. This substitution has the effect of converting the role of the leader from change-maker to mediator, of transferring the initiative for change from executive leadership to more or less leaderless constituencies pursuing self-interest. To the extent that such groups successfully pursue self-interest and obtain superior privilege, their defense of the status quo achieves priority over their impulse for change.

Unfortunately, the increasingly hierarchal and segregated structure of the national educational establishment injects the nation's class and race stratifications into the campus confrontations. Consequently, the freedom, justice, and reason issues on the campus almost always now involve class and race tensions. Moreover, although advocacy and confrontation are at the very core of Anglo-American systems for the determination and administration of justice, American education at all levels has kept the country's youth virtually illiterate about the techniques and skills of advocacy. Compelled to become a part of the confrontation political system, they have approached their problems with a meat axe instead of with a scalpel. This accounts for the low qualitative level of the disruptions, for the ineffectiveness of the student movement.

To this explosive situation the university brings a medieval conception of community government, traditions contrary to the democratic ethic and to modern notions of a representative, parliamentary disposition of community power. The medieval tradition champions a hierarchal arrangement of power on the basis of class and generally dishonors the principle of a separation of judicial, legislative, and executive prerogatives. The tradition, naturally, is feudal. And in a feudal sense, the contemporary college president (the chief executive) often finds himself acting like a supreme court judge in the ultimate stages of what passes for faculty or student due process; faculties increasingly find themselves sucked into or seeking executive powers, the power to execute and administer the laws they rightfully may enact affecting curriculum, personnel, budget, and so on; and the students, generally excluded as a class from the important executive, legislative, or judicial powers, are usually compelled to express their fondness for the democratic process through street action, trespass, or the ultimate device of the labor union, the strike.

The essence of the feudal tradition is status—the powers of each citizen fixed in time and place—the certainty of knowing where each person fits. The spirit of our time is the opposite. It is a time of uncertainty, a craving for equality, a disrespect for status, a special penchant for mobility. Never before has the quality of the *substance* of change been linked so solidly to the quality of the *processes* for change. With our educational institutions as with the individual learner, the cultivation of the capacity to think is related in a new and intimate way to the quality of action-opportunity. Curricular reform depends sensitively now upon renewal of the academic community. And this renewal requires a reconsideration, in light of our academic purposes, of the way power is matched to responsibility so that we may restore some accountability for the possession and use of power in the university.

Ghetto Demolition

The technology economy (anticolonial, consumer-oriented, urban, and overpopulated) presents two profoundly complicated and urgent challenges: (1) Given the growing shortage of resources, how to increase efficiency; and (2) How to *control* increasingly complex technology systems. These challenges obsess educational production in our country.

These are not now the obsessions of the brightest and the most concerned among the young in our high schools and colleges. They seem to be more concerned about how to operate and perfect a complex civilization, not merely for the sake of efficiency, but in behalf of being human in spite of the technology's ever-pressing demands for greater efficiency and more extensive control. Woodstock, the peace movement, the reactions to the campus killings, the use of narcotics, and the thrust for student power underscore deepening misunderstandings between those in charge of young America and those they are in charge of.

Hitler once told the German people (and those in charge of his universities) that if they would but leave the economic, political, and diplomatic decision-making power to him, they would receive in return their greatest support for the promotion of science and technology. In the short-run, the sciences—university-based—flourished under Hitler, and his regime, once under way, was not marked by significant unemployment problems. For a while many German teachers and students bought Hitler's package. Our students aren't in that marketplace now.

Education, by its very nature, is disruptive. Both the subject matter of education and the outlook of the humans to be educated mainly reflect the past. Very little that we teach in the university concerns the future or is future-oriented. We have many departments of history, but no departments of the future. And our students, arriving at the old age of eighteen, are usually consummate confirmations of the value systems represented by their parents, the communities in which they grew up, their churches. To disrupt what they believe, what they think they know for sure, is a herculean task too seldom undertaken with success.

The past is not to be condemned either because it is history or because it is old. At best the past is but a preparation for the future. To change anything, we must first know what there is to be changed. *Why* in order to know *how*. The danger of coming to know the past too well is that one can easily become overawed by it. When this happens (as it does all too often) evaluation stops and simple knowledge transfer becomes the end-all.

One of the principal advantages of being powerful, rather than powerless, is the privilege of defining who the disrupters are and what the disruption is. Knowing all the time that education is by its nature disruptive, we have defined disruption so that it is a dirty word. Confronted by students complaining about our miseducational conduct, we respond that *they* are the real disrupters. Instead of concentrating on the quality of our own disruption, we have taken steps to make sure that the performance of our students will be qualitatively inferior. Instead of coming to grips with the overbearing consensus, uniformity, and standardization of almost every dimension of the country's life—its mass media, its products, its schools and campuses, its political parties and options—we have moved aggressively to repress the clumsy and ineffective dissenters for whose clumsiness and ineffectiveness we are also responsible.

We have the obligation now to move aggressively toward improving the quality of the disruption.

Time

Time, more than ever, is of the essence in the educational process—not because there is so little of it, but because our uptight approach to it has led to the misuse of what there is. We have exalted institutional versions of time and of excellence at the expense of honoring the realities of human time and the excellence of individual people. Heretofore the burden of proof has been on the individual to persuade the institution to let him in. Institutional admission criteria have been used to keep people out in defense of abstract institutional standards of excellence. The burden of proof has shifted to the institution to convince society why individuals or classes should be kept out. This shift is the meaning of the extension of universal education beyond grade twelve. With the diminution of the importance of abstract quality judgments at the point of admission, the emphasis will naturally shift to the point of *exit* for the measurement of quality performance. Instead of the institutional assertion of excellence on the basis of who is kept out at the beginning, worth will have to be proved in accordance with the results produced at the end. Now the institutions will be compelled to demonstrate their quality through what happens between admission and graduation. This proof cannot possibly be made simply on the basis of standardized examinations. It can only be made on the basis of how well individuals realize over time a variety of human talents combined differently in each case. Quality performance in education necessarily will become (as it should) a much more subjective matter.

Therefore, more attention will have to be given to the facts of human biological development as these bear upon unfolding learning capacities. In the case of young people growing up in cities, this undoubtedly means that the ages nine or ten through thirteen or fourteen are far more critical than age eighteen. And with the national extension of the franchise to eighteen-year-old citizens, that age, for some purposes, will become more critical than age twenty-one. The political-bureaucratic line we have drawn at eighteen between secondary and higher education is no longer tenable for learning purposes, just as the line drawn at twenty-one is no longer tenable for separating the boys from the political men. For the mobilization and deployment of teachers, campuses, curricula, money, and other learning resources, we should look at time in terms of humans rather than in terms of rigid institutional accommodations of humans. Institutional assumptions about life styles, learning-capacity rates, the prior experiences and future aspirations of people run counter to the ways both students and teachers really are. Our institutions assume that almost everyone is motivated by the same things at the same time. Our academic programs, the criteria used to admit people to and evaluate their performance in them, link success to homogenized conformity. Among our programmatic offerings there is as much variety and real difference in substance as there is in the department where Macy's sells television sets to its customers. In Macy's department and in the collectivity of ours, there is but the flickering illusion of choice. But unlike our clients, Macy's customers may use time to their own advantage. If they are misled, cheated, or sold a defective machine, they may finally take their business elsewhere without fear that Macy's will issue a certified transcript to Gimbel, Lord & Taylor, or Bloomingdale that they, the customers, have screwed things up.

New institutional accommodations of formal learning time must be invented. One possibility is a learning framework ensuring continuity for a seven- or eight-year period between ages twelve or thirteen and twenty or twenty-one. But a rational adjustment of this kind will force a restructuring of what is now called junior high school as well as of the high school and of the internal functioning of what we call college. About the latter, the credit-hour time grid must be broken. But this change requires a different view of the organization of knowledge and the ways that "students" may be exposed to it. At the college level there is nothing magic about two years or four years, except the magic of institutional habit.

Different people learn at different paces. Prior individual life-experience counts for a lot. Life is not organized for most as enforced extended periods of contemplation as opposed to action. Learning is both disciplined and undisciplined, contemplative and active, and the components are naturally mixed up. Each person picks up a book and then puts it aside according to his own circumstances and style. Each gets whatever he does out of the book—or his perception of anything else—according to the state of *his* receptivity and capacity to perceive. There is nothing dishonorable in this variability among people. Only our rigid institutional approach to people has made this natural variability dishonorable. We honor conformity, shouting our alarm about the dissent.

Space

Our institutional prejudices about learning time are matched by those about learning space. Learning space is organized according to the principles for organizing urban ghettos. There is a proper place and time for everything and everybody, and it is assumed that we know where and when they are. We have built walls around them and programed the entire campus along the principles for programing the typical classroom, in rows with a blackboard and an authoritative desk in front. Finally, we have assumed for the whole campus an authority tantamount to that accorded to the teacher in the classroom.

Just as the classrooms have become more crowded, subverting conversation, discussion, and free exchange, lengthening the distance between teacher and taught, between those with authority and those subject to it, so campus conditions have become subversive of conversation, discussion, free exchange, and responsible contact between those in authority and those subject to it.

Once learning space is turned into a ghetto, those in charge of it will want those living in it to conform to the ghetto's way of life. They will favor talent, mobilize and use it, qualify and credential it with that in mind. In the modern city the university cannot possibly monopolize all of the best talents and places for learning. Often the best workshops for learning in the city—and the best teachers—will be found on the streets beyond the campus walls, in the theaters and museums, the industrial laboratories and the offices of government, the financial centers, and in so many other places. But the ghetto economy and mentality, tenured by the ranks, isolated and aloof, do not easily accommodate the use of these places and talents. The outlook of the ghetto toward what there is to know and how people learn is against such integration. The outlook of the ghetto essentially is monopolistic.

Having left the streets of Bologna centuries ago for the illusory safety of Oxford's fortress, the contemporary university finds itself once again facing the risks and dangers, the rich knowledge and learning opportunities of the streets. The state of our knowledge and the urban spirit of our society in effect amount to antitrust legislation. Fundamentally, the American aspiration is against the ghetto, against monopoly.

Content

The demolition of the walls around time and space is a first step toward the renewal of the learning community. Regarding the engagement of talent and the use of resources, the demolition of the academic ghetto means a redistribution of powers so that people may be *free* to learn.

The obligations routinely placed on the American citizen assume that knowledge and learning will guide his conduct far beyond his institutionalization for formal education. As a worker and a producer-consumer, as a voter and the head of a family, a premium is placed upon the citizen's intelligence, his *continuing* capacity to learn, to bring reason to bear upon his decisions. Indeed, life experience itself, properly explored and understood, is an educational force, a curriculum around which knowledge can be organized, as powerful as any contrived system for formal education. Ideally, the formal educational years are meant merely to incubate a capacity and a desire for life-long learning.

The adult ideal in America is a life of work *and* learning, of thinking *and* acting, of testing knowledge *through conduct*, an ideal too often unrealized and dishonored in those institutions through which we provide formal education for young adults. We have taken a very narrow view of where knowledge is and how it may be approached. It is as if we have become so bedazzled by methods for classifying knowledge in a library that the highly structured systems for recalling knowledge have become the primary purposes of learning rather than accommodations of it. Too often our institutions imprison the knowledge (just as academic libraries imprison the books) rather than setting it free.

Talent is differentiated and rewarded differently for many purposes in the larger American society. But in America *commingling* is normal and desirable. We expect the younger and the older to live and work together, the black and the white, the artisan and the professional, the artist and the businessman. Finally, at least officially, we do aspire to integration. We no longer can tolerate schools and colleges, knowledge and experience, organized and operated according to the principle of segregation. Our learning programs and places should bring people and things together, not only because integration is a more desirable way of life, but also because bringing things together is more conducive to learning.

We must invent new ways to put the young in the decision-making workshops of the country as a part of their formal education. We must discover new programs to demonstrate how the knowledge, tightly departmentalized and disciplined, bears upon the solution of problems which do not conform to the politics of the departments or the rationality of the disciplines. We must restore opportunities for the younger and the older to work and learn *together*. And we must do these things, deeply respecting the worth of different talents, the dignity of variety, the compatibility and symmetry that can emerge out of human diversity.

Finally, it would be a rather good thing if we could bring ourselves to be a little less condescending toward and resentful of the meaning of being younger.

> *He had entered the college but six weeks before, anxious, angry, and uptight. He had come from Harlem and Vietnam—a dropout, except on the college he had dropped-in. Elected chairman of the black students' organization, he was calling on the president of the college to serve his various and sundry notices. I asked him what he was learning. He said that, at the street academy uptown where they had fixed up his English and his math so that he could get in, they had told him over and over again that if he ever got in he should Listen. "Listen," they said. "That's the way to get through."*
>
> *"I've listened," he said, "and man, I've learned something around here! This faculty of yours—nobody has ever taught them to listen."*

In our struggle to get through all this, maybe we should listen, just a little bit more.

The Square Society and Mr. Birenbaum

ANDREW M. GREELEY

I SHALL NOT PRETEND that I like Mr. Birenbaum's paper. Although I agree with much that he says, I must categorically disagree with his perspective and his style. Indeed, if anyone cares to find a symbol for some things that are wrong with American higher education at the present time, he need only look at Mr. Birenbaum's paper.

I will mention only in passing some of the minor points to which I take exception. I pass over in relative silence the allusive, watered-down Norman O. Brown style of discourse. I will say nothing about the facile identification with the young and the black as carriers of special virtue, and of the equation of minority spokesmen for the young and the black with these whole population groups. I will say nothing about the scapegoating of Vice-President Agnew, save to comment that Mr. Nixon really did us liberal academics a high favor by providing us with a splendid inkblot as vice-president. I shall not comment at length on facile catch phrases such as "we have many departments of history but no departments of the future." The big difference, of course, between history and the future is that history has already happened. But if departments of the future are indeed to be instigated at our universities, I fervently trust that they do a better job than the present departments of history, because if they do not, we will then be producing students who know nothing either about the past or the future. I will resist the temptation to comment on the standard liberal guilt feelings (see the paragraph beginning "One of the principal advantages of being powerful. . ." [page 78]) which have traditionally paralyzed liberals in the face of the disruptions of the fascists of the left and the right. Finally, I will defer until the end of my comments Mr. Birenbaum's lack of awareness that there is anybody else "out there" in the larger society besides the young and the black.

I wish to take issue most particularly with what I would call the messianic arrogance of academia which Mr. Birenbaum has captured so notably in his paper. Mr. Birenbaum himself is a kindly and gentle man. He intends, I suspect, neither to be messianic nor arrogant, and if he is so, it is only because he reflects attitudes that are characteristic of academia and that, in the present paper, he has not exorcised.

One assumes from the paper that the university ought to be reorganized so that it can remake the class structure of society. I submit that the university is quite incapable of such an enterprise and that the destruction of the multitrack system as it exists in California and Maryland—as bold and radical and as politically unlikely as it may sound—would contribute little to egalitarianism in American society. Equality of opportunity is an extraordinarily complex problem about which we know relatively little. As of now, however, it seems safe to say that an attempt to enforce absolute equality of opportunity for all young people at the age of eighteen (even if it were technically and politically possible and even if it could be done by the university) would probably destroy freedom in our society in the name of equality, an event which Alexis de Tocqueville predicted over a century and a half ago.

At some point in our society, or indeed in any society in our complex, technological world (a world created by the academy, incidentally), young people of every color and every social class will have to be evaluated on their performance. This performance, in its turn, is affected by all kinds of background variables that colleges cannot erase—social class, ethnic background, early family experiences, cultural and social history. It is naïveté for the academy to assume that, simply by randomizing admissions, background differences will be erased overnight or even in a generation. For example, the research my colleagues and I at the National Opinion Research Center have done indicates that the differences between the Irish and the Polish immigrants at the beginning of the twentieth century have not been erased seventy years later. Holding parental background constant, the Irish have higher levels of educational achievement than the Polish. Holding educational levels constant, the Irish have higher prestige occupations than the Polish. And holding occupational prestige levels constant, the Irish make more money. This is not to argue that people are discriminating against Poles (though some discrimination may be occurring) and is certainly not to argue that the Irish are biologically, culturally, or socially superior to the Poles; it suggests, however, that, for reasons of cultural, social, and historical background—mostly having to do with language—the Irish came to American society with certain advantages which the Poles did not have and that these advantages have persisted for seventy years.

For the university to assume that it can eliminate background differences when their nature is not even fully understood is, in my judgment, the height of arrogance. It may refuse to evaluate the performance of students in the terms of those competencies which the larger society has declared necessary for its own functioning and, on the whole, such evaluation in terms of grade-point average may well be meaningless ritual. But the university would be engaging in sheer deception if it attempted to persuade young people that at some point their performance is not going to be evaluated in terms of the competencies that society values. It would be even greater deception to try to persuade young people that the university or any other educational institution can erase the impact of all the background variables that give some people advantages over others in the competency race. The best the university can do—and it hasn't been very successful even at this—is to say that no man will be prevented from developing his capacities for intellection and articulation merely because of his color or his social class or his ethnic background.

In the face of the almost overwhelming evidence that the quality of college attended makes only minor differences in educational outcome, it seems naïve for the academy to presume that if it could distribute students randomly, there would be no discrimination in the quality of the education. Mr. Birenbaum apparently thinks that because the University of California has more famous faculty names, with better publishing records, something more impressive happens to students there than happens at the two-year community colleges. There isn't much evidence, however, that it does. Academics would be better advised, in my judgment, to ask how they can facilitate the powers of thought and expression among young people, no matter where they go to school, rather than to ask how they can achieve neat, tidy population balances at all institutions. (I suspect, incidentally, that a better educational job could be done through a community college than by most of the institutions of the University of California system.)

In other words, as I read Mr. Birenbaum, he is saying that the academy, having fouled up badly in its assigned task of cultivating the powers and thought of the middle class, is now going to embark blithely on a messianic mission of remaking the American social class structure. By means that have not yet become specific, somehow or other the academy is now going to provide the children of lower class with a precisely equal start in American society. Having failed at its relatively simple task, it now assumes that it has every right to take on a fantastically complicated task (and to ignore the real contribution it could make of enabling all Americans who so desire—regardless of color or social-class background—to undergo an experience in which their powers of thought and expression are developed).

But my principal disagreement with Mr. Birenbaum focuses on a sentence that appears two-thirds of the way through his paper:

> And our students, arriving at the old age of eighteen, are usually consummate confirmations of the value systems represented by their parents, the communities in which they grow up, their churches. To disrupt what they believe, what they think they know for sure, is a herculean task too seldom undertaken with success.

How utterly awful! Young people have the values that their parents, their communities, and their churches have had! Obviously, these values are wrong because they happen to be divergent from those that are held by us in the academy, and therefore it is our job in the academy to disrupt their beliefs—and charge their parents either through tuition or taxation or both a mammoth fee for this labor of charity of ours. How dare Mr. Birenbaum or anyone else presume to disrupt what any young person believes?

Who has made us academics the custodians of the true faith of society; who gives us the right to judge that our values are superior to the values of other people? By what authority do we assume the prerogative of re-making the value systems of young people? Who has appointed us the grand inquisitors who will review each young person's value system upon arrival in college and determine whether it must be disrupted or not? Who has set us up as judges of parents, communities, and churches? Who has authorized us to say that the values of parents, communities, and churches are inadequate? By what incredible arrogance do we presume that our values are not merely the standards by which everyone else is to be judged but also the models according to which all young people are to be remade? And, indeed, which of our values ought the young people learn to imitate? Should they aspire to assimilate the charity and open-ness of discussion in our professional journals? Should they want to imi-tate the friendliness and camaraderie of our academic departments? Should they strive to model themselves after the capacity to suspend judgment that we have displayed in the Jensen or Moynihan cases? Should they follow our example in the use that we have made of public funds entrusted to our care? Should they imitate our careers as empire builders? Should they want to imitate the flexibility that we display when faced with a program of academic experimentation which threatens our course load, our departmental requirements, our rigid notions of curricu-lum? Oh, yes, indeed, by all means, let's disrupt their values so that then, having been deprived of the narrow, benighted values of their families, their churches, and their communities, they can imitate the superior morality of us academics!

Our young people should learn to be undogmatic and undoctrinaire just as we are undogmatic and undoctrinaire—free from phoniness, clichés, and busywork just as we are free from phoniness, clichés, and busywork. And, above all, they should learn how to be compassionate toward all men just as we academics are truly compassionate toward all men and not just toward those particular population groups that now just happen to be the special concern of fashionable compassion.

The best college can hope to do, and the most it should attempt to do, is provide an atmosphere in which young people can, if they so desire, think through their value commitments and rethink their posture vis à vis life. I do not think there is merely a verbal difference between this state-ment of purpose and Mr. Birenbaum's desire to "disrupt what they be-lieve." I think, on the contrary, the disruption of someone else's belief has no place in a democratic educational system. We respect every man's belief no matter what it is. We merely try to create for him an atmosphere for what Joseph Schwab calls "intelligent consideration of alternatives and intelligent conversation toward consensus." If, in the process of help-ing him develop these qualities, we also create an atmosphere in which he can think through, reorganize, and reformulate his own values and commitments, all well and good. Anything less or more than that I would argue is messianic arrogance.

It is also an arrogance with incredible political naïveté. Is Mr. Birenbaum—or any of the rest of us—willing to go before state legislatures or before the Congress of the United States or before alumni organizations and say that the purpose of higher education is to disrupt what young people believe? If that is really our goal, then not to make it clear is dishonest. But if it really is our goal and if we really do make it clear, then we can scarcely be surprised if our funds dry up. The 90 percent of the Americans who, according to most public opinion polls, constitute the square society are really quite benighted. For some ungodly reason, they do not see why they should pick up the tab while a group of people —self-righteously convinced of their own moral superiority—destroy the value systems of their children. The academy can't have it both ways. If it is really bent on its messianic mission to destroy young peoples' value systems, then let it be clear about it and take the financial consequences. It must abandon either its mad, messianic hubris or its naïve assumption that the square society is eager to finance the destruction of the values to which it is committed.

The Paradox of Community in Higher Education

JACQUELINE WEXLER

THE UNIVERSITY system and the constitutional democracy of the United States of America both depend on the continuing resolution of the paradox of continuity and change. But unless the change is radical, unless it is both rooted in tradition and capable of penetrating the very roots of that tradition, the change will be only on the surface and the life of our institutions will wither away.

The university world is indeed a citadel of traditions. It bears the full weight of the glory and the scandal of those traditions. But the university is also the citadel of innovation, of skepticism, of heresy, of protest, of radical change. Most of the technological advance of this century came out of this innovative spirit in the university. The face of the university itself was radically changed by these developments. The old liberal arts culture at best became a part of an expanded university, an important part—but only a part—of the education of each of its members. For better or for worse, we of the academic world must acknowledge the technological revolution as our child, even as we all too often watch that child use its power for both the salvation and the damnation of our fellow men and ourselves. The innovations of technology are still crucial to us if we are to humanize our cities. But the innovations of technology are harnessed and energized by the decisions of free men. Either that technology will continue to be used for killing in Cambodia or Vietnam, in Kent, Ohio, or Jackson, Mississippi, or Augusta, Georgia, or it will be used to sustain and nurture the physical, the psychic, and the spiritual lives of ourselves and our fellow men.

Like the tradition of the liberal arts before it, the tradition of the technological revolution must now make way for further innovation in our universities and in our nation. We must become as pragmatic, as action-oriented about making a free society as we have been pragmatic and action-oriented about making the technological advances that have both ennobled us and demeaned us. There was, for example, a real irony in President Nixon's suggestion that a new gasoline tax be the means of paying the budget deficit incurred because of stepped-up military action in Southeast Asia. Because this nation has not harnessed its energies to produce a transportation system free of the fumes of death, the very producer of the fumes will probably provide the tax base for other fumes of destruction. What is it that has caused this nation to escalate taxes for so-called defense at the same time that we refuse to escalate taxes for the development of life and dignity for all of our citizens? Every adult has made real sacrifices to invest in life and dignity for the members of his own family. Every mother and father has supported, as best they knew how, physically, psychically, and spiritually the development of their own children. In a very real way, all of us have personally taxed ourselves to the hilt to provide a kind of social welfare state in our own homes for our children in order that they may have the basis of opportunity to go on to make their own lives. Was it an inalienable right which gave them a head start over millions of other sons and daughters in our land who, by another statistical accident, were born into different circumstances? The very people who espouse bootstraps, rugged individualism for the human family are very careful to provide the best in food and in environment, in education and in trust funds for the children of their own families. Most of us know the special privilege as well as the responsibility of providing for our own children. Is it not possible that we can let that kind of responsibility —that kind of ability to respond—extend to the human family?

Every parent who recognizes the value of education works to provide the fullest possible educational opportunity for his children. Every parent seeks to find an open admissions policy for his child, for all his children. To the extent that admission is closed to his children by economic barriers, he seeks to create public support for higher education so that opportunity extends to them. To the extent that admission is closed to any one of his children because that child cannot cope with the academic hurdles of admission or retention, he seeks out programs designed to reinforce his child's talents rather than programs that reinforce his failures. I submit that Vice-President Agnew would be among the first to search for such a program if, by some statistical accident, his own child had such needs. When, instead, any of us see the world of higher education as a prize for good birth, good breeding, good schooling in earlier years, we are indeed supporting an elitist society in which the rich get richer—richer in economic power, richer in government power, richer in corporate power. The question is not whether we favor an open admissions policy for our own children. It is only whether or not we support an open admissions policy for *all* children of the human race. "Where your heart is, there is your treasure also" is a homespun but sophisticated truth. Unless we can begin to be concerned about the welfare of the children in our slums, as indeed we are concerned about the welfare of the children of our own families, our treasures will be guarded and we will never tax ourselves as a nation for the full life of the human family.

I obviously agree with Dr. Birenbaum's cry against the elitism that has nurtured our university system and that continues to be reinforced by the university system. I share his concern about the critical necessity of preventing the separation of technical power from moral responsibility. If a community of mankind is possible in these United States and in our world society, the best elements of the nuclear family must be transfused into the whole society. But let us not confuse the life-supporting elements of the nuclear family with its life-restraining elements. The nuclear family nurtures its members in its communal life. All too often it smothers its members within that community and fails to release them as the centers of their own lives, freed and forced into relationships with multiple and moving "communities" within the larger society.

When Dr. Birenbaum expresses a final concern that "the educational ghettos are a tragic retreat from the idea of the college as a community at a time when one of the deepest longings in the hearts of the young is community," I suggest that we skeptically examine whether or not a basically nuclear community is largely a nostalgic wish for any adult who is to participate in the making of a non-elitist society. A home-base college or university can provide more or less of the substance chosen by a "student" for his own pattern of personal integration. Some good colleges, and other institutions set up to share their mission, will provide competent advising services to help the students recognize and put together the elements of their personal-professional life choices. But such a university will not be or portray itself to be a "community of learning," a

campus community that attempts to govern itself in the simplistic democratic manner of a town meeting. If the individual is the integrating
center of his own education, the particular college or university is at best
one of the basic offerings to which he responds. If instead we allow it to
be the patriarchal-matriarchal symbol of the total demands of small children and adolescents, we will give them illusions of grandeur about the
great society, even as we delay their adolescence and prevent them from
the maturity which will free them to form it.

Minds Like Jefferson's

HARRIS WOFFORD, JR.

President Birenbaum's provocative paper itself illustrates his point:
Something for everybody is not enough. His fireworks are stimulating but
when the explosions end and the smoke clears, we are left where we were
—in darkness, except for a few flashes of insight to keep in mind.

Our academic institutions are indeed inadequate models for a revolutionary society, though Mr. Birenbaum hardly does justice when he
describes their historic role as anti- if not counter-revolutionary. If modern
science and technology constitute the cutting edge of world revolution, if
the source of that revolution is the awakening of people through education, if what makes our civilization the most revolutionary one in history
is the idea of dialogue, then for all their shortcomings—from the original
academy to the State University of New York—the universities of the
West have played and are playing a fundamentally revolutionary role.
The goals of universal education and political equality have been linked
throughout American history, not just in Jefferson's mind. Seeing how far
our society has fallen short of attaining social and economic equality of
opportunity, I do not understand how Mr. Birenbaum can counterpose
America's revolutionary political traditions against its academic traditions, and see a drastic disparity; instead, the aspirations and frustrations
of the one seem to be the mirror image of the other.

To be sure, issues of peace, integration, equality, freedom, and the humane use of knowledge—Mr. Birenbaum's touchstones—do seem today
to fall largely beyond the purview of the university, and this is a serious
indictment. We must admit that consideration of the war in Vietnam
started with teach-ins on the periphery of the university and that the dis-
putation remained one-sided and superficial. Even now the question of
war—whether in Southeast Asia or in the world as a whole—like other

life-and-death issues of race, poverty, urban affairs, and the environment, is almost nowhere at the core of a curriculum or a subject of central academic study. And recalling the picture of J. Robert Oppenheimer, then at the top of our intellectual establishment, clasping his hands above his head in a victory salute, with a hundred scientists cheering, at the news that the atomic bomb had wiped out Hiroshima, who can deny that a "crucial educational problem in modern technical civilization is how to prevent the separation of technical power from moral responsibility"?

But do Mr. Birenbaum's prescriptions provide a remedy? One hundred and twenty credit hours over four years is no description of the liberal education necessary for our modern complexity, but are they, or the million entombed books, or the president's office, eight centuries old, the Enemy? Most of our teaching and curricula do seem to be failing to awaken students to a continuing life of the mind, and seem unduly disconnected from the worlds of work and art, of sex, politics, and religion. But will "carrying learning beyond the walls of the institution, enlisting teachers unisolated by rank and tenure from the world, and . . . building action and interaction into the curriculum" be a good or sufficient cure?

The City of the Mind, in this age of flux, may rather benefit by some walls, even a gate. Perhaps what this nation and age miss most is an ivory tower. Where in the world does one find this higher learning Mr. Birenbaum complains about, that is "clean and perfumed, utterly contemplative." In most places it is difficult to find a theory in a carload of courses, and everywhere, including Mr. Birenbaum's paper, our pragmatism is showing.

Having pursued, in the Peace Corps and in a college of Mr. Birenbaum's own university, the possibility of education-in-action and a University in Dispersion, emphasizing learning by apprenticeship, I want to see such experiments continued, but the early evidence suggests that the right rhythm between theory and practice, withdrawal and return, contemplation and experience is very difficult to find. My present guess is that the periods of each must be longer and more concentrated. The spirit of our time is indeed "a special penchant for mobility." Instead of yielding to that spirit, the academy may need to counteract it. As Justice Brandeis liked to say, "The way to deal with the irresistible is to resist it." A physical and temporal island called a "college," claiming several years of a person's life, may be an important part of the antidote. Such islands for study and contemplation may in fact help meet two of our modern needs stressed by Mr. Birenbaum: "one of the deepest longings in the hearts of the young is for a community," and the need for opposition to "the overbearing consensus, uniformity, and standardization of almost every dimension of the country's life."

I appreciate "the rich knowledge and learning opportunities of the streets," but having seen how the adrenalin of action tends to take over in a work-study curriculum built around assignments in the inner city, I realize that the wall around Oxford had some educational justification other than "illiberal prejudice." The classroom has its limitations, but so do the streets. A student who witnessed the turbulence of the first years of the experimental college at Old Westbury, from a new vantage point now at Yale, observed, "If only Old Westbury's experiments had taken place in an institution with yards across which students had been walking for two hundred years, in buildings where the walls have been standing for over a century, where you could shake the structure and not fear the whole tent would collapse."

One of the wisest men I have met in Africa was taken at age seven to live and study for twelve years in an Anglican monastery because his father, a tribal chief, believed his son needed to be educated thoroughly in our pervasive modern civilization, in order to be able to choose from the old and new, or, as Mr. Birenbaum puts it, to "transform the old into something quite new."

After his many sallies, Mr. Birenbaum's proposed reforms finally seem to rely on a restructuring of the politics within the university. "Reform," he says, "means a redistribution of the credit hours and of the budget, . . . means a redistribution of the decision-making power and of the rewards and punishments." Having experienced one such redistribution of power in a college where students from the beginning were "partners," I am not against a large measure of student participation, but, ironically, it seems to result in an intensification of the committee system that already afflicts academia, with the likelihood that decisions will tend even more toward the lowest common denominator. Participatory democracy, as H. G. Wells said of socialism, takes too many evenings. There is also the tendency, seen last spring in the reaction to Cambodia and Kent State, for majoritarian waves to sweep over academia, with the very "overbearing consensus" Mr. Birenbaum dislikes in America at large.

It is difficult to understand how any of his proposals, or all of them added together, would lead to the higher education everybody needs. He gives us, nevertheless, some interesting clues. As he suggests, the quality of the present disruption must be improved. Colleges and universities can improve our national and international dialogue if they meet the longings of the young for a community that is not subversive of conversation—if they put questions of purpose, of value, of truth at the core of their curriculum and research—if they respect the distinction between training and education, and provide not only the varieties of special training different people need but also the high level of liberal education everybody needs. To deal with the technical difficulty that was a matter of life and death, the astronauts in trouble as they approached the moon needed all the special training they and their friends in Houston had; facing death they also needed to draw on the other kind of education in the meaning and purpose of life that all men need. To the best of their ability, they needed to be, as we all need to be, philosopher-technicians, philosopher-citizens.

Jefferson's proposition that reason and democracy stand or fall together is self-evidently true, and the evidence now calls for a new burst of reason. If reason is not soon applied on an unprecedented scale to the public problems piling up around us, democracy and modern civilization and perhaps the whole human race will suffer a tragic fate. Our academic institutions, responsible for educating the Guardians of the Republic, who are now all the people, need to offer everybody a better education than most people get now or have ever got. Nothing is more important than the search for ways to provide that kind of education.

Perhaps Mr. Birenbaum's most promising clue is found in his reference to Jefferson. "Although the mind of a Thomas Jefferson was anchored in Heidelberg, Oxford, Paris, Bologna, Rome, Greece, the early Christians, and the ancient Hebrews," he notes, "minds like his transformed the old into something quite new. . . ." How do we develop "minds like his"? Would "Because" not be a more accurate way to begin that critical sentence than "Although"?

The revolution we need today is a system of universal liberal education that will provide an opportunity for everybody to develop a mind like Jefferson's. That education may be helped by Mr. Birenbaum's "department of the future," but if it is not anchored in the Renaissance and medieval Europe, in ancient Rome and Greece, in the early Christians and the Hebrews, it will need to find an equivalent thereof.

Response

JAMES L. MILLER, JR.

Who Needs Higher Education?

NINETEEN SEVENTY MARKS THE END OF A TWENTY-FIVE YEAR PERIOD IN American higher education during which the outstanding characteristic has been unprecedented growth. Nineteen seventy also marks the beginning of an era. The precise characteristics of the new era are not clear, but some of the environmental factors that will shape it are discernible. From these can be inferred alternative policy lines available to American society as it responds to the social goal of equality of opportunity through equal access to higher education for "all who can benefit by it." The question "Who needs higher education?" is key to understanding the past and will be central to policy development in the decade that is upon us.

Between the end of World War II and 1970 higher education changed from an activity that was simply important in American society to one that was vital, as judged by the numbers of people affected and the dependence of society upon it. The era has had its subperiods, notably the veterans enrollments of 1945–50, the post-Sputnik reordering of program priorities after 1957, the spectacular burst of federal legislation during the mid-1960s, and the period of campus unrest beginning in 1964. However, the dominant characteristic throughout was growth—growth in enrollments and in university-based research and service. As a result of that growth, the relationships of higher education and society have been fundamentally altered. The investment of funds on the part of governments and private donors has been justified chiefly on three grounds: the providing of needed manpower in the economy, the discovery of new knowledge through research, and the maintaining of the nation's competitive position internationally. The preoccupation of college administrators during most of this time was to provide more of everything—space, facilities, and faculty—so that the growth of instructional and research activities might continue. Less attention was given to the changing values, interests, and needs of the individual student until after 1964, when their importance was brought forcefully to the fore.

The end of the present period has been heralded by the almost simultaneous, even though causally unrelated, reduction in the rate of enrollment growth, leveling-off of federal financial support for higher education, and shift in focus of attention to campus unrest and associated phenomena, including the search for better ways of sensing and meeting students' educational needs. These developments pose unfamiliar challenges to administrators whose earlier experiences had prepared them instead to cope with challenges of growth.

Whose needs will be met by higher education in the coming decade? New (or newly self-aware) student and community constituencies clamor for attention, as do the old constituencies also. Belt-tightening is the order of the day. What will the choices be? How will they be made? Who will make them?

If the 1945–70 period provides a single guideline for planners of the future, it is that change in educational institutions is more likely to occur as the result of the interaction of many elements of society than as a straight-line projection of the present or as the orderly carrying-out of a long-range, preconceived plan of action. Thus, the long-range social goal of equality of opportunity as expressed in the demand for higher education for everybody will be met only as we can satisfactorily understand what forces we are dealing with today and adapt our responses accordingly.

In what follows I shall review briefly the legacy we have inherited from the last quarter-century, emphasizing the needs higher education tried to fulfill; review some of the needs of students; attempt to summarize the present national consensus on higher education; and then try to anticipate its consequences. These considerations in turn suggest several areas in which new relationships among institutions, students, and society may be sought.

The Era We Are Leaving: 1945–70

In the period 1945–70, growth was especially evident in two functional areas—teaching (evidenced by enrollments) and research. The growth of enrollments and the growth of research did not necessarily stem from the same causes although they occurred simultaneously.

Research growth was closely tied to federal funding, which was usually mission-oriented. The wartime development of atomic energy had established a pattern for relationships between the federal government and universities, and in the early postwar period the Atomic Energy Commission became a principal source of federal research funds. Subsequently, the government developed major interests in other fields, for example, medical research, space, language and area studies, biological sciences, and the improvement of education. A list of major supporting federal agencies suggests both the wider range of interests and the growth in funding: Atomic Energy Commission, Department of Defense, National Institutes of Health, National Science Foundation, Department of Agriculture, NASA, and the Department of Health, Education, and Welfare. In 1967, the total federal investment in university-based research, excluding federal contract research centers, was approximately $1 billion, which constituted about three-fourths of all funds spent by universities for research. Certainly one answer to the question "Who needs higher education?" is that the federal government has needed it during the past twenty-five years. In addition, business, industry, and governmental and private agencies concerned with programs of social betterment also increased their use of higher education's research capabilities. These too can be counted among those who need higher education.

In the past twenty-five years, enrollment growth was even more spectacular than research growth. Enrollments rose from two million to nearly eight million. Even more important was the increase in *proportion* of young people going on to college—from 20 percent to 50 percent of the college-age population. Going to college has become a mass phenomenon.

In all states, the question of who "needs" the instructional aspects of higher education has been answered in much the same fashion during the past twenty-five years—more people need it than have had it before. Attempts to designate a precise number or percentage of the population have largely failed, as evidenced by the failure of policy makers to be guided by either of the two major national studies done early in the postwar period, one of which concluded that only 25 percent of the population could benefit from higher education [1] while the other concluded that 49 percent could benefit.[2] The latter figure (proposed in the earlier of the two reports) is closer to present proportion, but some states have far exceeded that figure and none has established arbitrary limitations. Hindsight suggests that policy makers—in individual institutions, in state legislatures, and in the Congress—periodically concluded that the number who "needed" higher education was greater than the number then able to get it. States with low attendance rates tended to justify expansion of opportunity on the grounds of catching up with the national average; high attendance states based their case on catching up with manpower needs and present or projected student demand. Individual behavior—enrollment in college—suggests that throughout the era just end-

1. Commission on Financing Higher Education. See especially the study prepared for the Commission: Byron S. Hollinshead, *Who Should Go to College?* (New York: Columbia University Press, 1952).

2. President's Commission on Higher Education [Truman Commission] Reports, Vols. I–VII (Washington: Government Printing Office, 1947–48). Also published as *Higher Education for American Democracy* (New York: Harper & Bros., 1948).

ing, a steadily increasing proportion of high school graduates and their parents came to believe in the desirability of or the necessity for higher education.

To meet these perceptions of need, state support, always the mainstay of public higher education, has increased over 350 percent during the past ten years alone, from less than $1.5 billion to approximately $7 billion. In addition, the federal government provided funds for the construction of buildings, the support of new or expanded teaching programs, and the financial support of students. By the late 1960s, there was no longer any question about *whether* the federal government would be significantly involved in financing higher education. The only questions concerned how much, for what purposes, with what restrictions, and through what channels the money would flow.

Pressures of growth brought about major structural changes in the national system of higher education, including the development of new types of institutions, notably the comprehensive community colleges and the regional state universities. The growth of these new types of institutions prevented American higher education from becoming elitist by default. Existing institutions, unable to cope with the demand, would have been forced into selective admissions policies. That would have denied higher educational opportunity altogether to an ever-larger proportion of our population. In actuality, many individual institutions became more selective, but community colleges and regional universities provided alternative opportunities, and American higher education as a whole became more egalitarian.

When one contrasts the situation at the beginning and at the end of the 1945–70 era, the transformation that took place in higher education is strikingly apparent. In 1945, a typical state supported one state university of modest size, a handful of state colleges (usually teachers colleges), a large number of private colleges and universities, and possibly a few scattered two-year colleges. In 1970, a typical state had two or more major public universities, a number of state regional universities, a rapidly growing system of public comprehensive community colleges, and approximately the same number of private institutions as it had in 1945. In almost every state, a state coordinating agency has been established to perform long-range planning, allocate functions among institutions, advise state officials on budgetary needs of the institutions, and administer those federal programs that federal law stipulates shall be state-administered. Although the private institutions collectively enroll more students in 1970 than in 1945, their proportion of enrollments is far smaller than in 1945.

The old structure of higher education is gone. In the new structure, the public-private balance has been replaced by public dominance and private uncertainty. The simple classifications of "college" and "university" have given way to an array of institutional subtypes. The number of institutions, the average size and complexity of each institution, and the size of the state appropriation have all increased. These, in turn, have led to an increase in public and legislative interest in higher education. As higher education has moved front and center, the public has begun to scrutinize it more closely.

Growth has been equated with success in higher education, just as it has been in other aspects of American life. Some institutions have placed greater value on enrollment growth, some on research growth, and some on a combination of the two. All have found a degree of satisfaction during the bull market of the past twenty-five years. Most of today's collegiate administrators and faculty grew up professionally during this period. Their attitudes and expectations have been shaped by it. They have learned to accommodate to the problems and frustrations associated with growth. Their experience, at least until the last several years, has given them less exposure to other types of problems and frustrations.

THE END OF AN ERA: EVIDENCES OF CHANGE

Evidence abounds that an era has ended. Changes do not all come in a single year, but 1970 is a good choice to mark the close of the era. In 1970, the Ph.D. shortages finally ended. The war in Vietnam brought an end to the rapid escalation in federal funding for higher education; federal programs already authorized were not fully funded; and a de facto moratorium was imposed on authorization of new programs. Competing societal problems requiring immense sums for their "solution" have captured public attention, so that even when money again begins to flow from Washington, it will not be easily available to higher education. Campus unrest is having an immeasurable but obviously great impact on public attitudes toward higher education, public confidence in it, and public willingness to support it. Enrollment growth—the most important single element underlying the changes of the past twenty-five years—is projected to slow during the 1970s. Enrollments will continue to increase, but they will increase at a less rapid rate. After the exhilaration of moving at top speeds on the equivalent of an interstate highway, it will require adjustments to accept the speeds on a two-lane highway. Some people will conclude that things are standing still.

Actions on the part of the Nixon administration during 1970 also suggest the end of an era. The tumultuous early days of the Johnson administration, when new programs came too fast for comfortable assimilation, were succeeded by the latter Johnson days when the cost of war drained away the ability to fund fully programs already enacted, and, then, by the early Nixon days when the administration did not even appear interested in full funding. Action to end the war has dragged, administration rhetoric has widened the gulf between students and the national administration, and the Office of Education has become a wasteland of vacant positions. New administration proposals for higher education turned out to be stripped-down versions of programs already on the books. During the first year of the Nixon administration there were rumors of limited new higher education programs in selected areas such as support for community colleges, but by mid-1970 even those discussions had faded.

The honeymoon is over for higher education in Washington for a variety of reasons. In fact, it lasted a remarkably long time. It firmly established the general proposition that the federal government will contribute substantially to the support of higher education. In some quarters, higher education's current problems vis-à-vis public support are attributed solely to the Vietnam war and campus unrest. Certainly these factors loom large, but their effect probably has been to hasten change and heighten its impact rather than to cause it. The slowing rate of enrollment growth and the competition of other societal needs would have been felt in time.

A NOTE ON THE YOUTH CULTURE

Young adults have become an identifiable and self-aware subgroup in American culture, just as have "teenagers" and "senior citizens." In all three cases the group identification is accurate and useful only for certain purposes, just as is true of racial, religious, occupational, or any other group identification. Obviously, the dangers in such group identification are stereotyping by those outside the group and peer-group pressure for conformity on those within it.

The root causes for the appearance of youth as a distinct subgroup suggest that as a phenomenon it will be permanent rather than transitory. Physical maturity is reached earlier than in the past because living conditions are better; and at least certain aspects of social sophistication develop earlier under the impact of modern communications media, especially television. However, the workings of the economic system are such that young people, though maturing earlier, are held out of the labor market longer. The educational system is where most of them wind up, by design or by default.

The group's basic "differentness" from either younger or older segments of the population is not likely to change. Its members are too old, physically and psychologically, to be teen-agers or adolescents, and are different economically and in life style from those who (with or without attending college) have entered the world of full-time employment.

The linkage of the youth culture and higher education is the natural outcome of the large proportions of youth going on to college. College is where they live. Colleges and universities inevitably become the *locale* for much of the youth culture's activity, the *target* for a portion of its discontent, and the *staging areas* for many of its forays into the larger society. The intertwining of higher education and the youth culture is less a matter of choice than the inevitable outcome of the fact that they are cohabitants on the college campus. Like members of a family, neither really has any choice in the matter.

Youth becomes yet another force in the already complicated political and social mosaic of this nation. The American political and social system has repeatedly demonstrated its ability to absorb special-interest groups in ways that respond to those special interests while also taking account of the interests of others. There is no reason to believe that youth will be an exception. Indeed, on the political scene it appears that the eighteen-year-old vote will soon be a reality (if not by law, then by constitutional amendment). On the social scene, the antiquated rules left over from an age when the college was a surrogate parent are crumbling. Students are being dealt with as free agents and as adults.

An analogy with the labor movement is instructive in two quite different ways. One is the society's ability to accommodate an initially militant, activist, and even violent group (which met its share of counter-violence) in a manner which benefited rather than harmed the nation. The other is the inability of labor leaders to block-vote their membership except when the group's identity or existence is threatened (which includes gaining initial group recognition and status) or when the issue is one which clearly pertains to the self-interest or individual predispositions of the membership. Student leaders will certainly find themselves similarly circumscribed, especially after accomplishment of the easy reforms —those that are overdue and therefore having strong appeal. Like all other leaders, student leaders and youth leaders will be influential only within certain limits.

The war in Southeast Asia is one issue on which a wide student consensus exists, and it has provided the most dramatic evidence yet that youth has arrived on the American scene as a potent political force. The toppling of the Johnson government (in the British sense of that term) and the uprisings against the Nixon government suggest the extent of student cohesion and student power, as well as their ability to work with groups representing other segments of the population.

Many today think that higher education needs an end to the war in

Southeast Asia even more than it needs new campus buildings, that it needs a solution to the racial crisis—another matter of widespread and legitimate student concern—even more than it needs money for faculty salaries. Buildings and salaries are important but the societal issues are even more important. They are intrinsically important, and they also are crucial to peace on the campus and to the well-being of higher education.

We are paying an extremely high price during this period of accommodation and readjustment in the form of our consumption of leaders and leadership talent. Presidents and deans of students provide the most obvious examples, but the toll has extended throughout the ranks of academic leadership. During other stages of American higher education we have seen presidents who built great institutions, and we have seen faculty leaders who built into our system—often at great personal cost—such valuable elements as academic freedom and the self-governance of the community of scholars. The contribution of the current generation of academic leaders will lie in their efforts to facilitate their institutions' successful accommodation to change. Successful accommodation to change means incorporating into the institution the best of what is new while preserving the best of the old—something which is simple to state, difficult to do, and likely to leave unsatisfied the most committed advocates of both the new and the old. The importance of this leadership contribution is apt to be slighted, because it is less visible than buildings and because it often involves making one's contribution and later being martyred.

THE SHAPE OF THE FUTURE

One of the important influences on the shape of the future will be the extent and nature of the social consensus concerning higher education. One method for gauging social consensus is to listen to the statements of conservative leaders on issues which at an earlier point in time were the subject of liberal-conservative debate. "Who needs higher education?" was a topic of sharp debate between elitists and egalitarians in the 1940s and '50s, the first half of the era now ending. An analysis of selected sections of President Nixon's March 19, 1970, message on higher education to the Congress suggests the degree of national consensus concerning many aspects of higher education's role in society. (I take the liberty here of classifying Mr. Nixon as a conservative.) Throughout the message, he used the term "college" to include all postsecondary education—including vocational schools, four-year colleges, junior and community colleges, universities, and graduate schools.

Concerning the increasing proportion of young people in attendance, Mr. Nixon said:

There is much to be proud of in our system of higher education. Twenty-five years ago, two Americans in ten of college age went to college; today nearly five out of ten go on to college; by 1976, we expect seven out of ten to further their education beyond secondary school.

Concerning the economy's need for higher education, he said:

One of the discoveries of economists in recent years is the extraordinary, in truth the dominant, role which investment in human beings plays in economic growth.

Concerning the contribution of higher education in sustaining a democratic society, he said:

. . . the more profound influence of education has been in the shaping of the American democracy and the quality of life of the American people. We are entering an era when concern for the quality of American life requires that we organize our programs and our policies in ways that enhance that quality and open opportunities for all.

Concerning individual growth and development, he said:

No element of our national life is more worthy of our attention, our support, and our concern than higher education. For no element has greater impact on the careers, the personal growth, and the happiness of so many of our citizens.

And regarding higher education's importance in providing national leadership, he said:

. . . no element is of greater importance [than higher education] in providing the knowledge and leadership on which the vitality of our democracy and the strength of our economy depends.

Although Mr. Nixon's specific higher education proposals left most leaders in higher education less than enchanted, his statements of principle and philosophy clearly indicate the extent of our national agreement concerning the need for and importance of higher education. His statements on the economic importance of higher education have the ring of Galbraith; those on higher education's leadership role bring to mind Walter Lippmann's argument that today's "spiritual and intellectual vacuum . . . can be filled only by the universal company of scholars. . . ." (although Mr. Nixon may or may not have intended it quite that way); and the present enrollment proportions in which Mr. Nixon takes pride are approximately those proposed as national goals by President Truman's Commission on Higher Education (the proportion projected by Mr. Nixon for 1976 far exceeds the Truman Commission projections).

The liberal proposals of the last twenty-five years have become sufficiently a part of the national consensus to merit incorporation into the messages of a conservative President. This consensus establishes the base line from which we move into a new era.

Sometime during the 1960s, higher education passed the "tipping point" in its development as a mass social institution, and with that change it became the potential victim of societal events, as well as the beneficiary of them. It is to higher education that society turns for many forms of services, often advisedly, but also often with unrealistic expectations. In return, society invests large amounts of money in higher education. A certain amount of bargaining takes place on both sides, but each side must be reasonably satisfied if the arrangement is to last.

The future of higher education will be determined largely by the boundary relationships (in the sense that social psychologists use the term) among three groups—the traditional collegiate power structure, consisting of the administration and faculty; the newly self-aware and sometimes militant young adults who make up the student bodies; and the rest of American society, consisting of a multitude of political, economic, and social groupings with widely differing attitudes about higher education and different degrees of interest in it.

A set of ground rules governs the relationship between colleges and universities and the society that supports them. These ground rules, like the British constitution, are not committed to paper (at least not in any single document), but they are widely known and understood, nevertheless. Although always subject to change, they have tended to change slowly, through simultaneous processes of accretion and erosion.

Today, however, a variety of factors have conspired to lead us into a period of fundamental revision concerning the conventional rules governing relationships among collegiate institutions, their students, and the rest of society. During such periods of constitutional revision, all things are possible. Therein lies both promise and danger.

Beyond the development of new working relationships between society and higher education and between the institutions and students, higher education and the society which supports it most certainly will be faced with the following challenges:

1. To reconcile a basically meritocratic system of higher education with egalitarian social goals and values.

2. To restructure the collegiate environment so as to recognize new life styles of students, especially to recognize that students in the 1970s are adults, not juveniles.

3. To accommodate to the fact that higher educational institutions have become so numerous that they necessarily constitute an educational *system* with all that implies in need for planning and coordination and the loss of some degree of institutional autonomy.

4. To secure adequate financial support. Implicit in this are alternatives concerning relative proportions to be paid by students, private givers, and the three levels of government: federal, state, and local. Also implicit are questions concerning the extent to which funds are earmarked for certain programs, and the channels through which funds move to institutions— whether through direct grants to institutions, federal grants to states for redistribution to institutions, or grants to (or through) students who carry them to institutions of their choice.

5. To maintain and improve educational quality. This is partly a holding operation, to maintain excellence where it now exists; partly it is a building operation, to foster quality in places where it does not now exist.

6. To provide manpower education, that is, the education of people to meet the manpower needs of the economic and social system. In many respects this function overlaps support for universal education and quality education, but it operates from a different motivational premise.

7. To provide higher adult and continuing education, in recognition of the need of adults in middle and later life for further education and periodic reeducation.

8. To secure adequate research support, that is, support for the search for facts, including "facts" in their theoretical formulations. Research has become the fuel of the modern economic and social machine, and for many purposes it must be considered separately from the function of providing education for students.

9. To secure adequate support for scholarly work, that is, the forms of such work that can be distinguished from empirical research because they go beyond it or utilize different tools. Scholarship frequently deals with the meaning of life and the quality of life.

10. To provide needed and relevant public services, including both those directed to the benefit of individuals and those directed to organized groups—government, industry, civic.

11. To restructure the learning and teaching environment of the campus, including methods of teaching and the structure of the curriculum itself. This need is not new, nor has it been completely ignored, but continuous attention to it becomes more urgent in the 1970s because the pace of change is faster. Restructuring the learning and teaching environment includes actions designed to keep up with rapid changes in man's store of knowledge, and it also requires an accommodation to new and changing goals of education—goals that give greater emphasis to education of the total personality and to education for social responsibility as well as to cognitive learning of traditional skills and disciplines.

These challenges may be thought of as expressing legitimate needs of one or more segments of our society. Successfully meeting them will require ingenuity, patience, and adaptability. Indeed, adaptability will be the greatest need of American higher education as universal higher educational opportunity moves toward realization and higher education becomes steadily more important to, and under greater pressure from, the rest of American society. How to adapt, and when to adapt, and to whom to adapt, and when not to adapt will be critical questions.

Whoever Wants It Needs It

BETTE J. SOLDWEDEL

IT IS BY *choice* that possibility becomes reality. In many respects, the word is particularly apropos of the position of institutionalized higher education today in answer to the question: Who needs it? This nation is not at one, but at a whole series, of the critical choice points in the development of our institutions of higher education and of our society as a whole.

Despite the importance of growth of universities in the last quarter-century, the lessons to be derived from an analysis of the recent past are far more consequential. Without committing ourselves to solid judgments about what was good, bad, or mixed in that history, we can do little more than "let the dead bury their dead." That phrase may seem no more than a metaphor until we recall the images of a Jackson State, a Kent State, and a University of Wisconsin. In the face of such passionate conviction and sorrow, it seems disingenuous to suppose that student dissatisfaction has no substantial basis or that its causes will be compromised away, perhaps, as higher education as an institution is pulled and hauled, adapting and accommodating, depending on the forces of change which may prevail. Professional educators must examine carefully the sources of student dissatisfaction. They will find that the values being most earnestly attacked by the university's own clientele are also those embodied in our traditional system of higher education. So long as those charged with the direction of higher education succumb to the temptation to regard it as a passive object of social forces, rather than as an active participant in the processes of social change, higher education risks crumbling at the moment of its greatest challenge. From that perspective, there can be little incentive for a national or institutional redefinition of goals, a restructuring of curriculum, an expansion of community services, the encouragement of responsible student participation, or even the imaginative search for new sources of funding. Unless we acknowledge some responsibility for the developments of the last twenty-five years, we cannot hope or expect that our institutions will act more responsibly in the future.

Precisely at this point *choice* and *responsibility* begin. At a similar point, the late Paul Tillich once remarked that the first word to be spoken on behalf of religion today must be a word against religion. Much the same thing must be said of institutionalized higher education in America, and, if we are to imitate his courage, we too must face the unpleasant facts.

"Who Needs Higher Education?" must be considered in the context of the university of today. A climate that lends itself so readily to shootings, bombings, and beatings did not develop overnight. The erosion of authority and respect in our colleges and universities has been a progressive wastage of the living spirit of higher education during the entire quarter-century and particularly during the last decade. But the loss of respect and authority also has its causes, and no accurate historical reading of this period, however deterministic, can ignore the growing discontent with the hypocrisies of a system that pretends to meritocracy, that has been found to neglect its essential teaching function in the search for grants and publishable research, that has abandoned its historical role as critic and teacher of society for that of accomplice and bondslave.

Moreover, while making pronouncements about the inclusiveness of higher education, we have done little to see that higher educational opportunities are made available to those thousands of students who are willing and able to learn but who are handicapped by an inferior public school education, which we have tolerated. Where "special" programs do exist, largely through federal funding, often the students are out of the mainstream of the university.

At the same time, we have excluded whole groups of people on bases no more substantial than their performance on tests that may have little relation to their ability to perform in the classroom or to the marks they would obtain if the validity of their teachers' judgments of performance were accepted. We even exclude because of age and sex.

The responsibilities and prospects of higher education are complementary to its past mistakes. To start with, we must decide that higher education in the future is no longer to be elitist, racist, closed off from the community and the issues of the day, and responsible only to trustees and boards of regents. Instead, we must decide that it is to become *truly* democratic, egalitarian, and integrated, increasingly open to more strata within the community. It must confront and debate the live issues publicly; it must become responsive and responsible to the whole society and its needs, admitting all citizens freely to the common dialogue while guiding them toward higher levels of achievement in ways that they themselves acknowledge as personally fulfilling and meaningful. I am saying that whoever *wants* higher education needs it.

In a diverse culture, not all institutions will meet these multitudes of needs in the same way and to the same degree. The aim, however, is for an educational system that is pluralistic insofar as it responds to the plurality of needs, goals, and abilities of its students at a given time, and insofar as it actively adapts itself to meet their requirements and those of the constantly changing body of knowledge. It means that higher education shall be "higher" not by virtue of serving the rich, the well-born, the academically able and advantaged, or those destined to fill the academic ranks; rather, it shall be "higher" because it takes any adult or near adult beyond his present level toward a fuller realization of his powers *to be*. Only then shall we have realized what Robert Hutchins has called "the learning society." Only then can we think of having an educational system that is fully accountable to an increasingly well-educated, less-stratified society. The object is nothing less than Jefferson's ideal of an intelligent and informed electorate.

As a matter of fact, there is no other acceptable alternative. There is no other acceptable *choice* if we hold ourselves accountable to increase the significance and value of *every* human life.

College and the Real World

JAMES S. SMOOT

WHEN EDUCATORS DISCUSS programs to expand opportunities for higher education, two thoughts come to mind repeatedly. First, the purveyors of higher education, as never before, are engaged in a soul-searching, hand-wringing, and agonized reappraisal of their students and their programs and services. Second, the sense of urgency generated by this reappraisal seems to be focused more on avoidance (don't expose our wrongdoings, don't force us to come to grips with this unmanageable assignment) than on the development of viable educational alternatives.

Professor Miller's summary of the growth of higher education brought to mind an awareness I gained while teaching at a placid college in the placid fifties: College attendance was being promoted nationally not only to develop essential manpower but also as a holding action to slow the growth of our labor supply. The growth in quantity of higher education was not characterized by growth in diversity of curriculum. Most students have been served a standard academic diet in a standard fashion. The response to needs has been quantitative rather than qualitative.

As we reappraise our conduct of higher education, we should question whether *all* the 50 percent of young people now going on to postsecondary education really *need* what they are offered in college. To what extent is the need manufactured—by employers, by government, by parents, by higher education itself? For example, many college graduates utilize only a fraction of what has been prepackaged in curricula, either on the job or in positive participatory citizenship. Again, many mature no further, personally or academically, as a result of their structured college experiences.

What do students need? They need instruction *in* the real world as well as *about* it: academe's "hothouse" laboratories and abstraction-strewn classrooms are grossly inadequate for learning how to cope with today and tomorrow.

It sometimes is heartening to hear educators ask, "Who needs higher education?" But the rising chorus of those asking this question also has a disheartening aspect. Is there a positive correlation between the rising doubt about higher education's need value (after years of overselling it) and the sharp increase in the numbers of new clientele (lower in class status, academic skills, and motivation than we're accustomed to dealing with) who want some of our educational goodies?

If we assess honestly the need for what is being provided by colleges, we might realize that about half of the students could be barred from enrollment. I refer not to the disadvantaged students (whom some educators still would like to bar, despite evidence that many of these "unprepared" students fare surprisingly well); they need higher education in order to become productive, participating citizens, and, therefore, they must have educational opportunities beyond the high school. Rather, acting on a basis of need, we might bar the "overqualified," those who could fare quite well in our socioeconomic setting with no more than a brief postsecondary orientation to the world of work.

We also might make a case for limiting college admission to those who show that they need college programs and services—not merely the degree it grants. For example, why not employ in our schools all college applicants who want to become teachers, allowing actual matriculation (or considering the on-the-job experience as an essential phase of matriculation) only when the neophyte "teacher" identified a specific need for help that the college curriculum and teachers could supply? This approach interests me: it not only might bring to campus students who know what they want but also might demonstrate that the teacher preparation curriculum could be pruned heavily. In addition, we might have confirmation of what many of us probably suspect but do not state openly: that there is no valid correlation between the ability to function at a specified level of competence and the number of credit hours and curriculum packages successfully compiled.

We all know how slowly change takes place in higher education. Perhaps those who need higher education most are the educators themselves. They need to learn how to deliver the innovative, creative teaching that is needed both by disadvantaged, atypical learners and by the academically able but socially alienated students.

Finally, higher education is needed by the nation. Upward mobility continues as a vital force in our nation. A society subscribing to this belief must offer its citizens enlarged life options. Enlarged options, in turn, call for enlarged educational alternatives. Educators have thrived on the belief that some cause-effect relationship exists between the progress of the nation and the provision of opportunities for higher education. We would be unwise to do anything that would dispel that belief!

Student Pressures and Manpower Needs

JOHN K. FOLGER

Dr. Miller has sketched a big picture that is changing rapidly and is hard to get in focus. Let me try to clarify some parts of the picture. He gives three major reasons for supporting higher education: manpower needs, discovery of new knowledge through research, and international competition. Actually, none of these is the major reason for support; it is student demand for higher education. Student demand and manpower demand have often been in harmony, but our system has grown by responding to the desires and pressures of the students, not by developing programs to train just enough men to fill job vacancies.

This point may seem small, but it is important. In the next decade, the relative supply of graduates in many fields will be much larger—in teaching, business management, social work, law, science, and mathematics. Only in the health sciences and to a lesser degree in engineering, applied sciences, and some applied social sciences do shortages seem likely to persist throughout most of the 1970s. In the last two decades college faculties could train a youth for almost any field and not worry about whether he would get a good job, even though it might be fairly remote from his specific training. But the future entry of college graduates into the labor force will be more difficult and more conditional. I am not raising the specter of the unemployed college graduate, for each graduate will be able to get some job—but it may not be a job in the professional or managerial category for which his college trained him.

The colleges will need to assume more responsibility for guiding youth toward the career fields where job chances are best. For example, occupational and vocational training at the sub-baccalaureate level provides skills that are fairly specific; therefore, such training is particularly vulnerable to shifts in the job market if the market in a narrow field becomes flooded with candidates whose skills are not transferable to many other jobs. In the past twenty-five years colleges have not had to worry much about manpower needs and the future demand for their graduates; in the future they will have to devote time to these matters if another major increase in student frustration and discontent is to be avoided.

A second point that the Miller paper fails to emphasize is the changing characteristics of the college population as we move toward universal postsecondary education. Although this movement is rapid, it is considerably slower than Mr. Nixon seems to think it is. In 1968, of each age cohort, about 75 percent were finishing high school and about 45 percent were entering college or were expected to enter after some years. By 1980, according to unpublished projections of the Carnegie Commission on Higher Education, about 85 percent of each age cohort will finish high school and about 56 percent will begin college, some after several years' delay.

Nearly all youth who have traditionally gone to college have been drawn from the top half of the family income distribution and the top half of the ability distribution. Humphrey Doerman has estimated that in 1969–70, 90–95 percent of youth who come from families with incomes over $10,700 a year *and* who score over 450 on Verbal Aptitude on the Scholastic Aptitude Test complete high school *and* enter college.[1] Very little of the future growth of higher education will come from this group, which is favored in both income and academic achievement, simply because most of them are already in college. What will be the implications for the private colleges and major state universities, which have drawn nearly all their students from this group?

If the percentage of youth attending college continues to rise, between 85 and 90 percent of the additional students expected in the next decade will either be below 450 on Verbal Aptitude or will come from families whose income is less than $10,700 a year, or both. These "new" students will be vocationally oriented, and although they may value autonomy

1. Information presented as part of a paper delivered at a College Entrance Examination Board symposium on college admissions, held at Wingspread, Wisc., in May 1970.

and the life styles of the youth culture nearly as much as current students do, the main goals of most of them will be upward social mobility and a good job. Colleges will not be able to provide the avenue to an upper-level job for all these students. Instead many of them will have to enter clerical or service white-collar jobs.

How can the colleges let everyone in, and still enable everyone to rise to the top of the social structure? Unless college administrators succeed in reconciling these two inconsistent goals, the result will be increasing frustration among college students.

PART TWO

PRACTICES: The Question of . . .

Access

Quality

Reform

Alternatives

Adults

ROBERT M. O'NEIL

Beyond the Threshold: Changing Patterns of Access to Higher Education

THERE IS MUCH TALK OF "UNIVERSAL HIGHER EDUCATION" THESE DAYS. The United States is far ahead of any other nation in providing higher learning for its citizens. Yet educational opportunity is far from universal. Half our high school graduates now begin college, but many other youth never graduate from high school. And of those who do matriculate, many drop out long before the baccalaureate. Thus the more meaningful datum may well be the proportion of college-age youth who are currently enrolled—roughly one-quarter.

BARRIERS TO EQUAL ACCESS

Even these overall figures conceal wide variations in educational opportunities. Nearly every youth who ranks academically in the top quarter of his high school class and comes from a middle- or upper-middle-class family will start college. But the prospect is vastly different for youth from urban ghettos and slums and the pockets of rural poverty. Several years ago Jencks observed that among high school students from the bottom socioeconomic quartile who ranked in the top academic bracket, only one in four could expect to attend college. The prognosis has improved somewhat in the late 1960s, but the correlation between wealth and access remains high. Of those who are excluded from higher education for nonacademic reasons, a disproportionate share belong to racial and ethnic minorities.[1] Yet many are Caucasian, and are simply very poor; indeed, educational opportunities may well be more remote today for Appalachian whites than for some ghetto blacks in Northeastern and West Coast cities.

The total capacity of the American system of higher education has grown dramatically in the last quarter-century, but demand for college education has grown even more rapidly. The result has been an increasing selectivity of two sorts: institutions that were already selective have

---

1. Christopher Jencks, "Social Stratification and Higher Education," *Harvard Educational Review,* Spring 1968, pp. 302–8.

been much more so as the quality of applications has risen; and many institutions that were relatively open in the past have now for the first time become selective. Save perhaps for the public systems of Ohio and a few other states, selectivity is entirely absent only at the bottom and at the fringes of the system—in the academically marginal proprietary colleges, and in the junior and community colleges. Within large public systems like those of California and New York City the very openness of the system to all residents with a high school diploma has produced sharp stratification between levels, intense selectivity at the top, and rapidly rising transfer standards.

These trends have had highly important meaning for two dimensions of access—race and geography. At the most prestigious of the predominantly white institutions, the increasing selectivity in the admissions process operated quite unconsciously to diminish educational opportunities for members of minority groups. In fact, from the postwar period, when the GI bill created educational opportunities for nonwhites, until 1968, these opportunities declined almost steadily. Take the revealing experiences of San Francisco State College: In 1959, black enrollment was about 12 percent. A decade later, largely as the result of the rising floor mandated by the California Master Plan, barely 4 percent of the student body was black.[2] Some of those excluded by the new selectivity may have attended junior college for two years, but undoubtedly many others who would have gone to college in the 1950s simply did not go at all in the '60s. Nor is the San Francisco experience unique. Egerton concluded his exhaustive study of nonwhite enrollments in 1968 with the ominous report that minorities, while gaining numerically on the large university campuses between 1940 and the late '60s, had "proportionately slipped further behind."[3]

A variety of factors caused the attenuation of educational opportunity for minority groups. In large part the barrier has been financial: a majority even of those blacks who do reach college come from families with incomes below $6,000, whereas only one-seventh of white students' families are below that level.[4] Moreover, many minority students come to college

2. Algo D. Henderson, "San Francisco State College: Dissension about Governance and Programs," mimeographed (Berkeley, Calif.: Center for Research and Development in Higher Education, n.d.), p. 3

3. John Egerton, *State Universities and Black Americans: An Inquiry into Desegregation and Equity for Negroes in 100 Public Universities* (Southern Education Reporting Service and National Association of State Universities and Land-Grant Colleges, 1969), p. 93.

4. David G. Brown, "Allocating Limited Resources," in *The Campus and the Racial Crisis*, ed. David C Nichols and Olive Mills (Washington: American Council on Education, 1970), p. 159.

with already substantial accumulated debts and heavy family financial obligations. Any realistic estimate of the "cost" of higher education for such persons must include not only tuition and fees, but forgone earnings as well. Even more culpable is continued reliance on the traditional measures of academic potential—high school grades and standardized test scores; whether or not these indicia are biased or unfair, their use has surely operated to exclude ever greater numbers of minority applicants. Of course, the minority experience has not been wholly different in states that adhere to an open-door policy at all state institutions, though it cannot be pure accident that Ohio State graduated more black Ph.D.'s during the 1940s and '50s than any other institution,[5] and that Ohio University today has as many blacks on campus as much larger schools such as Berkeley, Madison, and Urbana.[6]

It is not easy to assess blame for the exclusion of minority youth. Surely the predominantly white institutions (save in the Southeast) have not overtly discriminated against the poor, the black, and the Spanish-American. Indeed, in a variety of ways the most prestigious universities have tried to relieve the effects of poverty and discrimination: They have set aside special scholarship funds for disadvantaged students (sometimes unclaimed because there were no applicants). Their schools of education have devoted major energy and talent to improving teaching in the ghetto, barrio, and hill town classrooms. They have established extension centers and branch campuses to bring learning opportunities closer to those too poor or too timid to venture far in search of such opportunities. Yet until the last two years, when these efforts were augmented by intensive recruiting programs, massive commitments of financial aid, and explicit admission preferences for minority applicants, the inevitable consequence of increasing selectivity had been a slow but steady rise in de facto segregation in higher education. Only by becoming color conscious have admission officers been able to reverse the trend.

ACCESS AND RACE

Even now there is much uncertainty whether that reversal is permanent and substantial. During the past two years, to be sure, minority enrollments have been boosted sharply on many campuses by giving explicit preference to minority applicants. But there are fragile aspects to these impressive gains. First, minority enrollments and the recent in-

5. Preston Valien, "Improving Programs in Graduate Education for Negroes," *Journal of Negro Education*, Summer 1967, pp. 238–48.
6. "Black Enrollments Up in Freshman Classes at State Universities," National Association of State Universities and Land-Grant Colleges, *Office of Institutional Research Circular*, No. 150, April 1, 1970, p. 2.

creases are found disproportionately at two-year colleges, from which transfer opportunities remain uncertain. Take the City University of New York as a case in point. Even before open admissions took effect, total black and Puerto Rican enrollment was over 15 percent. But the students comprising that very impressive minority share have been concentrated in a few community colleges, notably Bronx and New York City. Many more nonwhites than whites were listed as "nonmatriculated," a status that cast serious doubt on their degree prospects. When one isolates the fully matriculated students at the four-year colleges of CUNY in 1967–68, he finds that, with the sole exception of Baruch, minority enrollments are about the same as the 4–5 percent typical of other large public universities, and are very far below the nonwhite or Spanish-speaking population of the city.[7] Much the same is the case in California: subtract black and Chicano enrollments at Laney, Compton, Merritt, and East Los Angeles, and the performance of the rest of the system—save perhaps for Berkeley —is far less impressive than overall figures would suggest.

Second, the minority share among freshmen is far higher than among upperclassmen. This disparity partially reflects the recency of vigorous recruiting efforts. But it also suggests that many minority students do not transfer from two-year to four-year institutions, and that others drop out along the way even if they matriculate at a degree-granting institution. (Attrition rates for minority students are virtually unavailable. Early in the Upward Bound program, 75 percent of the students dropped out, although the sample was admittedly a special one. ASPIRA reported recently a 60 percent attrition rate for Puerto Rican college students.[8] Other programs—including the seven-year special admit program at Brown University—yield much more promising conclusions, but wide differences among selection standards and program content make comparisons difficult.) Most of our current data deal only with matriculation; they reveal only the number of minority students who begin the freshman year. There is an urgent need for measurement of such vital indicia of educational opportunity as retention or attrition rates; transfer rates from two-year to four-year colleges; and reentry rates for those who drop out voluntarily and later wish to return.

Third, the very foundation of these recent gains may be in jeopardy. The future of governmental support for minority student programs is uncertain, as witness the cutbacks in federal work-study and other forms of subvention, and the callous crippling of the efforts of the California Economic Opportunity Program. Politically, it seems clear that special programs for minority students are becoming less and less popular. Vice-

7. *New York Times*, Dec. 15, 1967, p. 53.
8. *New York Times*, July 29, 1970, p. 39.

President Agnew knew his constituency when he charged the University of Michigan with a "callow retreat from reality" for agreeing to work toward a 10 percent black freshman class by 1973. And the regents of the University of Texas sensed the popular mood last fall when they banned further recruitment of any student "who cannot meet the usual academic requirements for admission."

Finally, there is much uncertainty whether recent trends really reflect net enrollment gains or simply describe the reallocation of a static student population. Clearly the percentage of nonwhites on the most prestigious campuses has risen much faster than figures for the entire system. Meanwhile, total enrollments at the predominantly black institutions may not have declined numerically. But there is evidence that some places once held by blacks are now being taken by whites, notably at Howard's graduate schools and at such undergraduate campuses as Lincoln, Bluefield, and West Virginia State, where whites have now approached or even passed parity with blacks. Integration of both types of institutions is, of course, an independent value of a high order. The chance to study and associate with students of a different color might well justify many of the efforts that have been made in recent years. But we must be careful not to claim too much credit for the recruitment efforts of the major white institutions until we know more about the extent of net increase in educational opportunity for the target group.

Whatever the dimensions of the recent gains in educational opportunity for minority youth, it is painfully clear that continued progress demands a continued adherence to explicitly color-conscious admission standards for some part of every freshman class. Many minority youth will, of course, be admissible without any ethnic preference. That number should increase steadily as the quality of ghetto and barrio schools improves through desegregation and other efforts, and as newly perceived educational and career opportunities raise the aspirations of disadvantaged youth. Yet a sudden return to the traditional policy of color blindness in making admission judgments would be disastrous; it would only frustrate the hopes and expectations of many thousands of youth for whom college appears for the first time a reality. Thus color has become an indelible attribute of that very selectivity in the admission process that brought the situation to such a critical pass.

ACCESS AND GEOGRAPHY

If *race* has historically been irrelevant to the admissions decision, the same cannot be said of *place* or geography. Concern about an applicant's residence has in fact produced sharply divergent trends in the public and private sectors. The private university, anxious to achieve greater diversity in its student body and to earn the designation "national," has eagerly sought students from distant parts of the country and lured nonresidents with special scholarships unavailable to local applicants. Indeed, geographical diversity of the student body may have become, more than any other single factor, the hallmark of such universities as Harvard, Yale, Wesleyan, Stanford, and Chicago—and the characteristic to which ambitious but less prestigious campuses most consistently aspire.

In the public sector, precisely the opposite trend has marked the most prestigious campuses. A century ago the University of Michigan, oldest of the major state universities, drew two-thirds of its students from outside the state. Gradually the percentage of nonresidents declined, and last year the legislature mandated a harsh quota of 20 percent. Similar if less dramatic trends are found elsewhere at the undergraduate level though graduate populations at the major public universities have remained cosmopolitan. The University of Wisconsin is now under regental injunction to reduce its out-of-state enrollment to 15 percent of the class entering next fall. Yet almost one-third of the current Madison student body comes from out of state and comprises the largest *number* of nonresident students at any campus in the country. The nonresident undergraduate enrollment at Berkeley is kept to around 10 percent, not by any rigid quota but by the equally effective device of a sharp differential in high school grades required of in-state and out-of-state applicants. Further, there is no way to tell how many nonresident students are deterred from enrolling by the tuition differentials that exist almost universally in the public sector. Here too the barrier against the nonresident is rising rapidly. From a 1967 base—an average nonresident fee more than twice that for residents—out-of-state fees rose in 1968–69 by nearly 10 percent while in-state charges rose only about 3 percent. Last year, the increases were 12 percent and 4 percent respectively.[9]

Hence the anomaly: while private universities have quite consciously become more diverse in matters of geographical representation, the public institutions—equally consciously if often involuntarily—are becoming more provincial. There are, of course, other reasons why public systems have become more local in character: the disproportionate increase in enrollments at junior and community colleges, to which most students commute; and the late but rapid growth of public campuses in the traditional "exporting" states of New York, New Jersey, Massachusetts, and Connecticut. But the central fact remains: the geographical mobility of

9. See Robert F. Carbone, *Resident or Nonresident: Tuition Classification in Higher Education in the States* (Denver, Colo.: Education Commission of the States, 1970); Robert C. Braun, "Resident or Nonresident—Legal or Illegal" (Berkeley, Calif.: Assembly on University Goals and Governance, 1970).

students who cannot pay private college tuitions or claim large scholarships has been drastically curtailed by the building of high walls in the form of tuition and grade-point differentials and strict nonresident quotas. The inevitable effect of these protectionist policies is to deprive both in-state and out-of-state students of opportunities for association that would measurably enhance the college experience and the quality of the institution. Meanwhile, the paramount educational concerns of most state legislators—campus unrest and high costs—will assuredly push these walls higher in the next five to ten years.

LAW AND MOBILITY

There is, however, reason to believe that both trends will soon be reversed by external and largely unforeseen pressures.

Let us consider the private sector. The very institutions that are most nearly "national" in character have made the boldest commitment to minority students; noblesse oblige has guided the reorientation of admissions policies. The demands of large numbers of very poor black and Spanish-speaking students on scholarship and financial aid budgets have already begun to be felt, with some private colleges devoting a third or more of these scarce resources to 4–5 percent of the student body. This redirection of resources may well impair the institution's capacity to attract even middle-class white students from the opposite coast at a time when all costs are rapidly rising. Moreover, even the ablest student from another part of the country may be unable to bring his state-awarded scholarship with him. The New York Regents and the California State Scholarships must, for example, be used within the state, although Pennsylvania, Connecticut, and other fellowships are exportable. Thus Columbia may now be forced to reject the brilliant Californian and take in his stead a less promising New Yorker whose regents award will free a corresponding share of the school's own resources for the Harlem black or Puerto Rican already accepted with acute needs. Southern Cal or Cal Tech may have to prefer the B-plus Californian to the A New Yorker for precisely the same reason. These pressures for homogenization in the private sector will continue unless the commitment to minority groups is abandoned or sharply reduced or unless the respective state legislatures make scholarships generally exportable—a most unlikely prospect in view of the critical need and the growing demand of the private colleges for indirect subvention from their own states.

If the private universities are to become more provincial in character, the opposite trend seems almost certain in the public sector, though for legal rather than fiscal reasons. Over the years there have been occasional court challenges to nonresident tuition and grade-point differentials, and all have failed. But the situation today appears quite different, and a different outcome predictable, for several reasons. No court has sustained a rigid percentage quota on nonresident applications—a device that absolutely precludes interstate migration rather than simply making it somewhat more expensive. Moreover, the barriers are much higher now than they have ever been; courts that sustained nonresident differentials in the past found no evidence of any serious deterrent to mobility. (In each case, in fact, the plaintiffs were already in the state and enrolled at the university before bringing suit.) It seems almost certain that the next cases will supply the heretofore missing proof of exclusion or deterrence of prospective students who wish to matriculate away from home.

Most important of all, there have been profound changes in the applicable constitutional law. In the past, the legal challenge to nonresident barriers rested uncertainly on the privileges and immunities clause—a constitutional provision of uncertain origin and meaning and infrequent application. There was much doubt whether higher education was even a "privilege" to which the clause applied; rather high standards had been set for invoking the clause at all. Moreover, states have long been permitted to assess a reasonable differential to nonresidents for the use of facilities supported by in-state tax funds—hunting and fishing licenses, occupational permits, and the like. Unless the tuition differential far exceeded the resident taxpayer's contribution to the support of the university (which has never been the case), the privileges and immunities argument was doomed to failure.

There is, however, a new element in the constitutional picture. Last year the United States Supreme Court struck down as a denial of equal protection under the Fourteenth Amendment the one-year waiting period which most states imposed on newly arrived applicants for welfare benefits.[10] The Court invoked two central propositions: (1) there was no rational difference, in terms of human need, between the newcomer and the long-term resident; and (2) the interests advanced by the states in support of the distinction—mainly the desire to cut the costs of welfare programs—were insufficient to defeat so compelling a claim. In a footnote, the Court expressly reserved for a later time the question of interstate tuition differentials in higher education. Since that decision, one lower court in California has found the welfare precedent inapposite, but the facts of the case were rather weak.[11]

10. Shapiro v. Thompson, 394 U.S. 618 (1969).
11. Kirk v. Regents of the University of California, 78 Cal. Rptr. 260 (1969). Some months later the very same court struck down on constitutional grounds the one-year California residence test imposed on voter registrants recently arrived in the state (*Los Angeles Times*, Oct. 8, 1970, p. 1).

THE CONSTITUTION AND THE NONRESIDENT STUDENT

The application of this new principle of equality to higher education is not automatic. The Supreme Court made clear in the welfare cases that only abridgement of a "fundamental right" would bring a state-imposed differential under such rigid scrutiny. Presumably the desire to travel between states for pleasure or recreation would not qualify. The need for welfare arises from the individual interest in survival and subsistence. Arguably, no claim to any other form of government largesse is as strong. Yet the courts have already accorded a very high priority to the student's interest in higher education. Two decades ago the Supreme Court declared that one could not be excluded from college because he was black. The lower federal courts have uniformly held that a student may not be expelled from a public institution without a hearing that contains the rudiments of due process. In other judicial contexts—as disparate as the treatment of educational costs under separation and divorce agreements—the courts have been building a very firm foundation under the interest in higher learning. Most recently, several courts ordered that campuses closed during the events of May 1970 should be reopened or kept open to ensure an uninterrupted education for those who wished to study.

Perhaps, therefore, it is already too late in the day for courts to classify higher education at a tax-supported university with sport fishing licenses rather than with welfare benefits. Of course the newcomer who seeks higher education will not starve if his application is rejected. Yet the long-range consequences may be quite harsh for the nonresident who is turned away, especially for the student who seeks a curriculum or a degree not offered by the public university of his own state. Hence the "fundamental right of interstate movement" on which the Supreme Court premised the welfare decision may well be found by analogy in the student's case.

Moreover, the nonresident quotas and grade-point differentials are more drastic in one respect than welfare waiting periods. The welfare seeker who somehow survived his first year—living off private charity or the generosity of friends and relatives—became permanently eligible. By contrast, the Arizona or Oregon student who graduates from high school with a 3.2 average can never get into Berkeley or UCLA, at least not as a freshman. And the Michigan or Illinois resident who applies next fall to Madison after the 15 percent out-of-state quota has been filled is permanently barred—unless, of course, he is able to move to Wisconsin and delay matriculation for a whole year. Thus, even if the two interests were not as comparable in importance as they appear to be, these irreversible effects of nonresident barriers would bolster the analogy.

There is, however, another part to the equation. Before a state classification can be held to deny equal protection under the laws, the basis of the distinction must be critically assessed. In the welfare residence case, the Supreme Court concluded that neither the desire to conserve welfare funds nor the wish to get newcomers into the labor force as soon as possible justified the disparate treatment of residents and nonresidents. Here too the case in favor of the out-of-state student seems comparable. The indigent person who migrates to another state is likely to continue to need public support. The contribution he can make to his adopted state is minimal at best; he is never expected to repay past disbursements even if he later becomes self-supporting. Thus the decision that a state has no constitutionally valid interest in barring indigent migrants is tantamount to saying that the state must accept a potentially permanent drain on its resources because ours is a federal system in which mobility is more highly valued than economy.

The position of the nonresident student is wholly different. President Robben Fleming has recently shown how much and in how many ways such a student may contribute to the state where he attends college or graduate school.[12] In many instances, his higher tuition and fees will in fact cover the incremental costs of his education. Sometimes he will also bring a fellowship or scholarship that will more than pay his keep. If he remains in the state to teach or to practice his profession—as many do who initially migrate for educational reasons—his lifelong contribution may be incalculable. Meanwhile, residents of the state to which he goes may wish to study in the state from which he comes; the interest in reciprocity is hard to measure, but surely warrants a higher measure of hospitality than is generally found today in the public sector. For all these reasons, President Fleming has concluded that "the net effect of changing the mix to enroll fewer out-of-state students would simply be to make necessary larger appropriations of tax money for the operating budget." These arguments appear, however, to have been uniformly rejected by the legislatures of the major importing states. The only remaining forum of appeal is the courts.

Even if the admission of nonresidents did place a net drain upon the state's resources, it would be far from clear that the Constitution permits the kind of barriers that are now rising rapidly in the public sector. The strongest case can be made against fixed quotas and the grade-point differentials, for they permanently bar from the state's campuses even those nonresidents who are quite willing to pay the higher tuition and fees. The validity of tuition differentials is more problematical. Typically the barrier operates much like the welfare waiting period: for his first year the student is classed as a nonresident, but thereafter if he remains in the state he is

12. Robben W. Fleming, *The Exploding Education Picture and the Case for the Out-of-State Student* (Detroit, Mich.: Economic Club of Detroit, 1968).

entitled to resident status. Perhaps the best that can be said now is that the interests on both sides seem weaker here than in the welfare context: the claim of the excluded individual is less urgent, and the justification advanced by the state is less persuasive. It may be only a matter of time before barriers of all three types are found unconstitutional as the result of test suits that are already in the courts.

What, then, would be the eventual impact of these several trends upon patterns of access to higher education? In the public sector, the easing of interstate migration would make more geographically diverse a group of institutions that are becoming ethnically and racially heterogeneous— some of them, in fact, returning to a condition that once existed in both respects. For the private university, the consequences are harder to predict. The costly commitment to minority students will reduce geographical diversity unless the federal government assumes major responsibility for supporting that commitment. Yet the reduction of diversity need not impair the cosmopolitan character of these institutions unless it reaches drastic proportions. And who is to say that the racial mix achieved at the price of localization does not contribute more both to the university and to the white students who now come from closer by?

Quality

WILLIAM W. TURNBULL

Dimensions of Quality in Higher Education

AMERICAN HIGHER EDUCATION IN THE DECADE JUST PAST HAS SURVIVED its greatest quantitative challenge, only to be plunged into a qualitative crisis without precedent. The wave of despair and disorder sweeping campuses in the spring of 1970 has no parallel in our history. The issues are embedded deep in the purposes of education and in the roles of its institutions in a society of pervasive and rapid change.

The facts of quantity are familiar: a student body that has doubled in a decade—an increase which, as Kerr has pointed out, equals the total growth of the preceding three centuries.[1] And a similar number of new students will be added to the enrollment in the 1970s. Today, some 45 percent of all eighteen-year-olds enroll in undergraduate programs offering degree credit, compared with 35 percent just a decade ago.

The rising percentage of the age group proceeding beyond high school poses obvious questions of possible change taking place in the mix of students on campus. Who are the "new" students? Where are they coming from, and with what kind of preparation? And what effect will they have on the "quality" of higher education?

QUALITY IN THE LARGER SYSTEM OF INSTITUTIONS

By 1960, 80 percent of students in the top quarter of their high school class were going on to college. The proportions from succeeding quarters were 54 percent, 32 percent, and—from the lowest quarter of the class— 19 percent. By 1960, then, we had begun to approach the ceiling on the proportion of the academically talented students (as defined by high school performance) who go to college. The expansion in the proportion of students continuing beyond high school is now occurring mainly in the second, third, and fourth ability groups.[2]

Higher education, then, is serving a new clientele along with the old. For many observers, the conclusion is that "quality is dropping," with the drop accelerated by institutional plans such as open enrollment. The specter haunting many a faculty member, not to mention an alum-

1. Clark Kerr, "New Challenges to the College and University," in *Agenda for the Nation*, ed. Kermit Gordon (Washington: Brookings Institution, 1968), p. 237.
2. W. W. Turnbull, "Relevance in Testing," *Science*, June 28, 1968, pp. 1424–29.

nus, confronting statistics like these, is of each campus inundated by new students of mediocre talents or worse, dragging American educational standards "in the dust." In such a vision of the results of open enrollment, the focus is on the individual college or university, and the assumption made is that open enrollment will become the policy of each institution.

The term "open enrollment" does imply that the individual campus will do what it can to encourage the matriculation of a sizable number of students of all economic and ethnic backgrounds who would have been discouraged in previous years, especially students who, without encouragement, might drop out of formal education for lack of money or lack of interest rather than lack of ability. The commitment of a number of institutions to this ideal is a new phenomenon.

"Open enrollment," in a different sense, has been approached by some state systems so that theoretically any high school graduate has been able to gain admission to an institution within his state. Where places were scarce, however, the open admissions principle has been modified to require higher standing. In some state systems, moreover, to qualify for entrance to certain of the institutions, a student has had to show a record of high grades in secondary school and thus, through some form of master plan, the state has maintained an academic hierarchy among its colleges and universities.

To a degree, the unregulated academic marketplace without master planning has given rise to a panorama of institutions that overall have provided relatively unimpeded entrance to all who could afford a higher education. Figures cited earlier indicated that, in 1960, 19 percent of high school students graduating in the lowest quarter of the class went on to college—a figure roughly the same as in 1950.[3] It has been commonly observed that there is a college place for any high school graduate *who could pay his way*—an important qualification. What we are discussing, then, is not the appearance on the higher educational scene of ability groups hitherto unrepresented: for many years students from the lowest quarter in secondary school have been going to college. Rather, we are now seeing a relative increase in the number of such students in higher education as a whole and their appearance on particular campuses where, until now, they have been represented only nominally, if at all. As individual institutions reshape their admissions policies to remove barriers of cost and to seek diversity in race and social class among their entrants, they are bringing about a concomitant change in the distribution of academic ability across institutions.

3. Ibid.

The question becomes whether each institution should try to provide a diversity of learning opportunities to match the diversity of talents and interests represented in its freshman class, or whether there should remain a substantial degree of specialization among institutions, for either philosophical or practical reasons. Do we want a diversity of institutions, each with relatively homogeneous people, as in the past? If so, the student sorting that has hitherto taken place through self-selection and admissions screening will presumably have to be achieved through high failure rates. Or do we want a more homogeneous set of all-purpose institutions, each with open enrollment and a commitment to try to provide a useful educational experience to all entrants? This option presupposes a remarkable broadening of the offerings of most institutions, with financial results that might well be unsupportable.

It might be argued that we could avoid the dilemma, that we could retain institutional diversity and combine it with open enrollment. The supposition would be that students (with guidance) would then choose their destinations. If they found their needs were not being met, they could transfer.

The first problem with this arrangement is that it might buy student freedom at too high a price in student satisfaction. Guidance is not strong enough in most places to do the job well. In the absence of extraordinary steps to give these students supporting and supplementary training and lighter course loads, the result would likely be higher failure rates, widespread student discontent with their programs, and high dropout rates.[4] The second problem is one of resources. How does a college with ten applicants for every matriculant practice open admissions? And thereafter, how does it maintain both its special character and its humane treatment of individuals?

If we want to maintain variety in postsecondary institutions, we may be forced to seek the answer in cooperating groups of unlike colleges that agree to maintain diversity and to work closely among themselves and with their students to make a heterogeneous system operate successfully. The state system of higher education may keep access to the system as a whole open to any secondary school graduate within the state, but with the proviso that the state may stipulate some broad-band qualifications for enrolling at institutions that are set up to foster particular kinds of learning. It might be possible to devise a similar arrangement through a consortium of private or combination of public and private institutions.

4. Alexander W. Astin, "Racial Considerations in Admissions," in *The Campus and the Racial Crisis*, ed. David C. Nichols and Olive Mills (Washington: American Council on Education, 1970), documents the relation of college GPA to voluntary dropout in addition to academic failure. Dropout is less highly correlated with predictive measures (test scores, school grades) than is college GPA.

Transfer among institutions within the consortium could be made routine. In this way, perhaps both institutional diversity and open enrollment could be preserved for complexes of institutions even though not for the individual, unaffiliated college. Inherent in the model, however, is acceptance of institutional specialization or patterning, which might be taken to imply a hierarchy of excellence and relegation of some students to institutions of lower quality. The basis for this concern may rest to a large extent in our historical view of quality as one-dimensional. We need to see other dimensions, which can be fostered within any institution. And we need to strive for a recognition, outside the academic community as well as inside, of the reality and increasingly critical nature of those dimensions.

Quality in the Individual Institution

The functions of a college or university may be discussed under the headings (arbitrary and overlapping, to be sure) of teaching, research, and service,[5] and controversies about quality rage within all three categories.

Teaching and learning: scholastic criteria

Traditionally, first thoughts about "quality" relate to the depth of teaching and learning that takes place on campus, most particularly in the academic disciplines. We, as a nation, have taken justifiable pride in the number of colleges and universities remarkable for the depth of scholarship of their faculties and of their students, who have gone on to become the core of the professional life of the country. The quality they represent might be termed "scholastic" inasmuch as it relates both to academic accomplishment and to the historical foundations of the modern university.

The most common indices of scholastic quality have been related to the selectivity of the institution at time of student admission; proportions of students from the top quarter of the class, level of admissions test scores, proportion of National Merit Scholars, and the like.

Choosing high-performance high school students has been a royal road to scholastic quality. At college entrance, the matriculants already know more than most of the graduates of other collegiate institutions. They think like the faculty, hence are a joy to teach, and make the institution attractive to scholars elsewhere. Institutional quality has meant academic talent in students, which has been quickly translated into all the concomitant marks of prestige in higher education.

Another traditional index of quality has been the learning exhibited by the collegiate graduating class. A university whose graduates go on to the

5. James A. Perkins, *The University in Transition* (Princeton, N.J.: Princeton University Press, 1966).

most selective graduate and professional schools, win high awards, and receive high-salaried jobs, enjoys a national reputation for academic excellence. Such indices of "exit achievement" correspond closely with the academic ability of the entering class.

The typical "exit achievement" of graduates, it should be noted, is widely different at different colleges and universities. The scholarship represented by the baccalaureate degree varies enormously among institutions, and the baccalaureate has many different levels of meaning in this country. If one looks at the performance of seniors on standardized examinations of academic achievement given in a reasonably varied sample of American colleges, it is clear that the lowest-scoring students in highly selective institutions would be at the top of the list in some four-year colleges and universities. This fact is unknown to, or ignored by, most of those who deplore the imminent decline of "the standard" represented by the bachelor's degree.

In principle, as already noted, any institution that so desired could move to open admissions with no change whatsoever in the standard of performance represented by its degree simply by flunking out large numbers of those who performed poorly in the traditional courses. Such an approach can buy quality in one sense, but there are those who would question any assertion that the institution was "better" than one that retained more students and gave them the opportunity to learn. A single institution of the latter variety is likely to find itself, over time, awarding baccalaureate degrees to people of widely varied accomplishment and thereby representing within its own graduating classes a broader cross section of the kinds of students already gaining a degree credential from institutions across the country.

Stretching the single credential to cover so many meanings may be a questionable practice, whether the variation in meaning runs across institutions or occurs within an institution. Should the degree be annotated to indicate the accomplishment it represents? Perhaps the answer depends on the function the degree is meant to serve. In the case of the professional degree, the function of proving competence to practice the profession is frequently invoked (and yet this certifying function has been passed increasingly to professional boards external to the institutions). The function of the baccalaureate credential today, other than its social labeling function and its function in providing personal satisfaction, is much less obvious. It is a passport to graduate study, but graduate schools have devised their own methods, through transcripts and examinations of accomplishment, to annotate the baccalaureate. The nonacademic world may want a similar accounting of a degree's meaning for any situation in which undergraduate accomplishment bears a valid relation to some career opportunity.

Even the best-annotated A.B., although it would speak to the attainment of quality by the student, would leave open the question of how much of the responsibility for his accomplishment could be attributed to the institution. The standard represented by summing up the "exit achievement" of all members of a graduating class similarly leaves unanswered the question of where credit is owed. A more defensible index of *institutional* quality would be the extent of the learning that took place during the years of a student's enrollment: the criterion of student growth or "value added." This criterion would recognize the institution's effectiveness as an agent of change rather than of either astute selection or discriminating elimination. In terms of "value added," selective universities as citadels of *learning* may be enjoying inflated prestige. There may be more growth, more "value added," in some struggling institutions whose students do not come well endowed either academically or economically. The question is how much the students change between entrance and graduation.[6]

The importance of the "value added" criterion leads to the institution's responsibility for teaching and learning. Clearly, a college adopting such a philosophy would accord greater value to evidence of results than to the completion of stages such as time spent on campus and courses completed. It would want to work with each student in defining his goals, devising alternative ways of reaching them, and establishing guideposts to mark his progress. Flexibility would characterize its calendar and its procedures. The degree would attest to an individual's final level of attainment, but evidence of the change brought about in students, rather than of their completion of requirements, would be the basis for the institution's satisfaction with its performance.

Still, the question remains, "What kind of change?" Traditional indices of quality suggest the answer: "Intellectual, of course." Quality, then, has typically been considered as scholastic progress: the greater the academic development, the higher the quality. There is more to the story.

Teaching and learning: secular criteria

If indeed students now come to college with a broader range of talents and goals than before, it may be instructive to move our focus from the institution's established program to the abilities and concerns of the stu-

6. Discussion of this concept, and empirical data relating to it, will be found in Alexander Astin, "Undergraduate Achievement and Institutional 'Excellence,'" *Science*, Aug. 16, 1968, pp. 661–68; and in Donald A. Rock, John A. Centra, and Robert L. Linn, "Relationships between College Characteristics and Student Achievement," *American Educational Research Journal*, January 1970, pp. 109–21.

dents as they perceive their needs and those of society. To the familiar "scholastic" criteria it may be desirable to add others derived more immediately from the outer world and its demands. Perhaps, then, institutional quality has a "secular" as well as a scholastic dimension. How broad is the array of student abilities, needs, and aspirations that the college is ready to recognize, and how well is it prepared to cope with them? It may be argued that insofar as an institution seeks diversity in its student body, it should be prepared to match that diversity with its courses of study. Such a secular goal, coupled with the aim of maximizing growth in each segment of the learning program, might be proposed as a worthy objective for any institution that wants to accommodate a diverse student body.

The secular criteria, however, are much more encompassing. The case for ends beyond scholarship has been stated by Pusey:

> Despite our long involvement in professional education it can be said that rational analysis and reserved judgment, the scholar's concerns, used to be our predominant, if not our almost exclusive preoccupation. Such qualities of mind ought always to be nurtured here. But now everywhere one turns within the University, among faculty as well as students, one senses a widening impatience with narrow scholasticism, that kind of scholarship which exists for its own sake. There grows among us, instead, a deeply-held conviction that it is not sufficient to pursue knowledge for itself, but that somehow knowledge must be put to work for moral, social, and political ends. What is wanted is an education which will recognize this and help to make it possible.[7]

The overwhelming message from campuses across the country is that higher education must go beyond scholarship and take as its aims the nurturing of social concern, involvement, and dedication. Here, indeed, is still another secular dimension of quality: its power to engender commitment. A campus may be characterized by its "climate" in respect to this and a host of other criteria: its respect for student self-direction, its provision for democratic self-governance, its sense of shared purpose and high morale, its respect for expanding and transmitting human knowledge, the strength of ethical belief and intention carried away by those who have been touched by it.

In this area lie some of the key distinctions and sharp issues between traditional and radical factions on campus. The differences center on the kinds of values to be sought, the actual effect the college is exerting on values, and the means by which values should be developed or fostered. In the view of many people, the whole university community should be the center of inquiry and debate about the great issues of the age, a center

7. Nathan M. Pusey, *Harvard University: The President's Report* (Cambridge, Mass.: 1970).

of constructive dissent from, and criticism of, the present social order, an institution sensitive and responsive to the significant movements in the nation and the world. In this view, the concept of a discipline-bound curriculum, a classical teaching technique, and a limited enrollment would define a failure of teaching and learning rather than high quality. The question of what is important to learn is the central and unresolved issue.

Teaching and learning, then, provide not one but several dimensions of quality. There are two other institutional purposes that may be drawn upon in the definition: research on the one hand, and service to the community on the other.

Research

Productive scholarship is the time-honored hallmark by which faculty (and particularly graduate faculty) recognize quality. The definitive summing-up of scholarly opinion has been provided by Cartter.[8] Although his report refers specifically to graduate education, the spill-over of recognition extends to the institution at large. The technique of relying on a graduate department's reputation in the academic world as an index of scholarly quality may not be wholly satisfying, but the results are highly indicative of an important segment of opinion. It would follow closely (or lead) an institutional index of federal grants for research. Its ratings would, one suspects, correlate closely with the indices of scholastic quality noted for the student body.

Just as there is a secular dimension to teaching and learning, so is there a secular dimension to research, and it may well receive increasingly insistent attention as an index of quality. As the flaws in the human condition become more achingly apparent, and as the growth in our capacity to blow ourselves off the planet seems in a race against our efforts to make earth unlivable, it is hard to say that research on any problem is as "good" as on any other. Would it be worthwhile to define an index of quality based on the probability that an institution's research output will better man's lot, and do so within the time that is likely to be available to us if the problems are not solved? [9] Such a question calls up such thorny issues as competing priorities of basic and applied research, of science and poetry, and also legitimate differences of opinion about the timetable of human events. But when the survival of our society and our world may be at stake, the secular dimension of research assumes overriding importance for all of us.

The importance of the secular dimension can be seen in the relation between research and teaching, as research informs and shapes teaching

8. Allan Cartter, *An Assessment of Quality in Graduate Education* (Washington: American Council on Education, 1966).
9. John Platt, "What We Must Do," *Science*, Nov. 28, 1969, pp. 1115–21.

and learning and as students and faculty work together to relate the business of the institution to the betterment of the world. Whether or not the aim of the research and teaching is visibly to enlarge man's chances and his humanity *does* make a difference in the real engagement of many students and consequently in what will be learned.

Service to the larger community

A final criterion of an institution's quality is the extent of its contribution to the community of which it is a part. Here the secular dimension is self-evident. As Enarson has said:

> Just possibly some institution of the higher learning in this nation is indifferent to its community obligation and only vaguely aware of demands that colleges and universities unleash their immense intellectual resources in an all-out assault on the problems of urban America. It seems unlikely. Stung by the goading of critics, the conscience of the academic community has been aroused, and in small towns and big cities our institutions are searching for ways to be "part of the action." And action there is—restless action that walks and runs and marches, sometimes timidly and sometimes recklessly, in all directions.[10]

The "community" of which the college or university is part may, of course, be seen as its immediate geographic environment. Almost all people would concede the institution's obligation to apply a high standard of civic and social responsibility in the way it conducts its affairs, although clearly this obligation has not always been discharged. But what is the institution's obligation to mount an active program to improve the quality of life around it? Are we to stand on a principle of scholarly detachment and disengagement? Or does the university have a duty to put its resources at the service of the host community? If the latter, how can it do so? The university's traditional organization by academic discipline virtually paralyzes it in the face of community ills that cut across scholarly fields. Should the institution match the real-world problems by organizing action-oriented "missions" through which the relevant disciplines can be brought to bear in community action programs?[11] And if the college or university opts for involvement in solving the community's problems, who is to define those problems and guide the processes of "improvement"? The contrast between academic freedom in scholarly pursuits and the sharp restraints on freedom of action when a university would seek to ameliorate community needs is a lesson that apparently must be relearned by each institution for itself in its own circumstances.

10. Harold L. Enarson, "Higher Education and Community Services," in *The Campus and the Racial Crisis,* pp. 126–39.
11. An interdisciplinary program of this kind is in effect at the University of Wisconsin's Green Bay campus.

We have been considering the institution's service to the proximate community—usually urban—but the perimeter of concern may be widened to the nation and beyond. Here the distinction between "research" and "service" is particularly hard to maintain. In the years since World War II, for example, the university's obligation to cooperate with the national government in research was largely taken for granted and the opportunity eagerly welcomed. But with the country deeply divided over the government's military decisions, the easy assumption of proper partnership was shattered as powerful voices in the academic community—faculty, students, and administration—cried out against any liaison through research that would support the aims of a governmental leadership that they felt was engaged in violating global decency. Thus, at a minimum, they distinguished between service to the nation and service to its government. Further, they have called upon their institutions to take activist positions in causes they see as contributing to social justice. For many people on today's campus, the concept of a university aloof from the human social, political, and economic crises of the day, on a global scale, is anathema. For them, the community to be served is the world.

Where the mission of the college or university is the primary unresolved issue, no question of quality can be addressed apart from the larger philosophy. That this philosophy must embrace respect for the secular dimensions of quality is being affirmed resoundingly in the wake of tragic convulsions on campus after campus, and often with greatest fervor in those institutions whose reputations have historically been gained through their scholastic eminence. The great problem is to define and strengthen the secular function without destroying the scholastic values in the process. The institution that can reconcile its many constituent voices with respect to the secular values to be served will best harmonize its functions of teaching, research, and service.

How does the issue of open enrollment relate to institutional quality in its secular dimensions? One may well question whether high quality—including breadth in that term—can be achieved by an institution or system of institutions that limits enrollment in such a way as to restrict sharply the representation in its student or faculty of any distinctive segment of those it aspires to teach and to serve. An institution or system of institutions that does so will face the herculean task of avoiding one-sided definitions of its purposes and narrow solutions to the problems it chooses to address.

Our concern is not, of course, simply with the learning that takes place within institutional walls. As educators, we are devoted to enlarging and deepening the learning of an entire people, in school and out, young and old, formal and informal. Our foremost responsibility, however, and the one to which this paper has been confined, is the primary responsibility of our institutions and organized systems to define and seek quality in all its legitimate dimensions.

We may look to history for the trends and precedents that will help us predict what dimensions of quality will be sought in the future in this country. But though it is useful to predict what will happen, it is more important to decide what we think ought to happen and take steps to bring it about. As McHale has said:

> There is . . . no future other than as we will it to be. If we conceive of a future state as desirable, we tend to orient ourselves toward it and to initiate the courses of action necessary to its attainment. Of course, willing a future connotes more than wishful thinking; it involves an action-oriented commitment to the future in ways that transcend past constraints and present obstacles. The latter are often more apparent than real in our current affairs, where lip service to change is the norm that conceals even the strongest investments in the status quo.[12]

Measurement and Relevance

EDWARD J. BLOUSTEIN

My comments are directed at some of the assumptions and presuppositions of Mr. Turnbull's paper, rather than at its conclusions.

1. I have the uneasy feeling that Mr. Turnbull's paper may be missing the point about "quality" in higher education for the reason that he seems to assume that "to be is to be measured." Without entering into the metaphysical question of whether nature is measurable in all its aspects, I feel that most of the measures of quality Turnbull adduces—percentages of high-ranking secondary school graduates, percentages of award winners, percentages of entrants into graduate schools, scores on achievement tests, and the like—are inadequate criteria of educational quality.

Although more adequate measures may not be available, even the best available may simply be inadequate to the task of identifying educational quality. I am not, of course, opposed to using such yardsticks as we have, but simply have doubts about their ultimate significance and warn against confusing such crude measurements with a satisfactory assessment of educational quality.

12. John McHale, *The Future of the Future* (New York: George Braziller, Inc.).

2. Another weakness in Turnbull's paper—or perhaps it is the same weakness in another guise—is that he seems to place exclusive attention on the educational product to the neglect of the educational process. What is most important about higher education is not what a student gets, but how he gets it. The experience of learning, rather than what is learned, turns out to be the most significant aspect of a college education, and what really distinguishes the better from the mediocre educational institutions is the nature of the learning experience rather than, in Turnbull's sense, "value added" as the product of learning.

What I am talking about are such characteristics as a skeptical turn of mind, intellectual detachment, wariness of all forms of provincialism, a love of the scholar's, artist's, or scientist's craft, attachment to humane values, respect for cultural diversity and a sense of the appropriate roles of reason and emotion in the life of man. It is these characteristics of the cultivated man that I look to the college and university to foster, and it is in these terms that I assess the quality of an institution.

3. In another sense, the process rather than the product is of crucial importance in assessing educational quality. I believe that our best educational institutions are those in which education is a rewarding experience in itself, rather than solely or predominantly a preparation for life. In the concern of many colleges and universities to be relevant and to fulfill, in Turnbull's sense, their "secular" mission, I fear they have neglected the importance to students and to the educational community generally of the immediate satisfactions of learning and teaching and researching.

This neglect takes place in subtle ways, in changes in a climate of opinion, in tone, and in attitude, but it has profound effects. Many undergraduate colleges have become preparatory schools for graduate education and for vocational achievement and have thereby lost their excitement and vitality as centers of culture and thought. One consequence has been that students and faculty alike have lost their emotional attachment to, and their sense of fulfillment in, undergraduate education. Another consequence—one which smacks of paradox—is that the more a college commits itself to graduate and vocational preparation, the less well it prepares its students for graduate education or for vocations. The best collegiate preparation turns out to be no preparation at all; or, to state the same thought without the overtones of paradox, a college that conceives of its role as a center of learning, and stresses the immediate satisfactions of its academic fare, does a much better job of preparing its students for the future than one which dedicates itself to preparing its students for the future.

4. Now a more general point concerning Turnbull's paper. One of the distinctions running through the paper is that between the academic

and secular missions of the college and university. The distinction he is making, as I understand it, is between the institution fulfilling its own ends in obtaining a high level of achievement among its students and a high level of research and scholarship among its faculty, as compared with the institution fulfilling social needs, that is, educating a student body with diverse needs and abilities and helping to remedy a variety of social ills. The point is that this distinction is an invidious and misleading one. If the academic goals of the institution do not fulfill a valued social purpose, they must fail as academic goals, no less than as measures of secular success. That which is of only academic significance is not really of significance, academic or otherwise. Any academic value must be translatable into the coin of social value or it should not stand as an academic value.

The important distinction one must make is not between academic and secular values, but between a shorter and longer historical range and perspective of time in terms of which academic values are to be assessed. The contemporary demand for relevance and fulfillment of the college's secular mission must be met, not simply by asserting or denying that it has such a mission, but rather by distinguishing between shorter and longer term social benefits which accrue from the pursuit of academic excellence. There are areas of our traditional learning which are socially sterile and unrewarding, which are academic in the pejorative sense. They deserve to be rooted out of the curriculum. There are, however, large segments of traditional learning which have no immediate relevance to the social problems which face us, but which are nevertheless vital to the abiding interests of our culture. This body of learning must not be sacrificed to the political exigencies of our time.

"Relevance," in other words, is a relative term, and in assessing the relevance of academic study, one must ask whether it is relevant to anyone, for any purpose, and over what period of time. Simply to ask whether or not it is relevant is senseless, in the strict sense of the word.

5. Although it is unfashionable to say so in these days of student demands and turmoil, it is of utmost importance to reassert that colleges and universities exist to serve the needs and purposes of their faculties, no less than those of students and society. To be sure, many faculty members have misused their positions and made a mockery of their professional obligations. We must not overreact to their failings, however, and thereby neglect their legitimate interests in the academic community. The quality of colleges and universities must be assessed according to the extent to which they satisfy these interests as well as those of our students and society. In fact, colleges and universities can only serve students and society well if they serve the faculty well.

Quality and Inequality for Black Americans

ELIAS BLAKE, JR.

TURNBULL'S DISCUSSION OF QUALITY in higher education is remarkably conservative in its analysis of the relationship between so-called varieties of "academically talented" students and quality. The paper is trapped within what can be called elitist assumptions: (1) Those who have been getting into the system are the correct people; by their performance they deserve to be there more than others. (2) Those who do not get into the system have defects or handicaps that make them less able to compete. (3) If too many of those now excluded get in, the system will be damaged, especially the "high quality" components. (4) Thus, one must create new alternatives for the new people, reserving places in the old system for those who have always gone into it.

The current social arrangements having developed from acceptance of these assumptions makes them all the more powerful. The higher the quality of the university, the more its products are found in seats of power and influence in the public and private sector. Those, however, who are outside the prevailing social arrangements, and doubt that they can abide being a part of them as they are, must press for a different analysis of the quality question. In this light, the following points need to be made.

Some other assumptions

Black Americans must reject the initial assumption of Mr. Turnbull's paper that there actually is less academic talent among those students not in the top 25 percent of the test score distributions or grades. To accept that assumption comes dangerously close to accepting racial inferiority, inasmuch as few blacks, Mexican-Americans, Indians, or Puerto Ricans are in that top quarter of "academically talented" students.

The enrollment of blacks and other nonwhites should be a separate issue from "higher education for everybody." The problem of blacks getting into college is not a function of a larger proportion beyond the earlier, "normal" proportions attending college (from 43 percent of the age group to more than half of the age group). The implication that the best talent has gone on to college in high proportions does not apply. No level of academic talent among blacks has been fairly represented in higher education. Actually, the poor functioning of the precollege system for nonwhites makes grade and test distributions an impossible means of accurate assessment of the *true* ability for academic performance.

There is an underlying issue of the moral quality of a system of higher education that has always been exclusionary along racial lines. White colleges and universities have been neither a neutral or positive force for racial equality, but rather a negative force. The words of the universities have, until the last three years, masked inaction and acceptance of the rightness of the selection and admission system. And the words were usually from individuals who were *not* moving to change the system of admissions or to develop greater responsibility for the teaching and learning of previously excluded groups.

Colleges and universities are part of a dysfunctional system for achieving racial equity in education (that is, equal levels of attainment, not just opportunity). They cannot stand apart from the racial inequities in the precollege system run by persons they trained. The Turnbull paper assumes the system is basically functional and leaves untouched the responsibilities of the older, most prestigious system of higher education that now, in 1970, creates this dialogue about new options. New options can mean simply that the old system will remain intact and thus escape responsibility for the teaching and learning of unfairly excluded groups.

Diversity means more than differences in student ability and interest groups. An institution that has a significant minority of blacks, Mexican-Americans, Indians, and Puerto Ricans from the top 25 percent of the score distribution must also change. Basic assumptions about civilization, culture, and aesthetic judgments inherent in the heavily Western-oriented curriculum must yield to a more diverse and accurate view of non-Western alternatives.

The current high-quality institutions are unlikely to meet the challenges implied in the above points in the near future, if ever. Alternative subgroups of institutions should, then, be developed into "high quality" institutions that do not accept the assumptions about various quartiles of ability. Thus, quality will reside heavily in the area of "value-added" to the entering performance of students from previously excluded student groupings. Some predominantly black colleges are prime candidates for such development inasmuch as they have fewer allegiances to the status quo in selection and admission. A mark of quality will be the extent to which performance in the precollege system does *not* predict performance in the college system. A large part of the research for this system will deal with the applications of technology and science to the problems of poverty and with knowledge of the role of motivation in the academic performance of the poor and the black.

Universities as a negative force in educational equity

In discussing secular criteria for quality as opposed to scholastic criteria, Turnbull overlooks some factors that bear on the impact of university "research" in the areas of education, psychology, and sociology. Much of the thinking about why blacks are not being educated flows from these institutions. The theorists of "disadvantage" come dangerously close to being apologists for massive institutional failures. There is virtually no research on the characteristics and bases of success, and thus new solutions are based on a prior reasoning versus empirical analyses. Yet the interplay between prestigious university professors and social policy-makers enables their solutions to be translated into reality in such programs as those labeled "community involvement," "performance contracting," and "voucher systems." They say they put these forward *because* of the massive failure to date. But the institutions where these new ideas originate are in no way as radical as the ideas in responding to the greater educational needs of able but poorly educated black youth. To date, the institutions are interested only in the small number of able and well-educated black youth.

Universities and colleges as part of a dysfunctional system

If one assumes that equal ability distributions exist in white and black youth, then instructional systems should be possible that would carry black youth through the most rigorous academic program. Rather than flunking out large numbers of nonwhites, the system would surface their abilities and develop them. In such a system it does not follow that the quality of a degree would decline. At any rate, what different people do now to earn their degrees, even in the most selective schools, sharply varies from mediocre to excellent.

It is the responsibility of higher education to deal with educating black youth who are turned out by a precollege system that it dominates through its training of teachers. To ignore the culpability of the old colleges as one discusses new options is to let them escape their responsibility to redress grievances. Again, this matter is a separate issue from the so-called expansion of the higher education population.

Dealing with this problem is a danger to the established system only if it does not perceive itself as a part of the larger dysfunctional educational system, for then its functioning is perceived as in no need of major readjustment. Other parts will change (precollege) and new options will develop (community colleges, technical schools) to deal with the problem of race and class. Since a natural process did not create the problem, natural evolutions are unlikely to make the necessary readjustments.

Diversity as more than students from different quartiles

An institution that has been 99 percent white in faculty and student population may not be able to absorb without change a 15–20 percent black, Mexican-American, Indian, and Puerto Rican population even if they have the highest possible test scores and grades. If significant numbers believe in the value of their distinctive heritage, there will be change or conflict. Who will work with them as they try to reject the pervasive white-Western-civilization-is-right dominance in a college or university? Nothing in the current reactions to small numbers of black youth indicates an effective reaction to this more complex problem. Will the problem be delivered over to the Ethnic Studies Department and leave the main line curriculum, dominated by senior scholars, intact? That is the most likely possibility.

A source of new quality in higher education

The predominantly black colleges have made the only stand against the tide of exclusive admissions criteria and a rigid system of instruction, unmindful of the weaknesses of their students. They could not use weaknesses in preparation as the standard by which students were eliminated. Such a standard only intensifies past injustice and educational neglect. Were the criterion of "value added" employed, this subgroup of colleges would likely be rated as of high quality. Some of the institutions can achieve highest quality also by the conventional criteria of faculty scholarship and research, and at the same time demonstrate that the undeveloped abilities of entering freshmen need not be viewed as conflicting with the quality of the degree achieved. Support for such a view is unlikely, however, unless much greater leverage for funds is generated among the poor and the nonwhites in the public and private sector. The conventional view of money being bestowed on the most selective schools for whatever educational or social goal is hard to break down. Support will come only by intense pressure from new groups not now benefiting from the current allocation of national resources for higher education.

Quality and the Black Student

VIVIAN W. HENDERSON

My comments will focus on black higher education as it relates to the dimensions of quality considered by Mr. Turnbull and emphasize two issues. The first is the role of predominantly Negro institutions in providing education for black youth, the worth of these institutions, and their future. The second is the question of what education should be offered to black youth, and where it should be offered.

One cannot speak of these issues outside their context. Growth in technology and the increasing dependence of society on the use and control of information require higher and higher levels of education for individual success. At the same time, black migration to urban areas— first to the North and now increasingly to Southern cities—has created centers in which social conflict and the maldistribution of benefits and burdens among the haves and the have-nots is increasing, but without the improvements in education which might ameliorate the evils. The national response has been a commitment to make equal educational opportunity a reality for all. Fulfilling the commitment will require adequate resources and the extension of opportunity particularly to the economically and educationally victimized ("disadvantaged")—the members of minority groups.

Colleges, responsible for carrying out a large share of this commitment, are already under other pressures from their students, who have developed into a special class of citizens, distinct from other members of society, with aims and objectives peculiar to themselves. Among their demands on colleges are a multitude of educational reforms, including open enrollments and the active participation of colleges in the improvement of their communities.

How do these circumstances relate to black colleges, black students, and the question of quality?

For well over a hundred years, black colleges have been the major resource for educating black youth in America. In recent years, the proportions have changed, and today about 45 percent of the 400,000 black students are enrolled in other than the traditional black colleges. Nevertheless, black colleges and universities still graduate about 75 percent of all black youth with baccalaureate degrees.

The discrepancy between enrollment and graduation percentages returns us to the two issues of what institutions and what educational programs are suitable for our black youth. There is no question that many black youth have imbalances in their preparation for college and fall educationally into the category of the "disadvantaged." As the Negro colleges have shown, however, substantial numbers of them can succeed in college and in later life. Thus, any standard of quality that excludes them from admission to college may preclude their success in society. The essential first condition is some form of open enrollment (to which I shall return in a moment).

For the college—whatever its predominant racial mix—the admission of disadvantaged students raises the question whether abstract standards of accomplishment (for example, Dr. Turnbull's "scholastic" criteria) should take precedence over standards based on individual need, motivation, and development ("secular" criteria). The statistics cited above suggest that the black colleges have been far readier than others to adopt secular criteria and to adapt their programs in ways that ensure the success of poorly prepared students.

The historical commitment of black colleges to special efforts for the educationally disadvantaged has, of course, created stereotypes in the minds of many, including established scholars. Most of the stereotypes equate black colleges with disadvantaged students and low quality, and carry overtones of racial inferiority. The stereotypes adversely affect the colleges, their students, and their graduates, as is evident in employment patterns, the distribution of training programs, the award of government and foundation grants, and in the common notion that black institutions are incapable of serving white students.

Nevertheless, for the black colleges to abandon the use of secular criteria and special programs in order to obtain the benefits that these stereotypes deny them is neither possible nor desirable. Instead, I suggest that the predominantly white institutions must adopt open enrollment and provide the required special programs for the disadvantaged.

Resistance to open enrollment is usually based on the assumption that quality education will be diminished and standards lowered. Spiro T. Agnew, in his April 3, 1970, Denver speech, based his unresearched attack on this assumption.[1] In fact, my own basic inclination is to look with disfavor on open enrollments.

But the facts do not support me. Open enrollment is not a new phenomenon in American higher education, nor is it now inflicting on colleges and universities educational burdens that they are "not equipped to handle." Several of our largest state educational systems of higher education have for years been operating what is essentially a policy of open enrollment. For that matter, many private four-year colleges have somehow been able to "handle" substantial numbers of students in the lowest ability ranges. Thus, open enrollment poses not a question of quality but of quantity: a larger proportion of seemingly low-ability students, rather than some new breed of "unqualified" students.

Furthermore, the intellectual development of the bright student, contrary to myth, is not impeded if he attends a relatively unselective college, nor is the development of the less able student adversely affected if he attends a highly selective college with an appropriate program.

Negro colleges give us the best—but not the only—evidence for these assertions.[2] For years, they have offered excellent education to both the

1. "Responses to 'Spiro T. Agnew on College Admissions,'" *College Board Review,* Summer 1970. Statements by Alexander W. Astin, Kenneth S. Washington, Herbert R. Coursen, Jr., Fred E. Crossland, Whitney M. Young, Jr., and R. M. Fleming.
2. Vivian W. Henderson, "The Role of Predominantly Negro Institutions," *Journal of Negro Education,* Summer 1967, pp. 266–73.

"unqualified" and the "losers," to the demonstrable benefit of both and of society. Their readiness to serve a clientele unhappily burdened with poor preparation but with the ability for success in higher education needs no apology. They have already demonstrated the appropriateness of Dr. Turnbull's suggestion that higher education for everybody will require secular as well as scholastic criteria of quality.

If the national commitment to equal educational opportunity is ever to be fulfilled, all institutions—not just the Negro colleges and a few other institutions—will have to adopt both kinds of criteria. As we in the black colleges have demonstrated, the expansion of criteria can be adopted without jeopardizing the success of any student.

Accreditation: A Means of Determining Quality

FRANK G. DICKEY

WHEN THE TURBULENT mid-twentieth century period is appraised in historical perspective, major significance may be attached to the national and international recognition of education as a means to security and survival. Thomas Jefferson, attaching great political importance to education, spoke eloquently of the need for a literate populace in order that our democratic form of government might be safeguarded. Until recent years, however, higher education in this country has been considered largely in the context of its importance to the welfare and success of the individual. It remained for the present age to demonstrate with dramatic effectiveness the imperative role of education as a means of social advancement and national survival, as well as individual development. The sweep of events on international, national, regional, and local levels during the past several years, reflecting profound cultural changes, largely accounts for the new reliance upon education as an instrument of social change. Obviously, when education is viewed as a vital element in social change, the concepts of quality in education take on new dimensions.

Perhaps the most significant contribution of Mr. Turnbull's paper is the attention given to the criterion of "value added" in the assessment of quality, for only when institutions recognize their responsibility for determining evidences of "change" rather than merely the "completion of courses" can quality be significantly improved.

Although Mr. Turnbull presents a wide variety of problems in his discussion of dimensions of quality in higher education, it is surprising that he makes no mention of accreditation as one of the more prevalent means of assessing quality in our educational institutions. He may have decided to omit this approach to quality assessment because accreditation, as it is currently operating, does not provide sufficiently valid information regarding the real heart of the educational endeavor, namely, the instructional program itself.

Unlike most other nations of the world, the United States has no ministry of education or other centralized authority that imposes quality controls on educational institutions. The states and other political units assume varying degrees of control but permit institutions of higher education to operate with considerable autonomy. As a consequence, institutions vary widely in the character and quality of their programs. In this country, we have developed a voluntary, peer evaluation system through which nongovernmental educational associations of regional or national scope establish criteria to apply to institutions and programs for the purpose of determining whether they are operating at basic levels of quality.

Our present procedure for assessing quality in higher education through the accrediting process needs to be restructured largely because the criteria, developed and applied by individuals steeped in the traditional approaches to education, no longer meet the needs of institutions serving a wide variety of students. Standards used today assume one kind of institution (basically of a traditional nature), but in reality these standards are applied to many different types of institutions.

Probably the most nagging and important question facing accreditation is that of the validity of present standards used in both institutional and specialized accreditation. We know little about the correlations between institutional characteristics and the quality of institutional output. In fact, we are not always sure what should be measured. It is encouraging to note research of the type being conducted by the Western Interstate Commission on Higher Education, for some of its findings may contribute to the improvement of quality assessment. However, relatively few of the standards currently used in accrediting have been framed on the basis of research.

Many of our present indices of quality are, in fact, quantitative and focus on the peripheral elements of the educational program. Accreditation now places more emphasis on the external trappings of programs or institutions than on the changes that take place in the student. It is not enough merely to say that a student has completed a prescribed program. We should know how far he has progressed between the time he was admitted to the institution and the time that he leaves. It should be obligatory for the institution to provide information regarding "change" and "growth" in the student as he moves through the institutional program.

If we are to improve accreditation, three areas of research and action deserve immediate consideration: (1) Criteria that are appropriate to different kinds of institutions must be developed. (2) Indices of quality which measure "value added" must be substituted for standards which emphasize the superficial elements of education. (3) Better balance in the composition of policy-making bodies for accreditation must be achieved in order that the lay public—so vitally affected by accreditation—can be included, along with students, employers, and practitioners in the various professional fields.

The opportunity for meaningful research on matters of accreditation exists, and studies should be encouraged and funded. Meanwhile, accrediting agencies must recognize the public trust they hold and make every effort to serve more than merely the education community itself.

If we do not have the courage and the foresight to undertake such studies, we may find that quality in higher education has suddenly become the business of government or some other noneducational agency, and institutions will have lost the opportunity to help determine their own destinies. Even though accreditation at the present time has serious flaws, potentially it is one of our best means for assessing quality in higher education. If accreditation should fall of its own dead weight, its destruction would seriously disfigure our nation's educational system.

JAMES A. PERKINS

Reform of Higher Education: Mission Impossible?

A T THE OUTSET, A NECESSARY DISTINCTION IS THAT BETWEEN CHANGE AND reform in higher education. Only the foolish would claim that there has been no change during recent decades and particularly during recent years. Even highlights of the 1960s give the lie to the idea that higher education is a stubborn and unchangeable establishment. In just over one decade, the numbers of students entering colleges and universities have doubled. Budgets have more than doubled. Financial support by the federal government has quadrupled. The two-year community college has flourished, to become a local necessity as well as a local status symbol. Significant numbers of black students have begun to arrive in predominantly white institutions. General education is giving way to individually tailored academic programs. And, not least, the power structure within the university is being changed.

The changes of the past decade do not, however, add up to reform. We think of reform as constructive change; obviously, change can destroy as well as improve. Any judgment about whether reform has really occurred depends on what one conceives the mission of higher education to be and whether recent changes support or damage the prospects for securing that mission.

There is a rub: most dangerous now is the absence in higher education of any master plan for its own development or for its contribution to society. For this reason, and because there is disagreement about concerns that are central throughout the system, higher education is not sure whether to label the changes it has undergone as reform or destruction.

A good example of the problem is the controversy over open admissions. A substantial body of opinion holds that higher education will be destroyed by open admissions. The argument is that education, particularly quality education, can be digested and appreciated by only a few— perhaps 10–15 percent of the college-age group, a relatively small proportion of the population. Martin Trow, one of our most brilliant analysts of higher education, believes open entry means that large numbers of unmotivated and unqualified students will be exposed to a style of education that they cannot understand or appreciate. He and others suggest that we must find a way to build enclaves of excellence for those (few) students capable of abstract and creative thought. To those of his persuasion, the changes of the last decade—the trend toward higher education for all— represent not improvement but destruction. Reform, to them, means combating, withstanding, and offsetting the effects of universal higher education.

The opposite view—that of the university as an open city where those who wish further instruction may have their needs met, whatever they may be—finds the changes of the last decade generally supportive of a notion of reform. Progress in this context is to be measured by steps toward equality of opportunity and the universality of experience. The only argument this group raises is whether change is coming fast enough to represent true reform.

To repeat the argument so far, higher education has been subjected to the most sweeping and violent change in its history. In numbers, costs and budgets, governance, relations with society, and curriculum, there has been more change in the sixties than in possibly any decade in the past. But higher education does not have any agreed-upon notion about reform and therefore is not able to pass judgment on the nature of the changes that have taken place. It only accepts them, lives with them as best it can, tries to survive, and hopes that the changes it must accept will in the end be considered needed reforms.

Such a stance is simply not good enough. Change without some idea of proper ends and means can be sterile at best and destructive at worst. We must indeed think hard about reform, by which I mean change guided by conscious purpose toward visible ends. We have only begun this task, and I am afraid that higher education has yet to take the initiative that will keep it from becoming a great mass of plastic clay shaped by political rather than educational standards.

Obviously, no paper can even attempt to cover in either breadth or depth the directions that reform should take and could take. Nevertheless, I should like to offer six balancing propositions for reforms that strike me as both important and possible. These cannot all be brought about unilaterally by institutions of higher education themselves. To make reforms possible, institutions will have to collaborate with those in the larger society who support higher education. But higher education will have to take the initiative in developing the appropriate stances and public policies that will help ensure that change is the servant of reform.

Size of Institutions

There must be a limit on the size of individual institutions, balanced by vigorous support for the development of alternative institutions and programs. The demand for access to higher education is with us and is not likely to cease during this decade. Till now this demand has been met substantially, but by no means entirely, by enlarging institutions. And most of these individual institutions have grown around a single-campus concept. The result has been a severe case of academic elephantiasis.

There is no general agreement about the maximum size of an individual campus, but there is considerable agreement that once a campus gets beyond 15,000 it loses that element of cohesion that makes it possible to deal with destructive forces on the one hand and reform on the other. It is difficult to see how campuses that now have 25,000 to 40,000 students can ever be reduced to the 15,000 limit. There are, however, a variety of ways in which decentralized living might be built into existing large campus complexes. Fortunately, there are signs of experimentation on this front: the exploration of the residential college concept at Cornell, the differentiated college complex at Claremont, and the new college—Hampshire—jointly supported by neighboring Massachusetts institutions.

Restraint on size is only one side of the suggested reform. If universities and colleges limit their size, they must be at the forefront of the effort to develop alternatives: both two- and four-year colleges, night schools, and also instruction at the higher education level using the new media of public broadcasting, cable television, and computer-assisted instruction. In short, it will not be enough to deny admission to the single campus. It will be necessary to think of ways in which higher education can be obtained off the campus, whether at home, at work, or at appropriate local facilities. The academic cities are already almost unmanageable, and it is inconceivable that they will be allowed to grow further in order to meet the continuing demand. But if they would exercise restraint effectively, they must help develop alternatives.

New Values within the University

A second set of reforms is the reduction of responsibilities assumed under in loco parentis, balanced by an increased concern for humane and social values. Few would assert that the exercise of parental authority on the campus is a constructive influence. Students are not willing to come to a campus in order to develop on their own and then subject themselves to surrogate parents. The institution cannot discipline young men and women for their behavior if that behavior is not disciplined either by parents or by society at large. The trend is toward recognizing that the student is a citizen first and a student second—not the other way around. He will be treated as an adult, not as a child of an institutional parent.

The removal of the university's role in loco parentis, however, only enlarges a vacuum caused by the adult world's lack of agreed-upon standards of behavior. And this vacuum has been reenforced by the insistence of scholars that value judgments should be rigorously excised from both teaching and research. They say that what ought to be is not a proper question for university inquiry. The university's task is to deal with what was, what is, and at best what will be, based upon projections of measurable phenomena. Any professor who makes a judgment about the choices ahead for society has to make sure the students understand that he is, in fact, making a value judgment and is, therefore, purposely acting outside the canons of scholarship. This notion is not unfamiliar to the student who comes through public schools because, there, neither religion nor politics is the proper business of the schoolteacher. Indeed, public education was conceived as being essentially neutral. It leaves matters of religion to the church and politics to the state and to political parties.

Students and teachers are now facing a backlash from those who do not believe that higher education can be neutral with respect to certain values. In the same breath, however, students are prepared to insist that the university accept *their* values as guidance for the institution as a whole if not for its individual members. This confusion lies at the very center of our current agony and can be resolved only by the reassertion of certain values as being decisive for an institution of higher education or a student as a member thereof. Honesty, objectivity, the right of dissent, skepticism about individual omniscience, the rights of the community as balancing those of the individual—a range of values that are important not only for the individual but also for the university and society as a whole is a necessary part of the university as a center of teaching and learning.

RELATION OF THE UNIVERSITY TO SOCIETY

A third set of reforms has to do with the need for restraint on institutional involvement in social controversy, balanced by a belief in the relevance of studies. Only the most extreme would argue that there are, or should be, no restraints on university involvement. It is fashionable, however, to assert that since the university is closely tied to society—particularly in areas of industrial and military research—it is in effect making implicit if not explicit social and political decisions. From this, some argue that these ties should be cut. Sometimes the same people add the argument that new ties with more constructive social purposes should be forged.

Even though the literature and forensics of the day are full of sound and fury, all but a minority would support the idea that the university must retain a modicum of autonomy, and that to do so it must maintain some degree of neutrality in partisan and social controversy. Neutrality is central if the university is to be a critic of accepted values and ideas as well as a developer of new ones. If it is to remain detached enough to have detached views, it cannot also be in a state of perpetual involvement. Clearly the burden of proof must be on those who would plunge the university into the public and social arena. Too many centuries of hard effort have gone into developing the idea of the university as a place of independent thought to abandon this view for all but the most extreme of necessities.

There is, of course, a direct relationship between the acceptance of institutional neutrality and the existence of a social and political consensus. Where the consensus is high, neutrality is not challenged. Where the consensus is low, the parties at conflict will try to enlist each institution—be it a university, a corporation, or a church—into supporting their points of view. The universities, of course, must resist moves that would destroy them. Yet, they cannot afford to be doctrinaire on these grounds; they will frequently have to bend with the social hurricanes, or they will be uprooted. In bending, however, they should keep in mind that they do so only for purposes of survival, not because the principle of institutional neutrality has been invalidated. One of the most terribly complex matters facing institutions of higher learning today is wise judgment about how far an institution should move from a position of neutrality in order, for example, to oppose the war, to deal with South Africa, or to advance the welfare of the surrounding community. Although it must remain outside these issues as an institution, there are three safety valves that will protect this neutrality.

First, there is, of course, the right of the individual members of the community to engage in controversial issues to the extent they feel it necessary and wise to do so. Naturally, it is not always easy to dissociate a student or faculty member or certainly an administrator from the institution itself; nevertheless, members of the academic community are still citizens, and they cannot and should not renounce their responsibilities as citizens because of their position in the university. The problem is particularly acute for the president, who has become the institutional spokesman. It is an interesting question whether the idea of the institutional spokesman is a good one at all. It certainly makes it impossible, or at least very difficult, for him to draw the distinction between statements he makes as an individual and statements he makes as president of the university. But as long as he is believed to be the spokesman for the institution, he will have to exercise considerable restraint within the limits of what would normally be expected of the rights of citizenship. The judgment to be made will be sensitive and fine, but cannot be avoided.

The second safety valve is that the university as an institution should enter the public arena when matters directly affecting or threatening its

REFORM: MISSION IMPOSSIBLE? *Perkins* 153

integrity arise. Nathan Pusey was profoundly right in leading the defense against Joseph McCarthy in the fifties. Kingman Brewster was profoundly right in his public concern for the impact of an antiquated draft system on university students and their academic careers. Yet it is a matter of some doubt that universities, as institutions, should attempt to influence foreign policy with respect to countries either on the right or on the left, or use the weight of their investments to influence policies in private industry. When the matter is of direct concern to the university as a university, institutional intervention is in order. When it is a matter of societal concern, then caution and restraint are in order.

The third safety valve that will make restraint on involvement acceptable is the most complicated of all, namely, the demonstrable relevance of academic studies to the development of the individual and to the needs of society. Where such relevance is obvious, the demand for university involvement will be reduced. Where relevance is questioned, university involvement will be demanded as the constructive alternative. The reason runs thus: Only a small fraction of students are motivated by intellectual curiosity alone, by love of learning without reference to its utility, by the pursuit of knowledge for its own sake. The largest number, and perhaps particularly those who are now coming to the universities from sectors of the population heretofore unrepresented, seek direct connections between academic experience and life after college, or between the academic experience and current priorities for social improvement.

Yet, if relevance is measured only by the relationship of studies to the most current concerns, the utility of knowledge and of the learning process in helping to solve the problems of society would be destroyed. For example, it is fashionable in some quarters to downgrade historical perspective. But surely one of the key questions at present is whether the student revolt is novel or historically cyclical. Seymour Lipset has demonstrated clearly by historical analogy that much of what we hear today was said in almost identical language forty years ago.[1] Others have pointed out that the pressures on higher education in the 1960s were similar to those on higher education in the 1850s. A sense of perspective helps in learning how to deal with even an immediate problem; knowing whether you have a new or an old problem on your hands makes a great deal of difference. Knowledge of the handling of old problems can often guide us when new problems arise.

In a sense, then, relevance is a word that applies to all of knowledge because all of knowledge is potentially relevant to the handling of current

1. S. M. Lipset and Gerald Schaslander, "Historical Background of Student Activism," *Passion and Politics: Student Activism in America* (Boston: Little, Brown, in press, 1971), chap. 6.

circumstances. But that relevance must be demonstrated and the connections must be drawn—this is part of what learning is all about. Relevance of this kind will not automatically be clear to all students. In times of great social upheaval like the present, that demonstration must be made continuously and repeatedly, for otherwise students will turn to direct involvement as the only test of relevance.

RESOURCES AND PUBLIC UNDERSTANDING

A fourth balancing set of reforms concerns, on the one hand, the efficient use of resources and, on the other, an improved public understanding of the nature of the academic enterprise.

As the cost of higher education mounts and absorbs an increasing fraction of the gross national product, the demand for the effective use of resources will increase. The demand will come not only from those supplying the funds—governments, parents, and students themselves—but also from the internal constituencies of the university. Faculty, for example, are particularly concerned when they find aspirations blocked because of the needs of other parts of the university. A department of physics, denied the increased funds it badly needs, will rarely hesitate to point out the inefficiencies in managing the bookstore, dormitories, and dining halls. A sociology department that discovers it is handling ten majors per faculty member will rarely be content with its neighbors in anthropology who are handling only three. When the size of the pie was increasing, the problem of efficiency did not seem vital to anyone's interest. Now, with financial limits the order of the day, efficiency at all levels is certainly on the high-priority list of those who are concerned with university reform.

But the very measures needed to ensure the best use of available resources to meet the needs of the physics department or produce equality between the anthropology and sociology departments will be measures that the academic finds distasteful. Some will find the imposition of the kind of budgetary and planning controls necessary to meet their needs "unprogressive" in nature; they will argue that these do not represent reform, but rather a degradation of the academic process. If the word "efficiency" is troublesome, the academic world could adopt a more comfortable synonym, such as "optimum use of scarce resources." It is only when optimum use seems to suggest that others will get scarce funds that the wisdom of the procedure that produces such a decision will be called in question.

Higher education is expensive, will continue to be expensive, and will probably continue to take a large fraction of the gross national product. And like most complex systems, it will never be as efficient as those who provide resources would like. Specifically, universities and colleges will always have difficulty in meeting tests of efficiency because results are qualitative rather than quantitative and can be evaluated only over time.

High costs and limited funds mean that while major efforts will have to be made to improve the allocation of scarce resources, universities will also have to devote more effort to making sure that the public understands, appreciates, and supports the central missions of the university. The university must give far greater attention to the media that report university affairs. On many occasions the media have been less than neutral reporters and have actually been problem inflamers.

Again we see the dimensions of the problem that was raised at the beginning of this paper, namely, the absence of a consensus within higher education about the nature of reform and the directions that higher education must take. It is the disagreement on these matters that is complicating the public's understanding and therefore reducing their willingness to put up with a certain level of inefficient use of resources. Perhaps the most one can expect is attention to the kind of balancing propositions for reform that are outlined in this paper. If the universities were to deal directly with questions of optimum size, values, restraints on involvement, relevance of knowledge, and efficiency in the academic context, public understanding of the role of higher education might be secured. Without reform and without public understanding and appreciation of the university program for reform, higher education is bound to sail on choppy seas.

CURRICULUM AND TEACHING

The curricula of both the professional schools and liberal arts are under pressure. Demands are made that the content of work in professional schools be more clearly in line with the new priorities of aiding the disadvantaged, improving our environment, and upgrading our cities. A social conscience has become as important as professional competence. Medical colleges, for example, are increasingly concerned with the problems of public health and patient care in addition to research and specialization. Schools of architecture are concerned with urban renewal as well as esthetic design, and engineers are concerned with problems of pollution as well as roads and bridges.

The pressures for rearranging curricula are producing some strains in the professional schools, but these strains are mild compared to the impact of the pressures on the liberal arts. After World War II, the notion of a general education as the keystone of the first two years of college was widely accepted: there were certain things every educated man should know, or at least there were certain ways of thinking to which every educated man should be exposed. But general education has always had to swim upstream against the powerful pressure for specialization. The balance was ever a delicate one at best, but with the upgrading of high school education after Sputnik, the idea of general education for the first two college years came to be seen as essentially repetitive. The coup de grâce came in recent years with the demand of students and younger faculty for relevance.

At this juncture, however, we do not know in which direction we should go under the banner of university reform. There are some who assert that general education is a necessary counterweight to the evils of specialization and professional education. Humanists argue this point with vigor. It would seem there might be a natural connection between the drive to have professional education socially relevant on the one hand and the desire of humanists to have the liberal arts an essential part of the academic curriculum on the other. The overlap of interest, however, breaks down when one takes a close look at the actual subject matter and point of view with which the liberal arts will be taught to those on professional tracks.

In all cases the problem is that most individual courses under the general rubric of the liberal arts, whether under the general education doctrine or not, have been taught increasingly from a specialist point of view. Rarely can students connect the subject matter, as it is currently taught, either with a track in a professional school or with the development of a professional career as a teacher and researcher in a particular discipline. Those who would argue for the maintenance of the liberal arts as a balance against specialization and professionalism cannot do so on principle alone. They must also demonstrate that the subject matter they teach and the way they teach it is in fact important and relevant to the aspirations of the student. Unfortunately, many who teach in the crucial area of the liberal arts are content to rest on the proposition that the subject matter is central and how it is taught is nobody's business.

The heart of the matter is that we must learn to join the content and style of the liberal arts to the content and style of professional education. The same student needs both. We have been content to offer a curriculum made up of disparate specialties and disparate styles. The assumption was that if the university offered all of them, the student would come out of it with a proper balance of professional and liberal arts points of view. This assumption has been one of the great self-deceptions of higher education. Reform, therefore, must take the route of giving less attention to formal systems of courses or of fixed curricula and far more attention to how a subject is taught, the experience of the teachers, and their willingness to make the connections between their subject matter and the professional career interests of those who would learn from them.

GOVERNANCE

Finally, not the least of the complexities in developing a program for the reform of higher education is that the very process of decision making both within and among institutions of higher education is being reformed. My last proposition for reform, therefore, deals with governance. Governance is both a means and an end. It is a means toward achieving the needs of institutional and curricular reform, but it is also an end in itself because it helps fulfill aspirations for democratic participation in the academic society.

Internally, the problem of governance is one of providing for the participation of constituent elements in the university that have not heretofore been heavily represented, namely, students and staff. Faculties and administration have arrived at a somewhat uneasy balance of forces. But the advent of students and nonacademic staff as parties of interest has forced a complete rethinking of the system by which the university should be governed. This process is further complicated because areas of governance cannot be neatly divided into areas of primarily student, staff, faculty, administration, or trustee concern.

Reform of internal governance, therefore, is taking the shape of wider and wider participation, leading to more generally representative structures such as university-wide assemblies or senates in which faculty, students, and administration are represented. Shortly, staff will join in this process. The problem of the role of the trustee or regent in this new mixture has yet to be resolved. Even more of a question is the role of public authorities, be they coordinating bodies or state executive and legislative establishments.

Clearly, the pressure of interest and internal power politics is increasing the demand for participation in decision making. This increased participation is, in itself, complicating the process of making decisions on the very issues that led to the demand in the first instance. Yet there is little choice. Unless there is some authority whose decisions are considered legitimate, decisions by any other route will be worthless. At this writing it is not clear whether the internal cohesion that may be achieved by university-wide administrative and decision-making structures can effectively tackle the complicated problems of limitation on size, allocation of resources, modification of the curriculum, and all the rest. Reform without participation is unthinkable while reform without decisions is unbelievable. Administrations must digest both necessities.

The question of reform and governance does not end at the campus gate. Many of the problems of higher education can be handled by arrangements in which the university is only a part. Limiting the size of the single campus, with the balancing responsibility to increase alternative systems of higher education, obviously requires state, certainly regional, and possibly and probably federal intervention. Planning that will make possible the reform of particular institutions must, increasingly, take place outside of institutions. This is the great dilemma of universities that would be both autonomous and systems-oriented. As a matter of fact, they must be both.

Just as internally we must have university-wide structures to make legitimate university-wide decisions, so also externally we shall have to have state-wide and nationwide structures to make state-wide and nation-wide decisions. Internally, reform is not easy to accomplish. But externally the problem is infinitely more difficult. The sheer variety of structures—for instance, public, private, two-year, four-year, etc.—makes the problem of legitimate decision making on the part of higher education enormously complicated. Reform, if it is to be accomplished at all, requires change in the notion of autonomy. Freedom from political control is certainly one aspect of reform, but the price the university will have to pay will be subordination of the individual campus to systems of higher education of which it is only a part. We are now in the infancy of this kind of reform and it is by no means clear that institutions of higher education will be able to manage their own affairs in a strong enough manner to forestall being managed in detail by public authority. Possibly one of the most important tasks ahead is to support educational systems as the best means of ensuring educational reform which individual institutions might be denied if they try to seek it on their own.

If educators and administrators are able to agree on these directions of reform, and if they are able to agree on essential systems of governance, both internal and external, then I think the mission is not impossible— higher education can be reformed rather than just changed.

Mission Undesirable

WARREN BRYAN MARTIN

ALTHOUGH IT IS PROPER to distinguish between change and reform, not all of the reforms proposed in Dr. Perkins' paper would likely effect changes deserving to be called "constructive."

For example, the proposal to limit the size of institutions, with concurrent support given for the development of alternative programs, must be weighed against another set of so-called balancing propositions. Governance within the institution, according to Dr. Perkins, should be reformed to achieve wider participation and include more representative structures, at the same time that systems-oriented planning affecting the institution will be carried out more and more by state and federal agencies.

Under the terms of these proposals, the smaller, more varied institutions would, in the future, implement by democratic processes policies determined oligarchically for larger, less varied systems of institutions. Dr. Perkins' proposals would reconstruct on a much larger scale the very situation from which students are starting to extricate themselves: a governance "system" where students have been privileged to cut pies baked elsewhere (the sizes, ingredients, and prices of which were, of course, determined at the bakery). Is it constructive change to encourage an environment where people within colleges and universities would have more and more to say about decisions that matter less and less?

Furthermore, to persons skeptical about the intent of Establishment reforms, these proposals may seem like a classical expression of the "divide and conquer" strategy: Split campuses into smaller units, set up alternative structures, create buffer arrangements which accentuate competing units, and distribute authority within each institution across interest groups. Then, apart from all this, organize systems of education, complete with planning coteries equipped with the latest technology, and commission them to achieve efficiency, order, and coherence for individual units as well as across the aggregate. Finally, to round out this strategy, announce that reform of particular institutions must increasingly take place from outside and that the notion of institutional autonomy must hereafter be accommodated to the authority of the system to which the institution is attached.

"Soft" arrangements for institutional governance—those more egalitarian and participatory, less hierarchical and authoritarian—are always inefficient and complicated to manage. Alternative programs that add substantive diversity to the system compound the complexities. If the name of the game is accountability and efficiency (now presently emphasized by societal spokesmen), structuring the situation as described here is to assure that "hard" systems-oriented management types will win control of rewards and sanctions in competition with those aforementioned "soft," "community" types. Reforms that set up such an apples-and-oranges competitive mix must be viewed with suspicion.

Dr. Perkins' proposals, taken together rather than viewed separately, promote changes that may not be constructive because they are halfway solutions. They encourage governance decentralization, human-sized operational units, and greater variety in program options at the level of individual colleges and universities. But they stop short of urging the same sorts of reforms where extrainstitutional *cum* superinstitutional planning bodies are concerned. Here centralism seems to be approved. It is almost as though, having lost control of individual campuses, established leadership now proposes magnanimously to delegate institutional governance procedures, while removing themselves (plus key rewards and sanctions) to foundations, centers, state capitols, or federal agencies where basic governance policies will hereafter be set amid circumstances and personalities likely to be hostile to significant change.

What reason have we to believe that the reform of particular institutions can best be achieved by distant system oligarchies? Dr. Perkins' confidence is expressed this way: "Possibly one of the most important tasks ahead is to support educational systems as the best means of ensuring educational reform which individual institutions might be denied if they try to seek it on their own." Bureaucracies may encourage efficiency and order, but seldom creativity and change. Assuming that reform requires more of the latter than the former, and remembering the nature of educational bureaucracies, it is unlikely that persons with the ideas and audacity to effect institutional reforms will ever get as far as the inner sanctum of such systems. The Russians talk of "dynamic centralism" but their example is hardly inspiring and, furthermore, they don't have to contend with our problem: people who are encouraged to participate in policy formulation for an institution scaled to a size and substance that has meaning for them do not take kindly to the discovery that their participation was an exercise in futility because the real action, the policy clout, is elsewhere. Black militancy and student unrest are consequences of just such revelations.

In another set of balancing propositions for reform, Dr. Perkins advocates that both individuals and institutions should have character—for example, honesty and objectivity are assumptions that, if accepted, would help to fill the present value vacuum; yet his next set of propositions, while acknowledging the social relevance of academic studies, emphasizes the need for institutional restraint in social controversies. Honesty and objectivity, at least for the institution, are as quickly explained away as they were briefly defined. Be honest, but don't be doctrinaire. Learn to bend with the wind, but be ready to take a stand if the survival of the institution is at stake.

But isn't significance more important than survival and, in fact, the only justification for survival? And in this day when individuals and institutions are being blown this way and that by rival ideologies, isn't significance to be measured by the ability of the person or group to stand? It is only a sure foundation that allows the tree to bend its branches without losing its place. Too much attention in this proposition for reform is given to the bending of branches and not enough to the vitality of the root system.

The institution is urged to embrace objectivity, but this commitment is explained away by the distinction drawn, if not explicitly acknowledged, between theory and practice. Espouse objectivity—but remain outside opposition to the war, conditions inside South Africa, and the human welfare of urban communities. But what if objectivity concerning these matters requires admission that the war divides this nation to the point where a community of shared values is impossible; or the declaration that South Africa is blatantly racist; or that no issue is more important now than the welfare of urban society? Honesty and objectivity require the institution to speak out on issues of social or political injustice. Failure to promote the practical application of relevant theories is a moral cop-out.

What is needed are reforms that will move the institution not toward neutrality concerning social and political realities but toward a position of institutional independence from which to evaluate existing conditions and probe alternative futures. The institution of higher education must be seen as a very special sort of place—the place of criticism and creativity; a place that, far from being distant or indifferent, serves society best as a center of independent thinking.

And can the people be persuaded to give the institution this privileged status? Yes. When they come to understand that there are fundamental deficiencies in our existing social system; deficiencies that promote racism leading toward genocide, competitive materialism that exploits and pollutes natural and human resources, militarism that raises the specter of nuclear or chemical death for all mankind. Yes, when they come to understand that no other institution in our society is as well qualified as higher education, despite all of its problems, to carry out the quest for new values for a new time. In the name of national defense the country supports the FBI and the CIA under terms that deny to the people knowledge of how, when, and where money allocated to these agencies is expended. Surely, in the name of the nation's future, the public could be persuaded to give the institution of higher education the independence needed to carry out its special responsibilities.

But how would we assure that the institution is not captured by some special interest group? By decentralizing and encouraging substantive diversity and value differentiation as well as subject-matter variation among the various units. The cluster college concept provides an organizational conceptualization in which the present heterogeneity of societal values could be reflected while the search proceeded for alternative models appropriate for a future that will be characterized by pluralism and process. Rewards, sanctions, the power of policy formulation, and the means for implementation should also be decentralized. This is the way to assure that wider participation in governance configurations will be meaningful for the individual and workable for the institution.

Dr. Perkins' proposals are another example of the moderals' (moderate liberals) willingness to negotiate, but under terms that promise to keep them in control of the institution. The paper offers "balancing propositions" which try to tap resources in present movements toward decentralization *and* centralization, character *and* compromise. Yet, beneath it all is the expectation that (although admittedly there is no agreement in the nature of the changes that must take place) moderals will be in a position to adjudicate differences and interpret conclusions.

It is too late for this little. Moderals, who have too often been on the exploitative rather than the exploited end of relationships, must learn that changes under way—changes not of degree, but in kind—demand sacrifices of them. Moderates and liberals who believe in substantive changes, and are willing to be changed by these changes, are now called "radicals." Moderals would make the institution of higher education socially accountable by having it participate actively, but at the level of theory, in reforming the values of society. Radicals would make the institution of higher education socially accountable by having it participate actively, theoretically and at the level of practice, in transforming the values of society. Because the need now is for transformation, not reform, for planners who look beyond the present period of reaction and have a vision of colleges appropriate for a new culture, we are obliged to conclude that, if the degrees of change proposed in Dr. Perkins' reforms are to constitute the contribution of the institution of higher education to our society in the coming decades, the effort must be termed mission undesirable.

Concepts of the Student and the University

SCOTT W. MAC COY

DR. PERKINS HAS ADDRESSED himself to several crucial issues in American higher education of such importance that they demand action if colleges and universities are to maintain an equilibrium, let alone make progress.

Several areas—some touched on by Dr. Perkins—are essential in any discussion or proposal concerning the future of our institutions of higher learning. The issues that I shall present are those with which I have concerned myself at my own university, namely, what the role of the student in the university should be, and what the concept of the university is and should be. Both items should be high on any list of evidences of disease in the system and indicators for cures.

Arguments about class size, enrollment, and costs are, to me, of little value when the structure itself rests on questionable foundations. Our society so emphasizes postsecondary education that social pressures and, often, school structure make it difficult for a student to pursue a high school curriculum that deviates from that goal. Today's high school, with its "college preparatory mill" orientation geared to high selectivity in college admissions, has increased the pressure on students. In fact, in some high schools the advanced offerings duplicate a good deal of the first two years of liberal arts curriculum. The university must not become a continuation of high school in any sense. An end must come to the era of broad liberal arts education, with its preselected curriculum and schedules, required on the theory that the student is not yet sufficiently "prepared" or "experienced" to choose what field of study he will pursue. In its place must come more "individually tailored academic programs" (Perkins' phrase).

Above all, students must be given more weight in determinations of university policies. Students realize how little say they have about the content of their education—both subject matter and mode of presentation; it is dictated to them, often by elements far beyond their control. The freedom of thought and expression that ought to characterize the American university has been supplanted by the hypocrisy of "Big-Business," holding concerns, and political machinery.

Gifts, grants, and allocations should be in the "spirit of free educational experience," sans strings attached. Learning through open questioning and experience (including the right to profit from one's own mistakes) are two opportunities that education has a responsibility to provide. Other needs are opportunities for expression of thought and criticism, experiencing life with those of other cultures and those of other social and economic levels within this culture, and the ability to pursue any course of knowledge or teaching deemed important to the education of the self. These must not be tainted or corrupted by repression or pseudo-cultural standards and ideologies.

When a student has been provided in the lower educational system with the tools and background experiences for higher education, he must be free to follow, alter, or create his own self-awareness and structure as he sees fit. He is obviously not fully free to learn if he is fearful that his verbal attacks on what he feels are unjust corporate or political practices may provoke harassment from those concerned (through utilization of monetary influence or pulling of political strings). Likewise, a professor who is similarly fearful is hindered in fulfilling his role as educator. To repeat, for added emphasis, what Dr. Perkins has said, "there is, of course, the right of the individual members of the college or university community to engage in controversial issues to the extent they feel it necessary and wise to do so." Completing the picture is the administrator who, continually reprimanding or lecturing his faculty or student body about their conduct in connection with controversial matters, is just the figurehead of a corroding, unstable structure.

The implications set out for change are clear. The first correction must be in the idea that today's college students must be protected from the realities of life. The college or university must not shelter its students. The diversion from real learning occurs in several ways: limiting or forcing certain course selections, and thus closing off open inquiry; forbidding certain issues to be taken up; and prohibiting certain behavior, such as participation in moratoriums or demonstrations, and so on. The student now leaving high school is far better educated, experienced, aware, and capable than in any other period in our history.

Course offerings must allow the student—and the professor—freedom of self-expression and individuality. Student evaluation must be free of mechanistic depersonalization. Requirements must be abolished, and in their place, if anything, should be only the goal of making classes (which faculty deem important) interesting enough that students will take them on their own initiative. Students must share equally with the faculty the power of making decisions concerning all academic affairs.

The imperative is that our institutions of higher education divorce themselves from their interrelations with corporate concerns and government where these connections can, or do, in any way interfere with their freedom and independence of operation. There is no place in higher learning for political "apple-polishing" or corporate manipulation. If independent operation is to exist, trustees who head large business concerns or political or governmental agencies and who might use their institutional position for corporate or political advantage must resign. The military-industrial complex must not envelop our schools. A university that does not wish to be institutionally associated with particular social or political views must think twice about engaging in research that will be used by government or industry to express these views.

Change as reform is obviously the only acceptable change in higher education. That point has been made very clear by Dr. Perkins. What has not been emphasized sufficiently is the acute state that many of our campuses are in at this time. If changes do not occur in the very near future, there will be disastrous results.

The Role of the Office of Education

DON DAVIES

Two ITEMS THAT I FEEL are missing from Mr. Perkins' paper will shape my comments. One is the role of the federal government; the second is the relation between school problems and college reform. Both omissions are disturbing, though they provide a convenient opening for me to chide leaders in higher education for looking to the federal government for money, but not reform, and for not looking to the schools at all.

The federal government plays an important and increasing role in education, providing over $12 billion in 1970. That role, in the context of the President's New Federalism, involves two missions: (1) support through distribution of federal tax revenues, and (2) leadership and reform. The first role will be carried out, I believe, in a variety of ways—revenue sharing, formula grants to the states for broad categories of assistance, student loans and grants, and institutional support without strings. Nearly everyone favors providing money. Differences arise over the means and ground rules for distribution, eligibility for aid, and the amounts that are necessary and possible to provide.

The second role—leadership and reform—is less well defined and accepted than the first. The case for it rests on the fact that the nation faces urgent and frightening problems, solutions to which require profound changes in our educational system.

The kinds of profound changes we need cannot take place unless we find ways to meet the growing demands on resources. Ever increasing numbers of people need more and more education in our technology-based, information- and knowledge-oriented society. We will need to discover more efficient and effective ways of providing educational services. An additional prerequisite is the development of a more pluralistic, extensive, and flexible system of education with a wide variety of institutions effectively linked together. National leadership, both in and out of the federal government, is needed to develop such a system. We are at a point where business as usual won't do.

We are caught between two crosscurrents—severe budgetary restraints, and profound dissatisfaction with the performance of existing institutions —both of which create pressure to cut back on support for what now exists. They also make the development of a strong reform strategy imperative. Development of such a strategy requires effective leadership at all levels. Execution of this strategy also requires a significant investment.

The Office of Education has a variety of the components of the strategy in place or on the drawing boards. These include the National Institute of Education, the National Foundation for Higher Education, and several discretionary grant programs for research, training, and demonstration.

The higher education community has an enormous stake in the decisions about resource allocations and reform strategy made within the federal government. They also have a tremendous stake in ensuring that the Office of Education has the strength and capacity to provide good leadership within the government and to work effectively with the various educational communities.

My second concern—which compels me to invade your turf—is the interrelation between reform, renewal, and improvement in elementary and secondary schools and in higher education. I doubt if anyone denies that reform in the schools is necessary, if for no other reason than that they fail to give adequate education to economically disadvantaged and culturally different children. However, we cannot talk about reforming one part of the system without talking about reforming the other part. What happens or fails to happen in higher education has a great impact on what happens or fails to happen in elementary and secondary education. The reverse is also true. Both "higher" and "lower" education continue to poison the well of the other. In fact, it turns out to be a common well. If we want our schools to teach youngsters to think, inquire, learn, and apply knowledge from various disciplines, we require a particular type of teacher. We require teachers who know a discipline as a way of thinking, not just as a body of facts, and who are emotionally, intellectually, and pedagogically equipped to work with students as individuals and with content in a way vastly different from the traditional "telling and testing." Such teachers are not now being produced by undergraduate teacher training programs. The teacher trainers (whether professors of history or education) are rarely equipped to do the job.

It is hardly novel to assert that graduate schools preparing those who will teach undergraduates are turning out researchers, specialists, and scholars ill equipped to teach, to be role models for future teachers, or, in short, to prepare the personnel who hold the key to future improvement in elementary and secondary education. Despite recognition of the problem, we have not devoted the necessary time, energy, and talent to do the job. Doing the job will require changing a lot of comfortable habits, learning new skills, and changing institutions.

To promote the betterment of teaching and learning at the elementary and secondary levels, the Bureau of Educational Personnel Development has created the Triple T (Trainers of Teacher Trainers) Program. The program is designed to do five things: first, to support those in higher education willing to give teaching parity with research; second, to support graduate schools which accept responsibility, in a deliberate and effective way, for preparing teacher trainers who will know what they need to know about teaching and the content to be taught; third, to bring together both educationists and academicians to train teachers and to train teacher-trainers; fourth, to bring together graduate school faculty, graduate students, and teachers in elementary and secondary schools in a parity relationship to teach and to learn about teaching in real, "functioning" schools. Finally, TTT is designed to introduce all of these parties to the communities that schools serve—particularly low-income, minority communities.

I mention TTT here because it is a good example of an Office of Education discretionary grant program used specifically—and, I think, effectively—to reform the educational system. Additionally, the discussion of TTT enabled me to elaborate on the initial two items that I felt were neglected by Mr. Perkins. These were that the Office of Education can and should contribute in a major way to reform in higher education, and that reform of the various parts of the system—higher and lower—are inevitably interrelated.

LOGAN WILSON

Alternatives to College for Everybody

A T THE 1970 ANNUAL MEETING OF THE COUNCIL IT HAS GONE ALMOST
without saying that American higher education has ceased to be a
privilege for the chosen few, or even an *abstract right* for the many.
Instead, the popular sentiment that our nation has an *obligation* to provide postsecondary schooling for virtually everybody has in the main been
reified. I have not heard anyone argue for compulsory advanced education, but I have noted the incongruity of frequent reference to the
supposedly "involuntary" presence of young people in our institutions,
alongside the intimation that somehow things will be better as we move
toward universal higher education.

As members of the establishment in higher education, we should all
acknowledge the necessity for change and improvement. More than that,
we should unite efforts to move ahead rather than merely defend the
status quo. Before we proceed further on the assumption that higher
education for all is both inevitable and desirable, however, I think we
must take a hard look at present impediments and future alternatives.
Various commentators in our sessions have touched on present obstacles
and have pointed out that the shape of educational things to come is not
likely to be simply a large-scale extrapolation of what we have known
in the past.

To begin, let me review in passing some of the impediments to universal higher education.

We need no reminder that the growing demand for higher education is accompanied by a mounting public reluctance to face up to the
costs entailed. In some states, the rate of increase in legislative appropriations is being reduced. Various federal programs have been cut, and
some have been phased out entirely. Private contributions to colleges
and universities continued to rise this past year, but many institutions
are pessimistic about the future. Blame is often placed on campus disruptions, public disenchantment with educational results, and increased
competition for funds to meet other urgent societal needs. With hard
questions now being asked about institutional outputs, or the dividends
yielded by the nation's huge investment in its educational system, opinion

is widespread that the bull market for higher education probably reached a peak in the 1960s.

Since the Council's Annual Meeting theme in 1971 will be specifically concerned with funding increased numbers of persons in higher education and more varied programs for them, I shall not comment further here on the financial problems to be solved and the issues to be settled.

DETERRENTS TO ENCOURAGING "EVERYBODY"

Aside from money problems, there is another difficulty that we are prone to talk about only indirectly and in euphemistic language. This is what John Fischer a few years back bluntly termed "the stupidity problem" in a book having that title. The real dimwits form a small fraction of any age group, to be sure, but if all high school graduates should go on to college, there is no gainsaying that the average level of intelligence among college-goers would decline. As Trow and others have mentioned, it would be a mistake to design and prescribe for all comers the same programs that are now offered to more selected groups.

Still another discouragement to higher education for everybody in anything like customary forms is an already discernible erosion of the certification functions of colleges and universities. We *now* make distinctions in the values of degrees according to fields of study and institutions awarding them, and, ironically, egalitarian pressures may increase rather than decrease such invidious discriminations. Moreover, if academic standards are compromised in an effort to equalize social privilege and status, existing modes of "credentialing" may lose much of their content and significance. The further possibility is that occupational associations and employing organizations will take over from professional educators the function of assessing educational outcomes.

The movement toward college for everybody may shortly encounter a deterrent resulting inadvertently from the relaxation of requirements and the growing tendency in some places to let everybody do his own thing. Although these measures may reduce campus tensions and make the higher learning a pleasanter and less rigorous enterprise, they may also have the net effect of reducing the marketability of much that is learned. This relinquishment of the institutional function of sorting human talent for socially valued forms of endeavor will tend increasingly to produce graduates who possess neither a mastery of any body of useful knowledge nor enough trained competence to fit them for gainful employment. Under such circumstances, it can be anticipated that individual and collective disillusionments will be reflected in the curtailed patronage of institutions themselves.

Finally, the principle of limits is already operating in the labor market's capacity to absorb college and university graduates and use their capabilities appropriately. This spring, new Ph.D.'s found themselves confronting a buyer's rather than a seller's market, and many employing organizations drastically curtailed their on-campus recruitment of young persons completing baccalaureate and other programs. Recent studies reveal increasing numbers of individuals in jobs requiring less education than they possess, and show that promotions in many occupations depend less on education than on experience, seniority, and various personal traits.

In brief, academic degrees are no longer—if they ever were—guarantees of upward mobility. To be sure, the malfunctioning may be the fault of the market itself; yet the mounting frustrations of college and university graduates in finding the rewards they expected from their educational aspirations and accomplishments not only causes the number of malcontents in society to multiply but also debases the values everybody attaches to higher education as a worthwhile individual and collective enterprise.

Almost everyone agrees that functional illiterates do not meet the minimal educational achievements needed for effective participation in our society, but there is no consensus regarding what is optimum. Some occupations now require twenty-four years or more of formal education as a qualification for entry, and hence the prospect that formal education may "eat up" the best years of our lives is already being realized. Aside from questions relating to the individual's benefits from education and its costs to him, there are also those relating to the society. Are there, for example, more benefits in reducing illiteracy or in improving advanced education? From the differing points of view of equity and efficiency, quite divergent answers may be given to the same questions. And apart from the utilitarian aspects of higher education, with calculated economies and diseconomies, there is also a host of considerations relating to learning for its own sake and the pursuit of truth because it is presumed to make men free.

To summarize, it will be a mistake for us to opt for college for everybody if this means neglecting other alternatives that might in many instances yield greater individual and societal benefits. Some of these alternatives are set forth elsewhere in this volume, but others have received little mention. Let me briefly list them for your consideration.

Some Alternatives and Options

First, the alternative of no further formal education after high school ought to be maintained. Is any useful purpose served by making social pariahs of those individuals who go directly into jobs and whose further education is largely self-education? If more and better education were infused into the K-12 period of schooling by cutting down on prolonged summer vacations, extending the curriculum, and improving instruction, two or more years of postsecondary education would be neither necessary nor desirable for some youth. We are told repeatedly that young people mature much earlier now than in bygone eras, and this would seem to justify shifting much of the subject matter of the first two years of college down into the last two years of high school. My guess also is that some of the vocational training projected for community colleges and technical institutes could be handled quite adequately and more economically in beefed-up and enlarged secondary school programs.

For those who change their minds after working at gainful employment, reentry to further formal education ought to be made easier at those institutions where little, if any, provision is now made for the beginning student who is not a recent high school graduate. Keeping open the individual option of not going to college or going later would undoubtedly free our campuses of the presence of many young people who either do not really want to be there or do not know why they are there.

Second, there ought to be more emphasis on equivalency programs that stress knowledge acquired and competence gained, under whatever conditions, rather than a continued insistence on arbitrary accumulations of credit hours, grade points, and semesters in residence. Taxpayers, customers, and clients—no less than students themselves—are entitled to complain when the increased time and money costs of unduly prolonged formal education are coupled to specious or arbitrarily imposed credential requirements that merely up the price of goods and services without enhancing their quality.

Third, I am of the opinion that individual institutions should strongly resist pressures to proliferate the curriculum endlessly. Reform of the curriculum is indeed overdue; deletions as well as additions should be considered. But students wishing to pursue their own lines of study need to be reminded that books in the library are often better suited to their particular demands than professors in the classroom. Campus nonconformists should be encouraged rather than impeded in their efforts to establish and maintain so-called free universities. In such places—and there are already at least 300 of them—the curriculum can be anything desired, with tests, grades, and credits ignored. Free-wheeling endeavors of this kind would be well-advised, furthermore, to find quarters off the campus and to forgo the inherent constraints of outside financial subsidy.

Fourth, if we really mean what we say about widening access and broadening opportunity in higher education, members of the educational establishment—including those on campus who attack the establishment —must cast aside the notion that they alone are entitled to decide the alternatives for and in postsecondary education. The greater spread of postsecondary opportunities as desirable alternatives to a monolithic structure implies an involvement of the outside public in policy making. Campus radicals no less than conservatives will have to concede that citizens in general also have a stake in what happens. More cooperative work-study programs and on-the-job training projects, not to mention community betterment projects, will necessitate a more effective mutual relationship between the campus and the larger society. Such a relationship necessarily implies some changes in traditional institutional autonomy.

Finally, I believe that further education for nearly everybody should be encouraged as one of the ways to achieve a healthier society, but that it should not be promoted as a panacea for most of our social ills. Undue preoccupation with mass education as the only road to social salvation can become an excuse for neglect in other areas. It can blind us to the complex interrelatedness of modern society. Indeed, requiring ever more formal education as everybody's purchase price for the better things in life can become a stifling rather than a liberating element in human progress. In our efforts to achieve greater equality of advanced educational opportunity, we should therefore examine with care every major proposal to make certain that it will aid rather than impede our long-range pursuits. In any event, we should strive for the kind of future in education that will keep individual options open and social alternatives freely available to all.

THURMAN J. WHITE

Adults: From the Wings to Center Stage

THE THEME ADOPTED FOR THE FIFTY-THIRD ANNUAL MEETING OF THE American Council on Education—"Higher Education for Everybody? Issues and Implications"—was reported to the Council's Committee on Higher Adult Education during a meeting in April 1970. After discussion, the committee was of one mind that the subject was worthy of its special attention. The committee determined that it should seek to have one or more of its members assigned to highly visible leadership roles in the conference, and that one of its members should do a critique of the conference background papers[1] from the viewpoint of continuing education.

The following discussion is offered as the requested critique. The first of its three parts is a review of the references to higher adult education by the authors; it begins with its conclusion: the authors had very little to say about higher adult education. The second part is a review of issues raised by the authors that are relevant to higher adult education; the position of this critique—again stated at the beginning—is that the authors have presented a number of issues which are fundamental to the future of higher adult education. The third part of the discussion follows the first two positions and asks, in effect, whether the authors have raised issues of substantial interest to higher adult education but have failed to follow through: What should the American Council on Education do in this field?

REFERENCES

The background papers give little explicit help to people who think about the problem of higher adult education.

A great many people do think about higher adult education, among them the administrators of community colleges, urban institutions, land-grant colleges and state universities, and most of the large private universities. Indeed, almost all administrators in higher education are con-

1. *Higher Education for Everybody?* (Washington: American Council on Education, September 1970; limited distribution). The papers are reprinted in the present volume and all page citations herein are to the latter publication.

cerned with higher adult education, even in institutions that do not
operate a centrally organized program. Administrators of institutions
with centrally organized programs of higher adult education are in institutions than control a major portion of all the money spent in higher
education—perhaps as much as 90 percent. They are constantly increasing the scope and number of programs for adult students, at a pace that
makes this area the fastest growing segment of many institutions. They
hear people with impeccable academic credentials—like Bentley Glass—
speak of the day soon when the budget for continuing education will
amount to at least half of the total institutional budget. And they are
reminded by the trusted observers of our time, like Paul Miller:

> It is just now that the importance of adult education is growing in those
> institutions of higher learning which formerly found difficulty in finding
> a place for it. Part of this new acceptance suggests the epochal passage
> of education over some great divide of social experience. Tumbling from
> that divide, the continuities of history seem scrambled, elusive, and some-
> times less than useful. To change skills and attitudes continuously has
> become as relentlessly important as acquiring them initially. Education
> in general is expanding in every direction and turning into a concept of
> human resource development. Therefore, it is becoming less the province
> of the young; it is moving from the learning space of the classroom to
> that of the community.[2]

Under the circumstances one might expect a great deal of attention
to the adult student body in a conference on "Higher Education for
Everybody?" And indeed W. Todd Furniss heightens the expectation
with his definition: "Equal access to postsecondary education programs
for those who desire them and are able to profit by them" (p. 4). Any way
you read that, several million adults move from the wings to center
stage.

What help do the authors give? Unfortunately, it is a short answer—
so short no one will become bored if all the directly relevant statements
are repeated here:

Furniss, "Educational Programs for Everybody"

> Should Meecham University's Continuing Education Program for
> Women require 30 semester hours of courses in the sciences, social sci-
> ences, and humanities as a prerequisite for a degree?
> Should Tom Wilson, who failed to go to college after high school, be
> given financial support if he wishes to return at thirty after holding a job?
> Should he be given degree credit for his work experience? [P. 4]

2. ". . .Moving from the Wings: An Introduction," in *Higher Adult Education in the
United States*, ed. Malcolm S. Knowles (Washington: American Council on Education, 1969), p. xiv.

> The traditional liberal arts college has no ready place for the student who must work outside the college community most of each day, the older student who cannot or does not wish to be part of a young community, the student whose skills are so deficient that special and time-consuming remedial programs must be provided, and the student whose purpose is to destroy the value system on which the college's program is based rather than to accept it. [P. 14]

We will make no comment on a sentence which gives adult students equal treatment with dunderheads and anarchists. But we will observe with almost unbecoming satisfaction that the Furniss chapter concludes (pp. 17–18) with an adult education story to illustrate "most of the issues America faces in providing higher education for everybody."

Miller, "Who Needs Higher Education?"

> Beyond the development of new working relationships between society and higher education and between the institutions and students, higher education and the society which supports it most certainly will be faced with the following challenges: . . . . To provide higher adult and continuing education, in recognition of the need of adults in middle and later life for further education and periodic reeducation. [Pp. 103, 104]

The statement stands like a lonely sentinel among eleven challenges. Miller seems to marshal the troops behind his earlier premise that

> The intertwining of higher education and the youth culture is less a matter of choice than the inevitable outcome of the fact that they are cohabitants on the college campus. Like members of a family, neither really has any choice in the matter. [P. 100]

Turnbull, "Dimensions of Quality in Higher Education"

> As educators, we are devoted to enlarging and deepening the learning of an entire people, in school and out, young and old, formal and informal. Our foremost responsibility, however, and the one to which this paper has been confined, is the primary responsibility of our institutions and organized systems to define and seek quality in all its legitimate dimensions. [Pp. 135–36]

The frame of reference for the Turnbull paper is "45 percent of all eighteen-year-olds enroll in undergraduate programs offering degree credit, compared with 35 percent just a decade ago" (p. 126). But an extended reference to the adult student body is a transparent possibility.

Trow, "Admissions and the Crisis in Higher Education"

> Thus, in our rapid move through mass toward universal higher education, we have brought into the colleges and universities large numbers

of students who are weakly motivated for the standard academic roles. These developments, coupled with an event that allowed them to become general knowledge, coupled with other parallel processes within the academic community itself—changes in the recruitment to college and university teaching, a weakening of faculty authority and of confidence in their special expertise, and deep confusion and conflicts about the central characteristics of the institutions themselves—these things taken together are making our leading colleges and universities unworkable. [P. 44]

Mr. Trow may be a pessimist; he may be a realist; he may be densely hardheaded; he may be a prophet.

> There may be an increased readiness to admit larger numbers of adults with broken or interrupted educational careers to the central university programs, rather than confining them to summer school and extension programs. [P. 46]

Pessimist, realist, hardhead, prophet, the author seems on the threshold of a thought about higher adult education. With only a slight nudge, he might see adults as people who continue educational careers as well as people who resume "broken or interrupted educational careers." But he might not if he views the learning enterprise as a race of hurdles fixed ex cathedra for all who want to compete.

Eulau, "Political Norms Affecting Decisions"

> The university's goals include not only educating undergraduate and professional students, but also giving expert advice to government, doing research for government and private industry or agriculture, training employees for all sorts of business, holding conferences for men of learning as well as for laymen, and participating in their communities' social and economic affairs. [P. 222]

Three of the goals lie in the area of adult education. Of four norms cited by Eulau (p. 213) as emerging from interviews with state legislators and executive officials, one seems most relevant: the norm of passivity in oversight. The results of the survey reported by Eulau show politicians so passive toward higher education for adults that it was not even mentioned. One must consider the possibility that the adult education goals of higher education were not a part of the politicians' gestalt when they were interviewed. But had they been, would the results of the survey have been different? Would Eulau need a new survey to be sure?

Birenbaum, "Something for Everybody Is Not Enough"

> The adult ideal in America is a life of work *and* learning, of thinking *and* acting, of testing knowledge *through conduct*, an ideal too often un-

realized and dishonored in those institutions through which we provide formal education for young adults. [P. 81]

The author knows adults. He knows the life of work is a life of learning too. He assumes educational opportunity, including opportunity for adults, as *pro bono publico*. He wants to join the issue on a different question: What shall be learned? His answer is equality, integration, peace, and humaneness. For him, the example is the premise.

Bolton, "Higher Education for Everybody: Who Pays?"

A remarkably quiet paper. Because it is remarkable, remarks are in order. Bolton missed the definition completely. Higher education for everybody means, to Bolton, only young people who get the expense money from somebody else without earning it by any effort except going to school. The concern is critical and therefore laudable. His concern is the adequacy of institutional aid as a means to higher education for everybody, and by that he means everybody just out of high school. Perhaps he worries about paying for postsecondary education for all— adults notwithstanding—who desire it and can profit from the experience. He missed a chance in this chapter.

Perkins, "Reforming Higher Education: Mission Impossible?"

It will be necessary to think of ways in which higher education can be obtained off the campus, whether at home, at work, or at appropriate local facilities. The academic cities are already almost unmanageable, and it is inconceivable that they will be allowed to grow further in order to meet the continuing demand. But if they would exercise restraint effectively, they must help develop alternatives. [P. 150]

This is a clear call to alternatives to "academic cities which are already almost unmanageable." One can wonder why the author feels constrained to offer it to young people only.

The position of this paper is that the background papers deal with the problems of higher education for everybody between the ages of eighteen and twenty-four; let the rest of the world—over twenty-four— do the best it can if it needs higher education. Thus far we have seen only the direct references to higher adult education. Two thoughts may be derived: (1) Anyone who includes adults in his concerns for higher education for everybody would be disappointed in the Fifty-third Annual Meeting of the American Council on Education. (2) After reading the background papers for the meeting, administrators who manage most of American higher education are still waiting for more constructive lights on higher adult education.

One final disconcerting observation needs to be reported here. The literature of adult education seems not to exist for the authors of the background papers. None of it is cited or listed among the references despite a Council publication of 1969, which Paul Miller said had the "quality of a bench mark" and Logan Wilson thought "because of the growing importance of higher adult education . . . [would] be welcomed on many sides." Malcolm S. Knowles authored the publication under the title *Higher Adult Education in the United States*. His subjects were the current picture, trends, and issues. Only an iron curtain of academic polarity could keep such a publication out of a national conference on higher education for everybody.

ISSUES

The background papers raise issues that are highly relevant to higher adult education. Perhaps the best way to introduce them is to cite the authors again.

Furniss introduces the concepts of "production models" and "ad hoc" models (pp. 8–10).

Miller all but names adults among those who "clamor for attention":

> The investment of funds on the part of governments and private donors has been justified chiefly on three grounds: the providing of needed manpower in the economy, the discovery of new knowledge through research, and the maintaining of the nation's competitive position internationally. . . .
>
> Whose needs will be met by higher education in the coming decade? New (or newly self-aware) student and community constituencies clamor for attention, as do the old constituencies also. [Pp. 94–95]

Turnbull discusses the concept of "value added" as a goal of institutions of higher education and as a measure of their quality (p. 131).

> There grows among us, instead, a deeply-held conviction that it is not sufficient to pursue knowledge for itself, but that somehow knowledge must be put to work for moral, social, and political ends. [Quoted from Nathan M. Pusey, *Harvard University: The President's Report*, 1970.]
>
> . . . the concept of a discipline-bound curriculum, a classical teaching technique, and a limited enrollment would define a failure of teaching and learning rather than high quality. The question of what is important to learn is the central and unresolved issue. [P. 133]

Trow looks into the likelihood of the breakdown of traditional forms of university education (pp. 28–29) and the growth of "consent units" (pp. 50–51).

Eulau has investigated the attitudes of state legislators and executive officials toward matters of higher education:

> four norms . . . emerged most strongly from the interview protocols—the norm of responsiveness, the norm of passivity in oversight, the norm of authority, and the norm of comparison. [P. 213]

Birenbaum makes a number of points that are relevant for those who are concerned with and about higher education for adults:

> The themes of peace, integration, equality, freedom, and the human use of knowledge are ones which, traditionally, fall beyond the purview of the university. [P. 66]
>
> *The most crucial educational problem in modern technical civilization is how to prevent the separation of technical power from moral responsibility.* [P. 70]
>
> . . . Around each geographic and temporal educational ghetto, we repair and fortify those walls segregating campus from community, academic professional from nonacademic talent, and acts of learning to think from the rich urban opportunities for thoughtful action.
>
> At the collegiate level, during the period in which we have used the four academic years, each of nine months, paced relentlessly by the credit hour system, mankind has enjoyed his most phenomenal knowledge growth. What we now try to fit into this obsolete system just doesn't fit any longer. [Pp. 73–74]
>
> . . . We have many departments of history, but no departments of the future. [P. 77]
>
> . . . in America *commingling* is normal and desirable. We expect the younger and the older to live and work together, the black and the white, the artisan and the professional, the artist and the businessman. Finally, at least officially, we do aspire to integration. We no longer can tolerate schools and colleges, knowledge and experience, organized and operated according to the principle of segregation. Our learning programs and places should bring people and things together, not only because integration is a more desirable way of life, but also because bringing things together is more conducive to learning. [Pp. 81–82]

Bolton sees public expenditure for higher education as based on concepts of social benefit, the redistribution of income, and the easing of loan finance for families and institutions (pp. 189–90); presents arguments concerning aid to institutions versus aid to students (pp. 194-95); and deals with the concept of balancing support from several donors (pp. 196–98).

Perkins points out that the many changes in higher education in the past decade do not add up to reform (p. 148). "To make reforms pos-

sible, institutions will have to collaborate with those in the larger society
who support higher education" (p. 149).

> Reform, if it is to be accomplished at all, requires change in the notion
> of autonomy. Freedom from political control is certainly one aspect of
> reform, but the price the university will have to pay will be subordination
> of the individual campus to systems of higher education of which it is
> only a part. We are now in the infancy of this kind of reform and it is
> by no means clear that institutions of higher education will be able to
> manage their own affairs in a strong enough manner to forestall being
> managed in detail by public authority. Possibly one of the most important
> tasks ahead is to support educational systems as the best means of ensur-
> ing educational reform which individual institutions might be denied if
> they try to seek it on their own. [P. 158]

All of the above references contain some yeasty implications for higher
adult education. The temptation is to rhapsodize, but explicitness seems
in order.

1. The Furniss contrast of production and ad hoc models speaks to
the adult educator. So also does the Trow proposal of consent units. The
adult educator has spent a professional lifetime with the ad hoc model
and in the development of consent units, terms that describe aptly the
creative pattern required for programs designed especially for adults.
The adult educator is a ready reserve to be called upon by any institution moving in the direction of ad hoc models or consent units.

2. Miller's missed opportunity is an open invitation to further discourse. He trains a big gun on "who needs higher education" by priority
to those who need manpower in the economy, those who need the discovery of new knowledge, and those who want this nation in an internationally competitive position. But his target shrinks to about 80 percent of the age group eighteen to twenty-two. He could have included
adult students, for he was pointed squarely in their direction.

3. "Value added" is a concept easily understood by people in higher
adult education. Unless the adult student believes a program is of
"value" to him, he votes to discontinue the program simply by staying
away from it. But when Turnbull raises the question of "how much
value added," he has caught our common concern for more precise
evaluative procedures. We would learn more.

4. Turnbull is attuned to adult education concepts in his concern for
knowledge that can be put to work and his skepticism about a discipline-
bound curriculum presented by classical teaching techniques. Higher
adult education is pragmatic and problem centered. If the rest of the
campus is moving in this direction, the extension people and the undergraduate faculties may have a lot to learn from each other.

5. The political norms presented by Eulau have potential usefulness for higher adult education. Do legislators feel public pressure for adult education (responsiveness)? Do they feel politics should be kept out of matters concerned with extension and continuing education (passivity in oversight)? Are they willing to go along with budgets for adult education as requested by the institutions and endorsed by their own committee leaders (authority)? Are they influenced by what other states do about continuing education (comparison)?

6. Birenbaum's observations about time and place have the hidden energy of atomic power, because the consequences of his remarks will be higher education for everybody at times when they are ready to learn and in places most favorable to learning. He would break the lockstep of the two- and four-year degree programs: the consequence is exit and reentry over a period of years, perhaps until senility. He would use the community resources as learning resources; the consequence is a new "campus" and a new "faculty," sometimes as an addition and sometimes as a replacement for the present institutions. Possibilities spring to mind: an advanced school for economists located in lower Manhattan taught by the now invisible faculty of the highest concentration of Ph.D. economists in the nation; an advanced school of nuclear physics in Los Alamos taught by the now invisible faculty of the highest concentration of Ph.D. nuclear physicists in the nation.

7. Birenbaum could also lead us to a monumental reassessment of the segregation practices in higher education, by which we do not mean racial segregation. We are struck by his principle of "commingling" the younger with the older, the artisan with the professional, and the artist with the businessman. It raises interesting possibilities. For example, would the distress of young people doing "involuntary servitude" on segregated campuses be relieved if at least a part of the time were spent in learning situations where half or more of the students were adults?

8. Bolton gives three reasons why the public so generously supports higher education: social benefits, the redistribution of income, and the reluctance of private capital to invest in human development. One wonders if the compelling argument he advances out of these reasons need be only for young people. Do adults not have the same call upon public help in learning the lessons they must learn? And if they do, is there any way to avoid the question of the form of the support, that is, to institutions or to individuals? And the further question of reward to the individual who is willing to invest in himself or a company that is willing to invest in its employees?

9. Perkins affirms that in order to make reform possible, institutions will have to collaborate with those in the larger society who support

higher education. Undoubtedly several millions in the larger society will be especially interested in collaborating—the several millions who are the adult students of the institutions of higher education.

Some of the proposed reforms have immediate implications for the adult student body. If a limit is placed on institutional size, is one alternative the development of higher adult education institutions? Would such an institution have any greater ability to foster the nurture of human and social values? Would it give greater attention to the relevancy of higher learning? Would it be less easily involved in social controversy? Would it be more responsive to budgetary and planning controls? Does it have a greater penchant for curricular and teaching innovation? Will student participation in governance be more productive? The answer to all these questions may be "yes." One is tempted to say that the possible advantages seemingly outweigh the disadvantages. In fact, the temptation to make such a declaration is so strong that further thought is surely in order.

MORE ISSUES—AND ACTION

Clearly we need further attention to the issues raised in the background papers as they apply to higher adult education. For example, what are the implications of a combination of the concepts of the "ad hoc model," "value added," and "consent units"? Or again, the question of who pays: the answer for higher adult education at the present time is markedly different from the concern of Bolton's paper.

There are other issues which, though omitted from the background papers, are of considerable, even crucial importance to higher adult education. Who shall teach? Where shall they teach? How shall they teach? When shall they teach? Who is to be taught? What shall students be charged? Who runs the program? Who is knowledgeable about higher adult education? How do they share what they know? What are the facility requirements of the adult student body? How are adult students recruited? How is adult learning made a part of the student record? Who worries about the adult curriculum? How can institutions specialize in one or a few of the dominant developmental needs of adults? If several colleges share potentially the same student body for their adult education programs, what coordinating mechanisms are needed?

The American Council on Education, through the Committee on Higher Adult Education, can make a much needed contribution if it puts some muscle into tackling these issues. *Pro bono publico.*

PART THREE

PRIORITIES: The Pressures of...

Money

Responsibility

Policy

ROGER E. BOLTON

Higher Education for Everybody: Who Pays?

I F WE ARE TO APPROACH THE GOAL OF HIGHER EDUCATION FOR EVERYBODY, we shall have to do it, first, by offering incentives for young people to invest more of their time and energy in education and, second, by increasing the resources that are complementary to the time and energy they invest in the process. Before embarking on a discussion of who pays, it should be made clear just *what* we must pay for education.

Higher education requires combining many different kinds of resources, and in our economy they must be attracted into institutions of higher education by the promise of remuneration, monetary or nonmonetary, immediate or deferred. Just above, I classified resources into two groups: time and energy of students, and complementary, or all other, resources. Time and energy of students are well explained by the words. Some think they are the more fundamental of the resources, but that view depends on which is easier: to change teaching to rely less heavily on students or less heavily on the other resources. A student spends time and energy on the particular consumption experience and the presumed capital good which higher education brings, but he or someone else sacrifices the different goods he could have produced had he joined the labor force. Economists use the term "forgone earnings" to cover all these opportunity costs; I use "time and energy" simply because it seems more expressive. Part of these costs are essential food and shelter, which the student cannot give up completely and which someone must provide him. The food and shelter costs are the time and energy costs most emphasized in popular discussion, but I shall mean by "time and energy costs" all forgone earnings.

In the other group I include everything else, from the time and energy of professors, secretaries, librarians, and janitors, to the bricks and mortar and books and computers in buildings, to the space of land the whole enterprise occupies.

I acknowledge a debt in writing this paper to Burton Weisbrod, Maureen Woodhall, and Robert Hartman; I alone am responsible for the result.

One may consider all the resources in the two groups as the costs of higher education, and certainly that is more sophisticated than looking only at the passing of money from one hand to another. It is even more sophisticated to reckon as costs the goods and services that the resources would have produced if they had not been enticed into higher education, but into some other industry. If a young man does not attend college and there use his time and energy to produce his own education, what other useful things might he turn out instead? Will he work in an auto assembly plant, or help supervise ghetto children in recreation? If a trained physicist is not teaching in a college, what will he do? Will he teach physics in a high school, or design cheaper color television sets, or will he design more economical antipollution equipment? If bricklayers and bulldozers are not hired to build a new university library, will they build more public housing, or a sewage treatment plant? Those other things, which might have been, all of them useful and valuable to someone and some of them valuable to almost everyone, are the true costs of higher education. Even the most dedicated educator must find contemplating some of the costs painful.

The true costs are not easy to predict, because to be precise we must guess in what alternative ways the resources would most likely be used. But the alternatives depend on what young people like to do and what jobs will be open to them, and how they and their parents will spend their income if not on education—will they buy more color television sets or will they be willing to pay more taxes to improve sewage treatment? What will the alumni or foundations spend money on if they do not donate it to higher education? And it depends on—hardest of all to predict—what alternatives governments will follow: Will they spend more money on physics education in high schools, or on public housing, or will they simply spend less, period? Higher education is a good thing, but producing it will cost other good things, such as better housing for the poor or a cleaner environment. No one's budget is unlimited. A scientist who spends some time teaching and sitting on his college's revolutionary policy committee will not spend as much time developing antipollution devices as if he spends all his time on the antipollution devices. Something must be given up.

Because there is uncertainty about what opportunities will be passed up by a commitment to higher education for everybody, there must also be some uncertainty about who will pay. In thinking and writing about financing higher education, I have been accustomed to dividing the payers into three groups: families (in which I include students); private donors; and public donors, or governments. But it has struck me that this glosses over the question of who the ultimate payers are when governments and private donors are involved. If a government uses tax revenue to subsidize higher education, who really pays? If taxes are levied without much question, and then allocated to higher education programs, the people who pay are the ones who would have benefited from the other programs that higher education squeezed out of the budget. Thus attitudes on public aid should rightly be shaped not only by how much money is spent on higher education and how it is spent, but also by opinions about what alternatives are sacrificed. I think it is a mistake, or at least not fully enlightening, to think only of the taxpayer as the one who pays for public aid.

Similarly, if a wealthy man gives money to his alma mater, who really pays? He does, if the only alternative he contemplates is a bigger yacht. But his real alternative may be some other worthy cause. And for a foundation, one assumes the alternative is *always* one worthy cause or another.

In the remainder of the paper, I shall examine the question of who pays in more detail. First, I shall review some American traditions in financing higher education. Next I shall refer briefly to some widely expressed doubts whether the traditional structure of financing makes sense. Finally, with the established traditions and criticisms of them in mind, I shall discuss what seem to be the main issues to be resolved in the future. All of them are connected in one way or another with who pays.

TRADITION

Although higher education usually means education beyond high school, I should like to start just beyond the compulsory attendance age, with the last years of high school. I do this because the last years of high school are the first years of *voluntary* attendance in education. These years are financed partly by students and their families, partly by private and public donors. The role of private donors is relatively limited, because only a small proportion of students are in private schools that rely on gifts and endowments. The student and his family largely finance time and energy costs, and, in the case of private schools, some of the other costs as well. Governments do little to finance time and energy costs, cheap lunches notwithstanding. They do finance the great bulk of the complementary resources; by far the greatest proportion of students attend public schools where family payments are limited to small amounts for some books and optional events like tours. Without much danger of oversimplification, we may say that in the first years of noncompulsory education families finance time and energy, and the public finances complementary resources.

The lines in undergraduate education are less sharply defined, although the family is still the dominant source of time and energy. And families also pay a large part of the costs of complementary resources by paying tuition. Public and private donors do help finance time and energy costs by giving scholarships to cover living expenses and by subsidizing residence and dining facilities. Needless to say, they also pick up the tab for a lot of the complementary resources as well.

Private donors are in general much more significant in undergraduate than in high school education, as individuals and charitable organizations help defray operating and capital costs and add to endowment, the earnings from which are important. Another difference is that here the federal government's contributions come directly to institutions and to students, whereas at the high school level they came largely through other governments. But state and local governments spend money on graduate education much as they do on secondary education, in the sense that they operate their own colleges in which they offer complementary resources to students at prices far below costs. Typically, a standard low-tuition package, carrying a very large subsidy, is offered to all students who qualify on academic grounds, and no means test is imposed. This point is extremely important: it represents a conscious choice and is not inevitable in the course of things, not even inevitable given that governments operate the institutions in the first place. These governments also offer some direct aid to students: to many for use at the institutions they operate, where it augments the standard package, and to some for use in private or out-of-state institutions, and means tests are often used for this aid. But direct aid to students is used much less by state and local governments than by other donors.

Not only is the pattern of aid to the (statistical) average undergraduate different from that he relied on in high school, but also the pattern varies widely among institutions within the undergraduate sector. There is the obvious public-private division: institutions that depend heavily on families and private donors but rely little on state and local governments, as against other institutions that do the opposite. The public-private distinction is the most important source of variation, but not the only one.

At the graduate and professional level, the same mixed pattern for complementary resources is evident. However, many institutions supply both graduate and undergraduate instruction, and it is difficult to separate the two functions in their budgetary data. As at the previous level, much of the federal money pays for resources for research whose value to education is controversial, to say the least. I do not enter that thicket. Time and energy costs are again shared. A graduate or professional student has already won an undergraduate degree and so his earning power is high; by continuing in training, therefore, he sacrifices a great deal in forgone earnings. At this level of education, both public and private donors give fellowships to defray living costs, and in some fields these are very generous. It is not clear whether relative burdens differ much from those in the undergraduate sector.

What explains the high level of public expenditure on higher education?

One answer is a long-held belief that higher education brings social as well as private benefits. The private benefits are widely recognized, and the state can rely on private tastes and financial incentives to induce a large amount of private investment. Some observers have grave doubts whether higher education really does create greater earning power or is merely an elaborate screening process that identifies the persons who already had the ability to produce. Clearly there is a difference, and it suggests important questions whether higher education at present serves the screening function efficiently. At any rate, success in the process brings benefits in higher earnings. There are much-valued nonpecuniary benefits to be gained too, both in college and later. Therefore, we can be confident that many families will finance some higher education out of their own pockets, even if there are no public or philanthropic subsidies. But there are assumed also to be benefits to society at large, which cannot be turned to his own benefit by the educated person himself. These are the so-called external benefits. A crucial role of subsidy is to induce the added investment which, although not worthwhile to the individual, is worthwhile to society as a whole. Private benefits are large, but they are not large enough alone to call forth the optimum investment. Subsidies are added to sweeten the deal—they are bribes, really, in a good cause.

A second explanation of public financing has been the desire to redistribute income. The ideal of equality of opportunity implies that investment in a child's education should not depend wholly on his parents' tastes and their ability to pay, but also on his own ability to profit. A large degree of inequality in consumption is tolerated in America, presumably to preserve incentives to work and save, but education is felt to be an exception, because the child is not consulted on whether or not he is born into a family which can afford an expensive asset like education. The state has exerted itself to make what is an exception in principle become one in practice, and even if not complete, its success has been considerable.

Finally, governments have aided higher education by easing loan finance for families and institutions. The imperfections of capital markets in financing human capital investment are well known. Guaranteed student loan schemes are an effort to reduce the risk to lenders, and now we are considering reducing the risk to borrowers as well, by substituting contingent repayment for conventional terms. In practice, governments have gone beyond guarantees of loans at market interest rates and have added explicit subsidies by making it possible to borrow at rates not only below what would have to be paid on loans without guarantees but also well below even the market rates on loans secured by safe assets. This added subsidy element is justified by the same arguments that support scholarships and outright grants to institutions.

DOUBTS

Even a cursory review of tradition would emphasize the increasing public criticism of some major theories and practices just described. Economists, college administrators, and politicians have all been heard from. The California system has certainly had its share of searching examination,[1] and the critics are criticized,[2] but dissatisfaction is more widespread.[3]

Some have never much believed the argument that higher education favors the creation of socially valuable attitudes in students, and their camp must have been augmented in the last few years of turmoil. Others reject economic reasons for subsidizing the training of manpower, saying we would do better by directly subsidizing the end products for which educated manpower is needed, rather than indirectly subsidizing them through education. I shall return to this point later.

There are also doubts about using the higher education system to redistribute income. Mishan, in Britain, has said that "this belief in the social merit of providing working-class children with the means of escape from a working-class environment is surely a peculiarly middle-class intellectual's view of the aspirations of the working class." [4] Here, one would say it differently, if one said it, but it is thought-provoking. One may ask why we are so specific about the national endowment, as some have called it. Perhaps it would be better to improve the distribution, if that is what we want, simply by giving every eighteen-year-old a large sum of money or productive assets other than education, such as a shop and set of tools for a trade of his own choosing.

Even those whose faith in education is not shaken have doubts that it

1. W. Lee Hansen and Burton A. Weisbrod, *Benefits, Costs, and Finance of Public Higher Education* (Chicago: Markham Publishing Co., 1969).
2. See papers by Joseph Pechman and Robert Hartman, *Journal of Human Resources*, Summer and Fall 1970.
3. There is also a debate in Britain. For a lively discussion, see Edward J. Mishan, "Some Heretical Thoughts on University Reform," *Encounter*, March 1969, pp. 3–15.
4. Ibid., p. 12.

still makes sense for public institutions to offer high-quality education indiscriminately and without a means test to students whose families are quite able to pay, and undoubtedly would be willing to pay, more than they currently do. The doubters may forget that the time and energy costs are even larger than the complementary ones, and they remain largely unsubsidized in public institutions. But those who still proclaim the virtues of "free" higher education also tend to forget the high cost of time and energy.

It is quite easy to argue that the large subsidies offered through the typical state university system are much larger than necessary to encourage attendance by middle- and upper-income families, but smaller than necessary to encourage poorer families who can little afford the time and energy costs which remain. And large sums of federal money are given to public *and* private institutions for facilities, given without means tests to all students; thus the issue is present for federal policy as well. Critics feel we should spend as much money as we now plan, but in a more discriminating manner; they are convinced that better-off families will pay more out of their own pockets when forced to do so and thus permit an expansion of total resources quite adequate to meet national needs and to increase equality of opportunity. Others may feel that indiscriminate subsidy drains too much money from governmental budgets and that other essential public programs are squeezed. In the context of my previous comments, they would argue that what we sacrifice now for education are a cleaner environment and housing and better elementary and secondary education for the poor, and that what we ought to sacrifice are color television sets and private swimming pools and other items of consumption. Officials of private colleges feel a responsibility to open doors to disadvantaged youth, but face the prospect of adding upper-income students at the expense of middle-income students to get the money—this is in the cause of greater diversity. They may be a bit bitter about the neighboring public institution which offers low tuition for all, but little extra for poor students who find low tuition not enough. They may agree with Truman:

> The willingness of many "private" institutions, at considerable sacrifice, to base undergraduate financial assistance on total need and to create in effect a sliding-scale tuition system supplemented by subsistence grants, accounts for the anomaly that these institutions have student bodies more representative of the income structure of the society than do most of their "public" counterparts whose low-tuition policies are defended as more "democratic." [5]

5. David Truman, "Autonomy with Accountability," contribution to a symposium on "Financing Higher Education," *Public Interest*, Spring 1968, p. 106.

But of course the doubters don't have all the arguments. There are powerful ones on the other sides. One argument is that the means test is degrading: it is better to give money to people who don't need it than to introduce the means test. And that argument may come from persons most interested in increasing access to higher education for disadvantaged students. There is the argument that quality of education is very important, and that even upper-income families need heavy subsidy at the margin to get them to accept higher quality. And there is the serious puzzle about the importance of financial barriers to college attendance, and attendance at better schools, as compared to other barriers. And finally, if tuition were raised selectively for those who can afford to pay, would legislators spend the money on improving opportunities for the poor? [6] If not, would they spend it on any other public program the critics feel was unduly sacrificed before?

These are the bare bones of the argument. Rather than filling out both sides of the debate fully, I shall confine myself to a few comments on some specific issues.[7]

How Big Are the External Benefits?

The question here is: What does a person's education produce for society that is not reflected in his own returns later in life? Even the external benefits that are economic, such as the favorable effects on economic growth through the discovery and application of new knowledge, are very hard to quantify in practice, and the noneconomic benefits are even more difficult to measure. The answer must come from some social consensus or, to be blunt, from the political process.

It will be natural for the subsidizers to credit some kind of education with *more* external benefits than other kinds: classics with more or less than nuclear physics, the small liberal arts college with more or less than the giant university. In our history, government long subsidized the mechanical arts and agriculture more heavily than the liberal arts, and it still subsidizes education in science more than education in the humanities. Until relatively recently state governments concerned themselves most with the external benefits to their populations from education in one or two state universities and a chain of teachers colleges, and gave little attention to any other institutions, to which they usually granted little more than exemption from property tax. Now states are increasing

6. See papers by Pechman and Hartman.
7. The remainder of this paper follows closely chap. 4 of my earlier paper, "The Economics and Public Financing of Higher Education: An Overview," in *The Economics and Financing of Higher Education in the United States: A Compendium of Papers Submitted to the Joint Economic Committee, Congress of the United States* (Washington: Government Printing Office, 1969), pp. 12–104.

the number of public institutions and increasing aid to students who go to private ones.

Public value judgments are inevitable. The state need not be preoccupied with evaluating private benefits; the responsibility of gathering information about earnings of educated people, the costs of various institutions, and the details of curricula are left to the student and his family. But the external benefits are public benefits, and governments must decide. They can hardly take for granted that the success of a university's efforts in creating or exposing earning power in its graduates is a good guide to its ability to provide education with large external benefits. Some institutions are reputed to be good at both, but the positive correlation may not be strong for the whole group. External benefits are benefits the market cannot value, so there can be no substitute for the political process.

A crucial issue is the value of quantity versus quality. Dollar for dollar, is it more valuable to society to give more education to a few or less to many? Are the external benefits of 1,000 students educated at a college which spends $2,000 per student greater or less than 500 students at one which spends $4,000? If 1,000 students complete two years or 500 four years? Do the costs incurred by institutions have much to do with the quality of education in the first place? The answers are needed to decide whether the rate of subsidy should be constant for all levels of family expenditure, or should increase or decrease at the margin as expenditure rises. If A will go to Harvard whether it is subsidized or not, but B will not attend any college without a subsidy of some kind somewhere, is it better to spend money to enable Harvard to improve an already good program for A or to spend it in a way that will get B in some decent institution somewhere?

I mentioned earlier a view held by some that we subsidize higher education as an indirect way of subsidizing other things, and that it would be better to subsidize the other things directly.[8] If higher education is socially useful because it is necessary for advanced research, or for elementary and secondary education, or for anything else that requires highly trained manpower, why not put more money into those things and then rely on private incentives to produce the needed education? In short, why not raise the salaries of scientists and teachers, and then count on people getting enough education to fill the jobs, rather than finance the education and then hope that the educated people enter the occupations in question, despite the low salaries which often characterize them? There is some debate over which is the better approach, and in this connection again we must think carefully whether higher education really

8. Mishan, "Some Heretical Thoughts on University Reform."

is a better device for sorting out talents and interests than, say, more on-the-job training. It is interesting to note that one scheme we do have for subsidizing the end product is forgiveness of student loans for persons after they enter teaching; it has not been popular with detached observers.

AID TO INSTITUTIONS OR TO STUDENTS?

Those who argue for aid to institutions often imply that only in this way will the aid produce higher-*quality* education, which they feel is especially desirable. They assume that the natural inclination of institutions which find themselves with funds available is to increase quality rather than keep tuition low and that the natural inclination of families is merely to substitute the aid for their own expenditure. Those who argue in favor of aid to students say it maximizes the choice open to families and subjects institutions to healthy competition. They argue further that incentives can be built in to ensure continued private expenditure, so that the competition need not be so cutthroat as to reduce quality.

Actually, if we assume the choice is either aid to a wide variety of institutions or aid to students who can use the aid at any of a wide variety of institutions, there may not be much difference for quality. Consider a hypothetical situation in which all institutions are private and compete vigorously for students. Variety flourishes; some competitors offer high-cost, high-quality packages; others low-cost, low-quality ones. The packages also differ in other dimensions which are important to some people but have no great importance for quality. Each institution appeals to a particular clientele. Now assume public aid is offered to those institutions, say, a fixed amount per enrolled student. Each one has a choice: it can use the funds to raise quality, or it may hold quality constant and lower the price it charges, or some combination. It must decide what its clientele wants and whether it should appeal to a different clientele. Not every institution need choose the same strategy, and there may be a variety of responses. Families, too, will have considerable choice, and their own responses likewise will be varied; some will be happy to get higher quality at the same price as before; others will prefer to buy the same quality as before at a lower price. Thus one would conclude that if most institutions do choose to upgrade quality, it is because families want it that way and would choose higher quality if aid were given directly to them.

Of course, it costs money to give money away properly, and the administrative costs are lower if aid is given to institutions. That saving can be a solid point in favor of institutional aid, especially if it is compared to student aid given as subsidized loans that are partly repayable and cost money to collect.

However, the picture changes if government aid is restricted to only one or a few institutions, as state and local government aid often is. Even in states that operate a number of low-tuition colleges and university branches, students have a narrower range of choice than if they were offered a scholarship which they could use at any school, in the state or out. The institutions, however, have more latitude than under the scholarship arrangement, for their freedom is limited only by the general characteristics of the market, not by price and quality competition from other institutions. An institution would then find it easier to impose a higher level of quality on the market than the market would choose in a more competitive situation, because the market does not have much in the way of alternatives. However, an institution could also more easily impose a *lower* quality than the population would choose if there were competition. When students can get aid only by attending particular institutions, they may be locked into a lower quality than they would choose if they received the same subsidy directly and could use it more freely.

Such restricted subsidies—to institutions—are open to objection on the general principle that they reduce choice. Some opponents also have fears about what sorts of educational programs will be shaped by the designated institutions. Against such shortcomings must be arrayed the advantages that concentration of aid may have, such as economies of scale and the creation of special kinds of social benefits valuable to a region, perhaps including the reduction of losses by emigration. A state government could never insist that its population buy education at only one place, but if it spends money to create social benefits, it may feel it should have at least some measure of control over the programs it aids.

Nevertheless, the dependence of institutions on the state raises more serious questions now than ever before, and critics will not fail to make connections between the way we finance education and the way our students behave. The public may view the state as a "generous and considerate patron of the spendthrift universities." [9] Some will call for substituting student aid for institutional aid in order to restore institutions to competition, and thus to more independence. Still others will go further and call for reduction of all kinds of public aid, saying that students and their families must put up more of their own resources and thus have more to lose by any disruptions. The present methods of aiding education are under attack, as is the whole concept of generous public support. Two critical questions are whether it is worse for institutions to be dependent on the state or on the market, and whether it is worse for students to be dependent on the state or on their parents.

9. Ibid., p. 5.

Federal Government and Other Governments:
How Big a Role for Each?

I have discussed two kinds of benefits from education: private and external. In a political system with several levels of government, there are two kinds of external benefits as well: the ones internal to some political jurisdiction and ones external to the jurisdiction, as well as to the individual. A state, for example, may be expected to discount the value of education if it expects the educated persons to leave for other parts of the country; it will also discount the benefits to the rest of the nation from the education of people who do remain. State universities charge more tuition to nonresidents, and some have specialized academic programs to meet the needs of the local economy. Jencks has noted that "Only a few public institutions have sought and obtained national constituencies, and none encourage this at the undergraduate level."[10]

One guide is: the fraction of the total public subsidy to be paid by a particular jurisdiction should be the share of benefits external to the person but internal to the jurisdiction. A local government should offer high subsidies if a large proportion of the external benefits are internal to the locality; a state's payment should depend on the benefits external to the locality but internal to the state. The federal government should assume responsibility for the rest. Unfortunately, the determination depends partly on migration, which cannot be known at the time of the financing. And migration is not the only reason benefits become external to the state and local governments, and, perhaps, not the main reason. Therefore, the principle is of little practical applicability.

The redistribution of income is a goal on a par with finance of external benefits, and is a goal that would naturally increase the role of the federal government. The federal government has traditionally accepted much of the responsibility for income redistribution in this country because much of the inequality is associated with regional differences. Further, the federal tax burden is clearly based on a steeper progressive rate system than are state and local tax burdens, so that financing education from the federal level also improves income redistribution.

One Donor among Many Donors

In addition to government subsidies, higher education gets philanthropic subsidies from private but public-spirited donors. Government must decide on its own strategy in light of these contributions. Should public aid be given without regard to the amount or extent to which

10. Christopher Jencks, "Diversity in Higher Education," in *Contemporary Issues in American Education*, U.S. Office of Education, Bulletin 1966, No. 3 (Washington: Government Printing Office, 1965).

the recipient attracts philanthropic aid? Or should government take the private gifts into account, either reducing its aid to students and institutions who get a good deal from others, or actually promising them more as an incentive to work hard to win it? The federal government faces the same kind of question—in perhaps a more important way— when it must consider its strategy in light of heavy subsidies by other governments. The problem stems from the unevenness of support from donors, who are quite selective. Should the federal government give less to a Harvard or a Rochester because it has a large endowment? Should it give smaller grants to poor students at a low-tuition state university than to poor students at a high-tuition private institution?

This problem is somewhat different from the usual one of whether or not to include a matching provision in a grant. The usual matching provision makes the donor's aid dependent on effort by the recipient, but here the question is whether, and how, the donor's help should be correlated with that of *other donors*. Philanthropic donors sometimes use the incentive feature; both foundations and individuals make "challenge" grants. Some federal aid programs, but not all, are on a matching basis. The institution is completely free to raise its own share from other donors.

In any event, some government subsidy may ultimately benefit those who are already heavily subsidized by other sources. This government subsidy may be hard to justify. The fact that the other donors are private and do not raise their money by taxation does not necessarily eliminate criticism: people may see little difference between the government levying sales taxes for education and private firms (or foundations owning their stock) paying out in donations a part of what customers pay for a firm's products. Yet if government tries to even out the distribution by granting aid inversely to what comes from elsewhere, it runs the risk of the other sources cutting back their own gifts. If a federal scholarship program, for example, makes the stipends a fixed fraction of tuition, many public institutions might be tempted to finance a greater part of their costs by tuition, knowing the adverse effects on students will be offset by more federal expenditure.

Not everyone would say that increasing tuition to gain more federal monies is a bad thing. Besides some unhappiness with the impact of income distribution through the public systems, there is uneasiness about the "crisis" in private education. For the federal government, the "crisis" raises very tricky questions. Private institutions have found it difficult to compete in the face of the enormous price advantages state schools offer. Should the relative decline of the private sector, and the absolute loss of some institutions in it, affect federal policy? In a federal system, states must have considerable autonomy in their budgetary policies. They have used their autonomy to subsidize education in different ways, and there are limits to how far a national standard may be imposed while preserving the system as a federal one.

The federal government may want to accept the present situation, making little effort to restore balance between public and private institutions or among institutions of various sizes and characteristics. This hands-off, or rather even-handed, policy would be consistent with confidence in consumer sovereignty and the market to reward the truly efficient, innovative private institutions. On the other hand, there is fear that unless the federal government deliberately offsets the unevenness of public subsidy, many of the private institutions will fall by the wayside, and the diversity so valued in American higher education will be lost. Diversity among public institutions will not count for much if most students are limited to choosing among a very few in each state. Is effective diversity enough of a national asset that the national government should strive to preserve it?

How Should Aid Vary with Income?

This discussion best comes at the close of this paper, for two reasons. First, it is interrelated with the preceding issues. Second, it is the question to which the official answers are most likely to change in the not-too-distant future. I doubt that the results of the debate on the other issues will cause much change, on economic grounds, in official policies. The chances are probably greater that, in the extension of aid to higher education, change will take the form of discrimination among students to be aided.

The question is interrelated with the other issues for several reasons. It is related to the issue of aid to students or to institutions. The public donor can offset inequalities in income distribution if it gives aid directly to students; it loses this control if it channels the aid through institutions and cannot at the same time control the institutions' pricing policies, which determine how the subsidy is transferred to students. Of course, if institutions have very homogeneous student bodies, then in choosing to help a particular one the donor can automatically limit its aid to a narrow class of students.

The income issue is also intertwined with other issues in that higher-income families may not need public aid as an inducement to buy a college education, but the aid may make a difference in the quality they are willing to pay for. If so, then an important issue becomes whether increased quality brings as much in external benefits, per dollar of cost, as the quantity of education. If quality is very important, helping the rich to pay for higher education may bring sufficient external benefits to offset any undesirable effect on equity.

Some have argued that any subsidies will inevitably go to the rich, in the sense that if aid allows a student to buy a lot of education, it will likely pay off in higher income later in his life. No matter what his family circumstances are now, he will be rich later, compared with many tax-payers in the previous generation who paid for his education, and com-pared with those in his own generation whose native ability and inclina-tions did not make it possible for them to be educated. There is a serious question about how much we should pin our redistribution strategy on aiding those with natural intelligence, and whether we should offer our endowment to the poor in the form of access to education.

It is not sufficient to reply that the educated pay higher taxes because they earn more, and thus repay the cost of their education. Because everyone with higher income pays more taxes—not just the person whose education was financed by the public—there is a lack of equity between persons of the same income. And if some of the educated person's taxes are going to repay the cost of his education, he must be paying *less* than he should for other public services that are financed by taxes.

An implication of the view that lifetime income is what counts is that governments should make loan funds available to students, but that the students should repay the loans. (A variation is that students as a whole should repay, but that each person's repayment should be contingent on his own earnings later, so that the loan scheme contains an insurance ele-ment.) This view would limit subsidies to those that provide benefits largely external to the student. If the external benefits are considered to be great, then students would repay only a portion of the amounts borrowed and grants to institutions would continue. If the external benefits are not felt to be large, students would be expected to repay loans at substantial interest rates and grants to institutions would be small.

Two very crucial questions (both of which need much more research) are the importance of quality versus quantity, and the importance of financial barriers to the poor. If greater attendance by the poor does generate as much external benefit as higher quality generates for those who would naturally attend college, and if financial encouragement of the poor is sufficient inducement, then the present system has not achieved the correct allocation of national resources. It is easy to call for an expan-sion of public expenditure, aimed specifically at lower-income groups, as the remedy. Less palatable is the conclusion that follows if it is as-sumed that budgetary constraints will not permit this expansion: subsi-dies should be reduced for the better-off and increased for the poor, quality being sacrificed for quantity. Attention to equality of opportunity, of course, strengthens these conclusions in a powerful way. On the other hand, if quality is extremely important, and if financial assistance is not the answer for the poor anyway, the present system passes with considerably higher marks.

It is perhaps useful to propose a plausible policy which a person can support if he feels that considerable external benefits accrue from higher education, yet feels that distributions from the public purse should vary inversely with family income but also give adequate incentives for quality education. This proposal attempts to reduce windfalls for better-off families and yet preserve some incentives for them to pay for quality. Let a student receive direct aid only as long as his family's own expenditure exceeds some minimum level. This minimum level would be higher for higher-income families, making them pay more out of their own pockets, than poor ones. So far the scheme is quite conventional. But also make the aid a larger and larger fraction of marginal expenditure as total expenditure rises. The student from an upper-middle-income family, merely to give an illustrative example, might receive no aid if he spends only $1,000 on tuition and fees, $100 if he spends $1,500; $250 if he spends $2,000; $450 if he spends $2,500; and so on. He thus gets no subsidy on the first $1,000; 20 percent on the next $500; 30 percent on the next $500; 40 percent on the next $500. This formula concentrates public aid at the margin, where it is likely to make a difference. For a poor family, naturally, the minimum family expenditure would be lower, perhaps zero, and the marginal subsidy percentages may be higher.[11]

In summary, higher education for everybody would force us to give up some other good things we could produce with the resources at our disposal. Knowing this, and pondering some of the particular opportunities we might have to forgo, we must examine critically the notion that higher education for everybody is a worthy goal. We must also examine critically the methods of financing we rely on, for they influence greatly just what we will have to give up. I have tried to suggest some questions still unanswered and the main areas of disagreement. I have raised only briefly questions about the worthiness of the goal in the first place, and have spent more time on financing. There is a serious question whether heavy institutional aid, especially as it is given very selectively by state governments, can still be defended even if it obviously restricts student choice and raises problems of institutional independence. And it is clear that the present methods, although they have permitted higher education for many, have not sufficed to give complete equality of oppor-

11. Bolton, "The Economics and Public Financing of Higher Education: An Overview," p. 76.

tunity—they have not *yet* brought higher education for everybody. Is it impossible for financial inducements alone to broaden equality of opportunity? Or have we failed so far only because we have devoted too many of our limited resources to offering very high cost education on such easy terms to some students?

Dividing Responsibilities in Paying for Higher Education

ROBERT W. HARTMAN

I HAVE NOT had access to the Indo-China planning papers that the National Security Council has prepared for the last two Presidents; I suspect they were inferior in quality but of the same genre as Professor Bolton's excellent essay. The documents would have raised the right questions, pointing out what information is needed to answer the questions. They would have dissected the overall problem into its component parts, indicating the appropriate spatial and temporal loci of decision making.

At the end, the policy papers would have conceded that the necessary information is not at hand ("external benefits . . . are very hard to quantify in practice . . ."), that most of the categories of analysis and associated rules are empty boxes ("the fraction of the total public subsidy to be paid by a particular jurisdiction should be the share of benefits external to the person but internal to the jurisdiction. . . .the principle is of little practical applicability") and that, as a result, some compromise proposal that gives a little weight to all (nonextreme) views is the only possible response ("useful to propose a plausible policy which a person can support if he feels that considerable external benefits accrue from higher education, yet feels that . . . [subsidies] should vary inversely with family income but also give adequate incentives for quality education").

Bolton's compromise student aid proposal gets high marks for encompassing the varied goals of public support for higher education [Asia for the Asians; the United States will not tolerate a blood bath in Vietnam]. But it is deceptive. When one gets down to the details of how much the maximum student aid should be and how much should be reserved for expenditure expansion at "the margin," we are back to some of the empty boxes of quality versus quantity in higher education [Our withdrawal shall not be precipitous . . .].

Author's note: The views expressed in this paper are not intended to represent the views of the trustees, officers, or staff of the Brookings Institution.

A different approach to finance analysis and policy for higher education seems to me both required and feasible. The approach would build on what we already know, derive conclusions from this knowledge, implement the conclusions, and proceed to more sophisticated, longer-term studies and proposals.

What do we know? We know two things about our present system of paying for higher education: (1) The structure of most public support for higher education cannot be defended as optimally satisfying any goal. (2) The higher education finance system is inherently unstable.

Bolton correctly lists the two primary goals of public financing of higher education as an expansion of higher education enrollments and an improvement in its quality. To achieve either or both of these goals, state governments enable public institutions to set low charges to students, and the federal government provides both student aid and institutional support.

Low-charge state institutions satisfy neither the quantity nor the quality goal. If states are trying to encourage enrollments by charging everybody the same price for higher education services and then rationing the spaces so as to exclude those who are most likely to respond to low prices, then certainly we can achieve this goal in a better way. If, on the other hand, state policies are intended to enhance quality in higher education, and induce external benefits, conceivably private institutions should receive no significant state support. Does the State of California believe that the external benefits of education at Stanford are that much lower than at Berkeley?

Federal college-based student aid programs (Educational Opportunity Grants, National Defense Loans, College Work-Study) confer handsome benefits on a lucky few who both meet needs tests and happen to attend institutions that come out as winners in the maze surrounding the allotment of these funds. But many equally needy students get nothing from these programs, either because the institutions they attend are losers in the allotment process or because they do not attend college at all, having lost out as high school seniors. This year another $150 million is being distributed as interest subsidies in the federal guaranteed loan program; these subsidies meet no discernible goal, considering the random process by which beneficiaries of this program are selected. Another several hundred million dollars is distributed by the federal government as indirect subsidies to instruction through support of academic research;[1] these funds may enhance quality in some institutions

1. For estimates of the instructional subsidy component in the federal budget, see David S. Mundel, "Distribution of Federal Student Subsidies," mimeographed (April 1970).

but no one has ever demonstrated why research support is the best correlate of quality. And research support is certainly not the best correlate for raising enrollments by attracting low-income youth. In addition, federal dollars are appropriated for construction of college facilities for studying, sleeping, and other less academic pursuits, but no funds are appropriated for college teaching as such. And yet, government officials, college administrators, and students would all agree that quality is more related to the unfunded function than to the funded ones.

The stability of higher education finances is threatened by the circumstance that we are asking the private sector to recoup from the market a substantial fraction of the costs of a product that state institutions are giving away.[2] The long-run equilibrium position of such a pricing system will have one of two characteristics: (1) There will be virtually no private sector in higher education as public institutions take over the bankrupt private colleges. A few very well-endowed or very innovative institutions may survive the low-price competition. (2) If public institutions fail to absorb the private institutions, competitive cost-cutting will ensure a dual, low-quality system of higher education.

What follows from this? Who should pay? The only possible guarantor of equal opportunity and of broadened enrollment in higher education is the federal government. The only efficient way for it to discharge this obligation is through student aid programs that discriminate in favor of students from low-income backgrounds. Student loans ought to play a significant part in a federal student aid package; but substantial grants will be needed for the disadvantaged. *The fulfillment of the goal of equalized opportunity through student aid should take precedence over all other federal functions in higher education.*[3]

Where would this leave state government support? States could play a vital role in enhancing the quality of higher education, once they drop the budgetary albatross of general subsidy for state institutions. With these released budget funds, states can and should offer to support projects that give some promise of yielding the external benefits to which Roger Bolton refers. Institutions, private or state-sponsored, should compete for these funds and should be held accountable to the public for results. Although the specter of retrograde state legislators evaluating

2. See Michael Clurman, "Does Higher Education Need More Money?" in *The Economics and Financing of Higher Education in the United States: A Compendium of Papers Submitted to the Joint Economic Committee, Congress of the United States* (Washington: Government Printing Office, 1969), pp. 632–51.

3. I do not intend here to denigrate the importance of federal support for research. But budget support for research should be as separated from support for undergraduate education as research activity on most campuses is removed from undergraduates.

higher education programs is just cause for alarm, the alternatives of no support or centralized evaluation seem to me even worse.

At some later date, after the revolution, it will be appropriate to ask whether state governments have failed to take into account benefits that spill over their own jurisdictions, and thus necessitate some degree of federal support for quality in higher education. Moreover, we shall have to grope our way toward finding the best package of student aid to ensure equal opportunity.

The restructuring of higher education finance broached here has the merit of at least addressing itself to the national goals in higher education, and its implementation would cure the instability of higher education finance. All that is needed now is a fixed schedule of state and federal withdrawal from pointless budgetary support and a concomitant commitment to new priorities.

The Choosers and the Chosen

FREDERIC W. NESS

ALTHOUGH ROGER BOLTON was considerate enough not to overwhelm us with sum totals, implicit throughout his paper is the ineluctable conclusion that universal higher education is going to be tremendously costly. Given the fact of limited institutional resources, the nation will be impelled to make certain hard choices. My observations will concern some characteristics of the choosers and the choices they can make.

Clearly the largest category of choosers in the foreseeable future will be the taxpayers. By a curious irony, our system makes infinitely complicated any assertion of taxpayers' priorities in such matters as the building of superhighways from Dubuque to Peoria or from Cape Canaveral to the lunar Sea of Tranquility. But, at least in our lesser political entities, the taxpayers can periodically protest such unrelated extravaganzas by voting down a school or college bond issue. They will continue to do so.

The corporate or private philanthropoid has opportunity for choice, for there are always eager and deserving hands rattling his gates. Whether he will be able to survive the added demands of higher education for everybody remains to be tested. But even if he does—and long may he thrive—his tribe's resources are not likely to increase to anything commensurate with the new demands. He will have to adjust to the humility of being but a drop in the bucket. We can only hope that the experience will not reorder his priorities.

The student, too, is ostensibly in a position to make choices. He can elect not only which type of college he will attend but also, in theory, whether he will attend at all. We are increasingly aware, however, that he has far fewer options than he may think. His actual choice of institutions has never been unlimited. It is becoming less so. Further, the draft and the drying-up of other channels leading into the economic mainstream virtually force him to become the universal collegian. He may be one of the chosen, but his choice is increasingly limited.

Among the list of choosers, one might conclude—from the consideration given the matter in Dr. Bolton's paper—that the college or university itself has virtually no choices in the new movement toward universal accommodation. Even though a few institutions might retain some choice, for the aggregate such a conclusion seems all but inescapable. I anticipate, for example, that a substantial increase of postsecondary technological training under the purview of the consumer industries will keep our academic recruiters calling "come one, come all," as our traditional institutions try to compete in a diversified educational marketplace.

Thus, it is hard not to agree with Dr. Bolton's prognostications of lean years. Even if we had no other problems, the prospect of a mounting demand for educational services of increasing diversity and sophistication against a backdrop of diminishing fiscal support is scarcely cheering. Bolton, if I read him aright, has questioned whether we can actually afford higher education for everybody. Or, even more important, whether it is necessary or desirable. Far less costly and potentially more satisfying for many of our young people would be the development of other means of access to the economy. Our academic institutions might well work with other agencies to devise a new type of apprenticeship under the aegis of unions or consumer industries or work to develop forms of national service that would lead directly to governmental or nongovernmental employment. In these ways some students who find little relevance in present collegiate patterns might become less frustrated or discontented.

But since the development of many acceptable alternatives to college training is not likely to happen in the absence of extrinsic changes of a cataclysmic order, we in higher education will have to examine with great care our already diminishing options. This planning cannot be done, I am convinced, solely at annual meetings of national associations, much as I commend the planners of such meetings. Work will have to be done as well through smaller regional groupings, and ultimately on the individual campus.

While I was reviewing Dr. Bolton's paper, with its assumption that we are moving rapidly toward universal higher education, I found in my mail a brief report on a major university from which I extract the following:

> During the ten years ending in 1966–67, the yearly increase in fall quarter enrollment averaged 327 students. This may not seem very much, but it was sufficient to finance the largest part of the faculty expansion that took place during this period. . . . Thus about 67 percent of the faculty expansion in the decade ending in 1967 was financed by increases in enrollment.
>
> In the last three years, fall enrollment has increased by 113, or 38 per year; at the same time the Academic Council has increased by 133, or 44 per year. . . . These 133 faculty members are adding at least $2.2 million to the faculty payroll in 1969–70 . . . , an amount that considerably exceeds the projected 1969–70 deficit.

The writer of the report then concludes with the following observation:

> While it is convenient to blame the federal government for our financial problems, the fact is that the present difficulties result in large measure from inadequate forward planning on our own part.

How much more forward planning will be needed as each college and university seeks to determine its own commitment to the new demand for expanded postsecondary education!

The message is clear. We do in fact still have some choices to make on campus. A college education is still the best way for a large portion of our youth to enter the economy, and it is up to us to devise the most effective and economically practicable ways of making it available to the largest possible numbers. Our reluctance to examine the whole question of faculty productivity; our changes in governance patterns, not enough of which contribute to demonstrable improvement or administrative effectiveness; our failure to utilize our own expertise (curiously, few of our faculty consultants to business and industry seem to have time to serve on college management committees)—all these give little encouragement to a hoped-for quick solution to the conflicting pulls of quantity, quality, and costs. But perhaps the onslaught of universal higher education will force us at last to become a genuine academic community wherein students, faculty, and administration will face together some of the hard choices laid out in Dr. Bolton's challenging but formidable analysis.

Responsibility

HEINZ EULAU

Political Norms Affecting Decisions
Concerning Higher Education

I F, AS IS SOMETIMES SAID, POLITICS WERE SIMPLY THE ART OF THE POSSIBLE, appraising the political component of options in choice making on public policies and their consequences would be relatively easy. At least it would not be more difficult than assessing options in economic decision making where standards of rational behavior are assumed to guide choice and thus permit reasonably accurate predictions of outcomes. But politics is not only the art of the possible; it is also a labyrinth of intangibles through which decision-makers must find their way, often by trial and error, if they wish to promote their own policy objectives or subvert the objectives of their opponents.

PATTERNS OF POLITICAL BEHAVIOR

The culture of politics, unlike that of economics, provides for rules, roles, norms, or standards which often tend to defy ordinary rationality and escape systematic comprehension, yet which in the long run are conducive to the achievement of political goals. To capture these rules or norms—frequently informal understandings—in models of the political process is difficult, but this very difficulty is reason for doubting the viability of the recently proposed models of political process which would treat political decisions as if they were only economic ones.[1]

Because we increasingly speak of the "economics of education" and the "politics of education" in the same breath, it does not follow that the

This paper draws in part on a survey of state officials conducted in 1968 by the author for the Carnegie Commission on Higher Education. Neither the Carnegie Commission nor Stanford University is responsible for this paper.

1. See, for instance, Anthony Downs, *An Economic Theory of Democracy* (New York: Harper & Row, 1957); James M. Buchanan and Gordon Tullock, *The Calculus of Consent* (Ann Arbor: University of Michigan Press, 1962); Mancur Olson, Jr., *The Logic of Collective Action: Public Goods and the Theory of Groups* (Cambridge, Mass.: Harvard University Press, 1965); R. L. Curry, Jr., and L. L. Wade, *A Theory of Political Exchange: Economic Reasoning in Political Analysis* (Englewood Cliffs, N.J.: Prentice-Hall, 1968).

behavioral patterns involved are merely two sides of the same coin. Politics is an arena of action in which the goals of policy making are generally more ambiguous than in economics. In fact, there may be no goals at all, at least at the level of the collectivity, so that politics becomes eminently concerned with goal setting as its primary activity. Examples are the economists' concern with *competition* and the political scientists' concern with *conflict*. Competition is a form of contention that is possible if goals are given or are reasonably clear: the contending parties agree on goals, and this agreement makes competition feasible. Both sides want essentially the same thing; for instance, economic firms compete for consumers and profits. There is, of course, competition in politics as well, as when two democratic parties compete for voter support and public offices. But, more often than not, political contention is conflictual because there is no agreement on goals; and when there is agreement, politics loses much of its luster. Further, where consensus exists, political actors may also entertain hidden agenda that make for tension and new conflicts. But the resolution of such tensions or conflicts may follow paths that need not be political, such as the specification of formal jurisdictions, the invocation of specialized expertise, the circulation of personnel, or the hierarchical determination of issues.

Politics certainly utilizes these pathways of conflict resolution. Especially it does so in decisional contexts which, like those in the Congress and the more modernized state legislatures of California, Illinois, and New York, have become increasingly streamlined as a result of executive influence, party discipline, specialization of labor among committees, and the emergence of professional staffs. But elected politicians, unlike appointed administrators, cannot easily be contained by management practices. Although the norm of seniority, for instance, is a powerful control device, Young Turks are always ready to rebel; although a committee structure based on a functional division of labor may be present, it can be —and often is—circumvented in the assignment of bills by a wily speaker or reference committee; although the party organization may threaten the insurgent with nonsupport at the polls, the rebel's constituency relationships may be good enough to make party discipline an empty threat. Politics is, above all, a collegial game in which conflicts are resolved by strategies of behavior—strategies of bargaining, exchanging, compromising, persuading, and negotiating—that assume power differentials among the players. Let us listen to a Congressman who was asked, "What would happen when the Senate and the House have different views about higher education?" He replied:

> The House usually wins. I say that facetiously. We like to think we do. I guess the Senate likes to think it wins and I guess in a conference no one

wins. You have to finally subordinate your views. No one can lose, no one can win. There have to be compromises. Senators because of the size of their constituency and because of the diversity of the areas that they must cover in their Senatorial service usually can't be expected to be informed on the details of these programs as can House members who have . . . smaller constituencies and less demands upon their legislative time to do a great, wide range of things. So most House members, not all, but most become more highly specialized in the particular area that they work in. And when you get in conference that begins to show up. The Senate has to rely on staff to make decisions. House members usually rely more upon their own expertise than the Senators. It is just the nature of the institutions as much as anything else. But really no one side wins all the time. I think the Senate is usually pretty generous in accommodating the House in its requests, but it is based on that understanding that House members do have an opportunity to see more of the details of the operation or programs than does a Senator, and I find that true in most conferences. While Senators will stick tenaciously to good things they believe in, they do recognize that there is a difference in the way we approach problems. No reflection on them at all. A Senator has got to be a great generalist and he has to place great reliance upon his staff, because he has just got too many decisions to make, while we are confined to narrower fields, comparatively speaking.

There is, of course, coercion as well, but it is a strategy that politicians risk only if the pay-off will likely be greater than the price of retaliation. It rarely is. Politicians are past masters in the fine art of decisional cost accounting. Partisanship as a hidden form of coercion will be avoided by the clever politician. A congressional committee chairman is speaking:

I simply never have been as partisan as some of my Democratic friends. I know that they disapprove of this. They do not like it and criticize me for it. But it seems to me that in regard to long-range goals you must have bipartisan support, and it just makes no sense to do otherwise. And I frankly think that Congressman X is just as much interested in good education at the college and university level as I am and he's got a lot of good ideas and it is pretty sad not to bring it out on the floor without the bipartisan support; so I just stay in the committee and don't try to get the bill to a vote until we have that.

The impact of political norms, standards, or criteria conducive to conflict resolution on choice of policy alternatives and assessment of consequences is difficult to harness in a model of the political process that links content of policies with decision-making procedures. The parties interested in educational policy making—educational associations, lobbies, college and university administrators, faculty, and even students and their parents—are likely to see the educational arena as more or less self-contained. For politicians, however, education is only one item on the agenda of issues that call for the specification of goals and the setting of priorities. Within education itself the field of higher education is only one component. The politician's frame of reference is necessarily larger than that of any particular interest, and he cannot afford to neglect a variety of interests that may be germane to his political needs. As a result, the politician is involved in a complex maze of negotiations over diverse political issues. A Republican U.S. Senator from a Mountain state expressed this sensitivity to the play of interests in the educational field alone:

> The higher education interest groups obviously are diverse. They also have an internecine warfare going on between them which is sometimes very extraordinary. Generally speaking, people think of the Catholics, for example, as being more or less monolithic in their efforts to promote a certain type of educational support. As a matter of fact, they are not. There are about four different groups in the Catholic educational process, and they are fighting between themselves, but they only have one spokesman here, and he is for the group that is militant and trying to get aid. There is a group of people in the Catholic educational field who don't want it or want it in a different form. Then you have the problems of the land-grant colleges versus the state-supported institutions which are not land-grant. Land-grant colleges, by and large, want to have the only direct aid of anybody in the educational field. And then, of course, you have the public-supported universities versus the private institutions, but this is not as extreme as I thought it might be. It was very bitter for a while between the public schools and the Catholics in particular. I find, however, that you also have problems with the Lutheran schools, you have problems with some of the Jewish, and I am sure we have problems with some of the Episcopalians, although they are not quite as vocal about it. . . . Therefore, on the whole, we recognize on the committee, I think, that there isn't one educational bloc as such, although they all want to get more funds. That's about the only thing that they really agree on.

In order to protect himself from undue exposure to pressures and commitments in any one area of public policy that may get him into trouble in another area, the politician has invented standards of choice and norms of conduct that serve this purpose. He jealously safeguards his freedom of action. The political requirements of being involved in a host of policy arenas call for strategies that make the political process appear kaleidoscopic, diffuse, and intangible. These strategies and accompanying norms have the effect of making politicians appear men of virtue somewhat less than most of them probably are. The American politician suffers from occupational role strains that make his status more ambivalent than that of most professionals.[2]

Much has been written about the roles that politicians play in legislating public policies and representing their constituencies,[3] the styles of response they adopt vis-à-vis interest and pressure groups,[4] the norms by which they regulate their conduct toward each other,[5] the informal relationships that bind them together,[6] the strategies they follow in seeking to obtain their objectives,[7] and the significance they ascribe to expertise in the making of decisions.[8] But these studies have dealt with the behavioral patterns involved either in general terms (independent of particular policy arenas) or (at the other extreme) in the context of specific case studies

2. William C. Mitchell, "The Ambivalent Social Status of the American Politician," *Western Political Quarterly*, September 1959, pp. 683–98; and "Occupational Role Strains: The American Elective Public Official," *Administrative Science Quarterly*, September 1958, pp. 219–28.

3. The leading work still is John C. Wahlke et al., *The Legislative System: Explorations in Legislative Behavior* (New York: John Wiley & Sons, 1962). See also Roger H. Davidson, *The Role of the Congressman* (New York: Pegasus, 1969).

4. John C. Wahlke et al., "American State Legislators' Role Orientations toward Pressure Groups," *Journal of Politics*, May 1960, pp. 203–27; Betty H. Zisk, Heinz Eulau, and Kenneth Prewitt, "City Councilmen and the Group Struggle: A Typology of Role Orientations," *Journal of Politics*, August 1965, pp. 618–46; Lester W. Milbrath, *The Washington Lobbyists* (Chicago: Rand McNally, 1963); Harmon Zeigler and Michael Baer, *Lobbying: Interaction and Influence in American State Legislatures* (Belmont, Calif.: Wadsworth, 1969).

5. Donald R. Matthews, "The Folkways of the Senate," *U.S. Senators and Their World* (Chapel Hill: University of North Carolina Press, 1960), pp. 92–117; Wahlke et al., "Rules of the Game," *The Legislative System*, pp. 141–69; Allan Kornberg, "Rules of the Game in the Canadian House of Commons," *Journal of Politics*, May 1964, pp. 358–80; Ralph K. Huitt, "The Morse Committee Assignment Controversy: A Study in Senate Norms," *American Political Science Review*, June 1957, pp. 313–29.

6. Samuel C. Patterson, "Patterns of Interpersonal Relations in a State Legislative Group: The Wisconsin Assembly," *Public Opinion Quarterly*, Spring 1959, pp. 101–10; Wayne L. Francis, "Influence and Interaction in a State Legislative Body," *American Political Science Review*, December 1962, pp. 953–60; Alan Fiellin, "The Functions of Informal Groups in Legislative Institutions," *Journal of Politics*, February 1962, pp. 72–91.

7. James D. Barber, *The Lawmakers: Recruitment and Adaptation to Legislative Life* (New Haven, Conn.: Yale University Press, 1965); Richard F. Fenno, Jr., *The Power of the Purse: Appropriations Politics in Congress* (Boston: Little, Brown, 1966); Ralph K. Huitt and Robert L. Peabody, *Congress: Two Decades of Analysis* (New York: Harper & Row, 1969).

8. William Buchanan et al., "The Legislator as Specialist," *Western Political Quarterly*, September 1960, pp. 636–51; Heinz Eulau, "Bases of Authority in Legislative Bodies: A Comparative Analysis," *Administrative Science Quarterly*, December 1962, pp. 309–21; Nelson W. Polsby et al., "The Growth of the Seniority System in the U.S. House of Representatives," *American Political Science Review*, September 1969, pp. 787–807.

of low generalizability.[9] Even if these patterns and their consequences for public policy making are sufficiently irregular to make lawlike generalizations difficult, they are not as random as the case studies in particular arenas of public policy seem to suggest.

Unfortunately, studies that connect patterns of political behavior, including standards of choice and norms of conduct, to broad areas of public policy rather than to specific instances (say, trade legislation or defense appropriations) are rare. In the field of educational policy they are even rarer, and in the field of higher education they are almost nonexistent.[10] One may speculate about the impact of political norms on the content of public policies and their implications for policy making in higher education, yet the speculation would probably only obfuscate what is likely to be the case. I shall limit myself in what follows, therefore, to some limited findings of a survey of American state politicians, chiefly legislators but also some executives. These findings fall somewhere between general statements that might fit the educational arena, and the recitation of instances in which political standards or norms affected the choice among policy options and possibly their consequences.

NATURE OF THE SURVEY

In 1968 I was commissioned by the Carnegie Commission on Higher Education to survey how state legislators and certain state executive officials perceived the problems and issues of higher education, their attitudes toward various aspects of higher education, and their expectations of future developments.[11] As a result, we conducted fairly intensive, mainly taped interviews with a highly selected group of respondents in California, Texas, Illinois, New York, Pennsylvania, Iowa, Kansas, Kentucky, and Louisiana.[12] These states were selected because they are located in different regions of the country and are characterized by variously complex systems of higher education. The respondents, about twelve in each state, were selected for their importance in policy making in higher edu-

9. The classic and still one of the best of these case studies is Stephen K. Bailey, *Congress Makes a Law: The Story Behind the Employment Act of 1946* (New York: Columbia University Press, 1950); among more recent studies, see Raymond A. Bauer, Ithiel de Sola Pool, and Lewis A. Dexter, *American Business and Public Policy: The Politics of Foreign Trade* (New York: Atherton Press, 1963).

10. See, for instance, Nicholas A. Masters, Robert H. Salisbury, and Thomas H. Eliot, *State Politics and the Public Schools: An Exploratory Analysis* (New York: Alfred Knopf, 1964); Edgar Litt, *The Public Vocational University: Captive Knowledge and Public Power* (New York: Holt, Rinehart & Winston, 1969).

11. Heinz Eulau and Harold Quinley, *American State Officials' Attitudes Toward Higher Education* (New York: McGraw-Hill Book Co., 1970) is a condensed version of the survey.

12. Ten intensive interviews were also conducted in the Congress by Dr. Robert L. Peabody. Some excerpts from these interviews were used earlier in this paper.

cation, such as speakers, floor leaders, or chairmen of education and finance committees. Fifty-six respondents were Democrats and forty-six were Republicans. The limited, but by no means arbitrary, nature of the sample precluded making exact distributive statements. We were interested in discovering qualities of expression and themes. Although none of our open-end questions was designed to probe for standards of choice or norms of conduct, observations with regard to at least some of them can be made. In particular, I shall deal here with four norms that emerged most strongly from the interview protocols—the norm of responsiveness, the norm of passivity in oversight, the norm of authority, and the norm of comparison. I shall, in conclusion, deal with the respondents' reactions to the central question of the theme "Higher Education for Everybody?"

THE NORM OF RESPONSIVENESS

Politicians are prone to protest that their policy positions are dictated by "conscience," by their convictions of what is right or wrong. But the luxury of this role orientation is readily sacrificed if constituency pressures are sufficiently strong to preclude the consideration of alternatives. In the latter case, the norm of independent judgment is readily displaced by the norm of responsiveness, which is probably the norm taken more seriously by politicians themselves as well as by their publics. Yet, this norm seems to be of limited relevance in policy making concerning higher education because constituency opinion (rather than constituency interest, which may or may not be articulated) is of relatively low political salience most of the time. Of course, constituency silence may be due to the politician's ability to anticipate reactions to what he might do, and this "law of anticipated reactions" makes it difficult to trace the flow of cause and effect in the educational policy-making process.

Our evidence suggests that the public does not communicate much with state politicians concerning higher education, and that such exchange as occurs tends to be sporadic and unorganized, usually dealing with some specific matter but not with higher education as an institutional concern of society. A respondent confirmed the lack of interest in higher education policies on the part of the general public:

INTERVIEWER: We are asking you all these questions because we know that legislators hear a good deal about education from their constituents and interest groups. From whom in your district are you most likely to hear about higher education?

RESPONDENT: Well, that's a false assumption. We hear from the voters only about the [secondary] schools, damn near don't hear from anybody about higher education. The only time I can think of we've heard anything much was when the new campuses were proposed, and that was mainly not from people in my district, but from the private institutions and from some people who had an interest in getting the campus one place or another. But that's very unusual.

When legislators do hear from constituents, it is rarely from the average citizen. Respondents almost unanimously reported that most of their contacts at home, if there are contacts, are with people directly connected with the colleges and universities. A Texas legislator with a junior college and a respected private university in his district reported:

We never hear anything from ordinary citizens about higher education. I never have. I have never gotten a single letter from a single constituent asking me for an opinion about anything in higher education.

A member of the Illinois House Appropriations Committee indicated a similar paucity of correspondence:

I would say that 95 percent of my correspondence or communications from my district on education deals with grammar schools and high schools, not with higher education—although I think in my district a very high percentage of people do go to college.

The reason for popular silence, in respondents' views, is simple enough —people outside the field of higher education simply do not think about it. As a result, some politicians equate constituent silence with satisfaction. A Louisiana respondent expressed this position well, as follows:

Well, I think that the parents are well satisfied, so there are no real comments—or bad comments. Their children are getting into the schools they want to go to—we've been accepting them. So, I don't think they're aware of the real problems in education—whether we're getting the proper education or whether our dollar is being spent properly. . . . They see their child go through school, they see him graduate, and they're pleased. And so there's not much comment. They're satisfied.

A New Yorker said very much the same thing:

Very few members of the public have the slightest knowledge of what is going on. The mother and father are concerned about whether their son is going to get into college; that is what they are concerned about. As long as you are making that available, and you are making it possible for them economically, that's it.

Unfortunately, our interviews were conducted prior to the disorders at Columbia University in the spring of 1968 and the subsequent escalation of student unrest throughout the country. Recent events in Congress and some state legislatures have shown that campus disorders do have an impact on legislative policy making in higher education. An Iowa respondent, who thought it was "appalling how little people really worry" about higher education as such, described the kinds of things that stimulate constituent complaints and, presumably, legislative response:

> They are concerned when the students burn their draft cards, when kids take the law into their own hands, and a few get out of line. Some of them are upset about hippies and a few about the kind of kookie fellows and kookie professors who get into the press. But they aren't, I'm afraid, concerned with higher education as such.

Yet, if complaints do occur and the mail is heavy, legislators are not necessarily impressed. "Just because you get a pile of letters doesn't mean that everybody is thinking that way," a Californian stated; and invoking the norm of responsiveness, he continued: "It's the people that aren't writing to you—you have to evaluate their attitudes too." Another respondent argued:

> You hear usually from people who do not have a four-year institutional experience. They are only reacting against the use of four-letter words. . . . These are people who are religiously oriented, and they object to the taxpayers' dollars being spent for things they don't believe in.

These and similar remarks reflect what is well known about a politician's response to communications and pressure. If what he hears agrees with his views, even if it comes from a minority, his response will be favorable; if what he hears disagrees with his views, his response tends to be unfavorable. His own freedom of action depends on the balancing of diverse viewpoints that he can discern, but the norm of responsiveness is likely to be invoked only if it suits his predispositions or if he feels threatened at the polls.

Higher education, it appears, has low salience in the perceptual world of state politicians because the conditions of high salience—articulated demands from a broad section of the electorate or from highly intense special interests—are missing. As a result, the average legislator is likely to give his attention to other matters that loom more prominently in his mind as he sets his own legislative priorities. While this indifference deprives the legislature of significant inputs, it frees higher education of some political constraints that might otherwise be present. Higher education policies or appropriations are less likely to be subject to the kind of bargaining that takes place in policy areas where the stakes are seen as significant for political survival, especially for politicians from districts that are highly competitive in either primaries or general elections.[13]

13. See Heinz Eulau et al., "The Role of the Representative," *American Political Science Review*, September 1959, pp. 742–56; Kenneth Prewitt and Heinz Eulau, "Political Matrix and Political Representation," *American Political Science Review*, June 1969, pp. 427–41.

THE NORM OF PASSIVITY IN OVERSIGHT

Oversight of administration is generally accepted as a legitimate function of legislative bodies. This function is difficult to distinguish from control, but the distinction does not matter here because, whether oversight or control, the behavioral patterns, as far as higher education is concerned, appear to be dominated by a norm of passivity. Nor does it matter whether the norm is deliberate or itself the consequence of other circumstances in the legislature's environment. Most legislators in the nine states of the survey felt that legislative oversight should be limited to the most general budgetary matters and to the broadest policy guidelines. For instance, the particulars of admission, curriculum, and even construction are considered essentially "academic affairs" best left to executive supervision or to the institutions themselves. A California assemblyman made the point:

> If you start controlling the curriculum you control the end product. I'd sort of back away from that. I think that . . . the Legislature should determine to what extent it wants to finance specialized kinds of education in the professional areas and law schools, medical schools, and that sort of thing. But it should be on a basis of evaluating recommendations made by the institutions themselves and by the Coordinating Council itself. I think the initiative ought to come there. And we have to evaluate these in terms of our set of priorities. What we can afford and what we can't afford.

When the norm of passivity is rationalized, it seems to derive either from a belief that "academic freedom" should be protected by legislative self-restraint and that "politics" should be kept out of higher education, or from a realization that legislators are not really qualified to make decisions on matters that call for "professional" determination. In part this deference to professionalism in higher education seems to stem from a profound sense of reality. Legislators recognize that their environment is characterized by too much work, too little time, and not enough staff to permit more than perfunctory attention to the oversight function.

Like all norms, of course, the norm of passivity may be broken. At least some respondents revealed that the legislature does not always follow the principle of nonintervention in academic affairs. Instances of legislative retaliation against university officials who, in the legislators' judgment, are reluctant to control student unrest and radical activities were cited as examples of situations in which the legislature had been "forced to act" because professional university administrators were neglecting their responsibilities to the best interests of the state's taxpayers. Our respondent put it this way:

I generally subscribe to the view of autonomy as far as the academic community is concerned, and I feel that we must rely on the people in education to make the decisions which affect education. That's about the best answer that I can give you, and I've tended to oppose efforts to use the pursestrings to force the academic community into courses of action which it was reluctant to take. I do think, though, autonomy means responsibility and I think that if higher education doesn't function responsibly and doesn't deal with these problems in a way which satisfies the public, which convinces the public that it's getting its so-called taxpayer dollar's worth, then there will be pressure on the legislature to involve itself in higher education.

In general, it appears, passivity in oversight is the norm in the state legislature's stance toward higher education. This self-restraint on the legislature's part is probably conducive to academic self-determination. In the view of some legislators, the norm is broken if the institutions of higher learning act "irresponsibly." The stress that legislators are inclined to place on being "forced to act" under certain conditions is perhaps the best proof of the norm's significance. They evidently prefer quiescence to turbulence in their relationships with the academic community.

The Norm of Authority

Closely related to, and in some respects a corollary of, the norm of passivity is the norm of authority. In many state legislatures specialization is highly institutionalized, so that effective decision making, in contrast to formal voting, is in the hands of individuals who occupy the crucial gatekeeping positions in the legislative hierarchy—particularly chairmen and senior members of committees or subcommittees. Not only are these gatekeepers of the legislative business the best informed on matters of higher education, but also the flow of communication to the legislature as a whole seems to cease at this point of the decision-making process. The small amount of information on higher education matters available to the rank and file in turn induces them to depend on the recommendations of those in the know. The norm of authority emerges as an important variable affecting educational policy decisions. A California legislative leader stated the predicament of the rank and file as follows:

Let me put it this way. I'm a senior member of the Senate. I'm now in the upper quarter of the men here on the basis of seniority, so I'm put into committees where the needs become more obvious to me. But to the men who are not, I think they have real voids [in information]. The men who have never served on the Education or Finance Committee, that's the majority of the Senate, I don't think they know enough about [higher education]. I don't think it's brought to them enough.

The rank-and-file perspective was articulated in detail by this respondent:

> The budget as originally prepared at the department level doesn't have any possible way of getting to us. . . . We hardly have any idea of what it was in the beginning. What did some professor or some department head have in mind when he was preparing his budget perhaps eighteen months or two years before the document ever arrives to us? What really are the desires and the ambitions and the plans of the people down at the department levels in these various schools? Surely, somebody has some imagination; somebody is offering some dramatic new programs. These things are all weeded out before we ever get them.

Asked if there were some way to change the situation, he continued:

> We seem to be enmeshed in the established bureaucracy. The bureaucracy works fairly well, but it does seem to make the transmission of information between the legislators and the people out in the field difficult. I don't know. . . . I just feel frustration that the lines of communication are so long and they have so many obstacles. It is very difficult to see the real picture if you have to get it after all these siftings.

Although most rank-and-file members of the legislature probably share this respondent's predicament, most have learned to live with it. Not surprisingly, therefore, most legislators want guidance from, and are prepared to accept the authority of, their colleagues who are on the inside of policy making concerning higher education, and they are willing to rely on the recommendations that come from the governor or special administrative bodies such as boards of regents or coordinating councils. Indeed, there appears to be a general feeling that these agencies, rather than the legislature, should be the primary governmental force in the state's system of higher education. Reliance on the authority of expertise may at times be resented, but it is a norm of conduct that under modern conditions of specialization cannot be readily dispensed with.

The Norm of Comparison

A Supreme Court justice once referred to the American states as "experimental chambers," suggesting that innovative policies might be tried in one state and, if successful, imitated in other states, and failure in one state would not have dire consequences in others. The evidence from our study is overwhelming that legislators pay close attention to what is happening to higher education in other states. The norm of comparison appears to be well institutionalized and to affect educational decisions.

Although most legislators, in making comparisons between their own state's system of higher education and that of other states, tended to view their own in a favorable light, they discriminated among the states which serve as standards of comparison. Legislators in California and New York most often compared each other's systems; they seemed to agree that the New York schools were rapidly approaching the excellence of California schools. Needless to say, the New Yorkers were pleased, while the Californians were concerned. According to a New Yorker:

> Yes, we make that comparison with California all the time . . . during the whole debate in the early '60's, the question of California and New York came up. . . . I think we are keeping up with them. We weren't for a long time, but we are now.

On the other hand, California respondents admitted that their state was losing ground to New York. For instance:

> I think we're number one, but New York is catching up with us. In the next five years we will be number two. . . . I don't think the Senate knows how fast New York is moving. . . . At the rate we're going, we will not be able to keep up. We're going to have to be cutting back. Instead of talking about growing in California with population demands, we are talking about back-paddling.

Legislators in the other relatively wealthy states—Illinois, Texas, and Pennsylvania—also paid heed to New York or California. An Illinois official stated, for instance:

> We look at the leading states of the nation—the large states, the wealthy states, the industrial states, with which to make our comparisons. . . . We ask if Illinois is doing as much as California. . . . We don't compare with other states. We don't use national norms to make our comparisons. Except if we fall below them, we feel that we really are behind because we should be far ahead of the national norms.

Although respondents in states with educationally less developed systems also often cited California or New York as models, they tended to make comparisons with states that were similar to their own in the level of development of higher education or of economic wealth, or that were geographically propinquitous. In doing so, many different criteria of "relative indulgence" or "relative deprivation" served the purposes of comparison. A Kentucky respondent, for instance, applied the yardstick of economic capability:

> Now, from my knowledge of what exists in other states and Kentucky, I don't know of any area that we're lagging behind in higher education. Oh, true, we could pick out some states with heavily endowed colleges and that sort of thing, and some states with heavier taxes, such as California, that are perhaps doing more than Kentucky as far as ability to pay

goes, than Kentucky is doing. Certainly for a state like Kentucky, not the richest of the states by any means, we're making, I think, maximum effort in higher education.

A Texan, making a regional comparison, was

highly pleased. At least as far as with what we would classify as the Southern states or the Southwestern states. . . . I would say that we rank number one.

But another Texas respondent was more somber:

You have to talk about higher education in Texas in two completely different frames of reference—one is the University of Texas at Austin and the other is everybody else. If you talk about Austin, I think you would have to say that we are up with the top ten or fifteen public institutions in the country. Perhaps I am over-optimistic about that, but I get the impression that we are making some very important strides at that institution. If you talk about the rest of them, I think that they are sadly substandard. If you compare them with California, it is just ludicrous. If you compare them with the state university system in New York, it is just—well, there is not any comparison. . . . The basic problem here is that we have too many schools, too little central coordination, and too much politics involved in who gets what.

There can be no question that the norm of comparison is a powerful stimulus in guiding development in higher education, as it is in many other policy areas.[14] Comparing one's own state with others makes for imitation and the diffusion of innovations. The norm of comparison has clearly a significant influence on the policy process as well as policy outcomes in the field of higher education.

Higher Education for Everybody?

The norms I have reviewed so far are essentially procedural rules which are especially germane to decision making concerning higher education. What of substantive norms—those basic policy positions on which a broad consensus might be expected to exist or which, on the contrary, may be sources of conflict? It is appropriate, in the context of a conference which seeks to shed light on the question of "Higher Education for Everybody?" to conclude with a résumé of legislators' orientations in this matter. It is a question on which polity and university may be disagreed. Yet, surprisingly, only relatively few of our hundred-odd respon-

14. Jack L. Walker, "The Diffusion of Innovations among the American States," *American Political Science Review*, September 1969, pp. 880–99; see also Wayne L. Francis, *Legislative Issues in the Fifty States: A Comparative Analysis* (Chicago: Rand McNally, 1967).

dents supported unequivocally the idea of universal public higher education; many more either rejected it or stated important qualifications.

Endorsement of universal higher education came primarily from legislators in the largest states with complex systems—Texas, California, and New York. In general, universal higher education was seen to benefit state and nation as much as the individual student. A California senator responded enthusiastically to the question "Would you say that everyone is entitled to a college education at public expense?" as follows:

> Absolutely, absolutely. I believe that the nation benefits from this. I don't think that everybody would end up going to college because some people are obviously not going to go. But for those who want to go, there should be an opportunity.

A Texan felt that at least a junior college education should be available:

> I think that society has gotten sufficiently complex that everybody should be entitled, at this point, to a junior college education. I'm not prepared to say that everybody ought to be entitled to a four-year education.

Most of those favorable to universal higher education stressed that young men and women should have the "opportunity" to go to college, though not necessarily at public expense—"I will say that I think every student in this state who wants to go to college should have the opportunity. I didn't say free," one respondent put it. Some legislators emphasized that, with opportunity given, the initial responsibility for seeking a higher education should be up to the individual student. For instance:

> I said at the beginning that I didn't think the state necessarily should furnish everyone with a college education. I think it's the obligation of the state to furnish every boy and girl an opportunity to get an education. But I think they should do it and must do it on their own initiative.

At times, opportunity was linked to the problem of student ability and desire, as in this response:

> Everyone who has the desire and the ability [should be able to go to college]. And the two go together. I think the question of abilities is a very difficult one to solve. Again, it is a mixture of motivation, ability, and previous training. . . . But the area of opportunity lies in higher education in our society. You cannot make it in our society . . . unless you have gone to college.

A few respondents opposed college education for everybody at public expense. Most of them thought it infeasible because of financial problems, and some felt that some young people might simply not be qualified. Others felt that students themselves should contribute to financing their education, on the ground that they would then have more of a stake in it and get more out of it. Loan programs were seen as an alternative to free education. A Pennsylvania official stated:

> I would place the burden of repaying on each one who would secure the benefits of higher education. Through that method I think they will get much more out of it. The other day at an educational conference one man spoke up and said he had sweated blood to get a little education on his own and now he's sweating blood to get an education for his boy and girl and he believed that that was wrong—that the boy and girl should be doing their own sweating.

The variety of responses to the question on universal public education, ranging from enthusiastic support to bitter opposition, pinpoints the ambiguity of educational goals. Curiously, ambiguity concerning goals is something that legislative bodies and academic institutions characteristically share. It makes them similar in some respects; yet it is also a continuing source of tensions between them, for goal ambiguity may tend to impede communication. Higher education for everybody may mean a great many different things to different legislators and different academicians.

Higher education is expected to provide a multiplicity of services for society. The university's goals include not only educating undergraduate and professional students, but also giving expert advice to government, doing research for government and private industry or agriculture, training employees for all sorts of business, holding conferences for men of learning as well as for laymen, and participating in their communities' social and economic affairs. In part, this heterogeneity of objectives and activities stems from the university's diverse constituencies, just as the legislature's diversity of positions on all kinds of public issues derives from its diverse constituencies. University administrators, faculty, and students have different conceptions of the mission of higher education; so do governing boards, political officials, private donors to the educational enterprise, and taxpayers in the general public. As a result, decisions affecting higher education, inside the university and outside in the legislature or elsewhere, are all influenced by different participants' own definitions of the role of higher education in society and its relation to other societal or private goals.

When goals are ambiguous, contention over objectives and their instrumentation is likely to be conflictual. Legislatures are, of course, institutions that are partly rooted in conflict and their operations are predicated on the crystallization, clarification, and resolution of conflicts involving both the means and ends of policy. Universities are not generally thought of as political institutions; yet anyone familiar with the internal workings of higher education institutions will probably agree that the conflict model of politics provides a fairly satisfactory fit. When legislatures and universities come into contact, as of necessity they must, the goal ambiguity characteristic of either institution is surely a source of misunderstanding and, possibly, controversy. On the other hand, the very flexibility in policy formulation that goal ambiguity permits is, over the long haul, conducive to the resolution of disagreements and the emergence of a democratic consensus, provided the participants in this political game play by its conventional rules.

The Normalcy of Politics

PATSY T. MINK

IT IS A PRIVILEGE to be given the opportunity, as a working politician on the state and federal level for the past fourteen years, to comment on the paper by Heinz Eulau.

To the extent that norms of a "labyrinth of intangibles" can be defined, Dr. Eulau has done a creditable job in setting forth the components of the crisis facing educators today. Yet his success in identifying these factors serves to upset his thesis that politics is all that murky and mysterious. In truth, the operation of politics is no more unfathomable than the operation of our higher education system—this is from one who has tried to understand both. I am struck by the similarities of the norms followed by college administrators and those identified by Dr. Eulau as applying to politicians.

It is surprising, in fact, that the recent wave of resignations by university presidents and the agonizing reappraisals of campus unrest policies have been accompanied by strident blasts at political meddling and interference. I do not dispute the merit of such criticisms, but only the apparent lack of understanding among the educators of the norms that brought it about. Perhaps, if the educators were more closely attuned to their own modes of behavior, they would have realized that such reactions to violence on our campuses were entirely predictable, and immediate steps should have been taken on the campus that would have averted predictable political intrusions.

Dr. Eulau says that "more often than not, political contention is conflictual because there is no agreement on goals; and when there is agreement, politics loses much of its luster." I submit that in the field of higher education, there is general agreement on goals, but that the conflict arises because there is no agreement on the means to accomplish those goals. This conflict, in turn, leads to a disinterested body politic which rightly assumes that the most elite intellectually in our society must settle among themselves on how best to pursue the goals of education. Educators cannot expect the general public to provide the inducement to action in an arena that is cloistered by intellectualism. Public apathy is no justification for lack of aggressive goals.

I further submit that there is no politicians' stratagem in the field of education. It is an arena which is largely vacant of leadership, and this void has forced initiative upon politicians. When the university community makes no effort to encourage the education of the poor, the politician must find a way to force university interest and participation. When the university community makes no effort to formulate study that is relevant to the needs of the real world, the politician must find a way to coerce the university to alter its curriculum. When the university community makes no effort to revise its teacher-training programs to fit the needs of our elementary and secondary schools, the politician must find a way to break the system from its rigors of the status quo. When the university community makes no effort to provide impetus to early childhood development programs, the politician must find a way to provide for these programs outside the university.

I do not believe there are any "undue" pressures, economic or otherwise, that cause the politician to "invent" the "standards of choice and norms of conduct" identified by Dr. Eulau. What Dr. Eulau has enumerated are simply standards of conduct that I would hope guide administrators as well as legislators.

For example, if politicians decry student violence and take a hard-line stance against destruction of property, their statements should not, necessarily, be interpreted as expressions against the university. Similarly, overreaction by the university in curbing lawful dissent is viewed by politicians interested in higher education as a sign of inherent weakness of university administrations to meet controversy and change.

I cannot believe that the destruction of property on a university campus is any different from the destruction of a bank or church. All such actions must be condemned, and the rule of law must be imposed in each instance. The difficulty we face is in the minds of university administrators, who confuse steps against this destruction as an assault on academic freedom. They do not seem to realize that freedom can flourish only in an atmosphere of open discussion, and that the use of violence forecloses the opportunity for unrestricted interchange of ideas and negates the purposes of the university. We must ensure a reasoned response to campus violence so that complete order is not achieved at the price of no interchange of ideas; yet administrators have all too often failed to initiate even modest correctives. This lack of immediate institutional response, without need for the police and without need for tear gas, is what has contributed to demands for restrictions in federal funds.

It is unfair to the politician, as well as inaccurate, to relate his stance on such issues only to what is dictated by the polls or by public outcry that fits his predispositions. The issue in campus unrest is not law and order versus academic freedom. Legitimate protests must be met by considerations of what is good for the student constituency rather than what fits the education establishment. Administrators must thus be receptive and willing to change.

You can see the norm of responsiveness, in this light, as a standard of conduct which must guide the administrators of higher education institutions as well as politicians. If the administrators respond well enough, there is no need for the politician to do so. But the politician's role in creating this receptivity to change in the academic community is often attacked by the academists as unenlightened outside influence.

Passivity in oversight is cited as a political norm by Dr. Eulau. Again, it is only when the university defaults badly in the area of self-examination that the politician feels he must interject his own opinion.

It should be noted that the politician does not remain a passive onlooker because of constituent pressures. Such an interpretation of nonintervention would suggest that, given such pressures, the politician must and should act. Rather, I believe that the policy of nonintervention is a laudatory policy established not by the expediency of politics, but because it is recognized that the institution has the first responsibility to determine the directions and emphases in programs. To regard passivity in the oversight function as politically motivated is to demean the role of the politician. Passivity on the part of the legislators should be the signal for greater emphasis on internal accountability by the institution itself, not less.

In any discussion of the norm of authority, it should be obvious that expertise is a major factor as a norm not only in politics, but in academic fields, business, and industry as well. It is simply a way of interaction. This norm of authority also contributes to the passivity of oversight. That politicians rely upon others with greater expertise within their own ranks is simply a norm of all human behavior and provides no unique insight into political behavior.

The norm of comparison found by Dr. Eulau is, again, nothing more than the normal examination of peer relationships found in every part of our life. No institution in our society can advance and improve unless it is in constant self-scrutiny, and decisions on performance can be based only on relative values. I hope that university administrators are no exception. It is simply good common sense to know how you stand among similar institutions.

I would conclude that indeed universities are political institutions whose internal workings fit the conflict model of politics advanced by Dr. Eulau. He does not, however, set forth any unique insight into political behavior. His norms fit all of human behavior in leadership roles.

I do not agree that "the culture of politics . . . provides for rules, roles, norms, or standards which often tend to defy ordinary rationality and escape systematic comprehension." The norms which Dr. Eulau has set forth are simply rational job specifications for any good administrator who is interested in public opinion (responsiveness), internal audit (oversight), expertise (authority), and standing (comparison).

If, therefore, those in higher education would like to discover the norms of politics with which they may be confronted, they should first consult their own operations. The two are amazingly similar.

Reality of Legislative Reaction to Higher Education

LYMAN A. GLENNY

Mr. Eulau has undertaken the difficult task of clarifying certain political theory, using higher education as his context. He also attempts to separate political theory from economic theory. The basic analytical framework derives from the general field of political science, which he selectively draws upon to provide his emphasis on "norms," or operative standards. He eliminates all but four norms. The four are then ascribed to legislative behavior at varying levels of validity.

To be helpful in this theoretical endeavor, I offer several suggestions that also derive from research by political scientists and certain other scholars.

A prominent weakness of the survey technique is its tendency to represent as respondent opinion what the surveyor wants to hear or else to reflect popular myths. Apparently even politicians do not detect trends in their own behavior or trends portending change in the society. Their responses to the survey seem not to comprehend recent practice.

Mr. Eulau's four generalizations, which he labels "norms," are responsiveness, passivity in oversight, authority, and comparison. Of these four, the survey methodology failed to show that the first two norms—responsiveness and passivity in oversight—were already passé for higher education at the time of the survey two years ago. Two major phenomena support this conclusion: (1) the doubling and more of the proportion of state general income expended on higher education from 1958 to 1968, and (2) the legislative establishment of state-wide coordinating and planning boards in the majority of states during the same ten-year period.

The great increase in state funds for higher education grew out of direct responsiveness to the demands of the society, that is, constituents. Although economic theory is not political theory (as Mr. Eulau clearly points out), economic phenomena resulting from the political process cannot be ignored. Legislators and governors authorized appropriation increases of 337 percent from 1959 to 1969.[1] These authorizations were in direct "response" to constituent desire, albeit the legislators did not receive thousands of letters and postcards demanding new levels of funding. Mr. Eulau too readily dismisses the "law of anticipated reactions." Legislators are usually reacting to some public stimuli. Those stimuli may be press releases by the state chamber of commerce expressing need for more trained manpower or may be speeches by leaders of the space and defense industries decrying the shortage of scientists and engineers. Or the stimuli may be almost covert—the rising expectations (as shown by Gallup, Roper, and other polls) of parents for their children's level of education. These stimuli fail indeed to fall within a narrowly defined responsiveness definition which requires direct verbal or written contact with legislators. In an area of mass communication, national and state opinion surveys, increasing sophistication of legislators, and subtle, soft-sell persuasion, the definition must be more realistic. Mr. Eulau himself indicates that this norm may have "relatively low political salience." This is so because high salience factors have been defined out of the norm. Omitted are the vicarious stimuli that constitute the real basis for legislative responsiveness.

The second norm, passivity in oversight, also suffers from definition constraint. Mr. Eulau concludes that legislators are circumspect in intervening directly in academic affairs. However, even omitting consideration of the myriad experiences of the last year or so, one can argue that the supervision and control of higher education was a matter of great concern to legislatures by no later than the mid 1950s.

The fact that only 5–10 percent of legislators consider higher education as the basis for their power and reputation should not mislead us to conclude that "behavioral patterns, as far as higher education is concerned, appear to be dominated by a norm of passivity." The work of

1. M. M. Chambers, *Appropriations of State Tax Funds for Operating Expenses of Higher Education, 1969–1970* (Washington: Office of Institutional Research, National Association of State Universities and Land-Grant Colleges, 1969).

Moos and Rourke and others in the late 1950s revealed that actions of legislatures belie the idea of passivity.[2]

The creation of state-wide coordinating boards and councils, as well as extensive professional staffing of executive and legislative budget offices through legislative initiative, can hardly be considered passive gestures. In 1955, only four states had a legislatively authorized coordinating agency for higher education. Today twenty-seven states have such agencies, many of them with extensive power to control major aspects of public college and university development.[3] Although these boards and councils are not direct arms of legislatures, the conditions that caused them to be created and that continue to increase their powers at almost every legislative session are those which deeply concern legislators and governors.[4] With one or two exceptions, coordinating boards have been established despite opposition by the leaders of the state's major institutions. The directors of these boards can testify to legislators' interest in specific problems of higher education through their numerous requests for information or for appeals to intervene in some current college problem.

Finally, on the norm of passivity and on the survey as a research technique, one should note that a Commission on Higher Education was established *within* the legislature in Illinois in the same year that Mr. Eulau's survey was made.[5] Its purpose was and is general oversight and supervision of higher education.

Mr. Eulau's survey failed to reveal the obvious fact that since World War II higher education has become too important for the well-being of society to allow for political passivity. Legislative concern with current student unrest is merely indicative of how far we have come. It is by no means a new political concern that higher education become more accountable: coordinating boards manifest it. So do program budgeting, management information systems, student-teacher contracts, and other devices geared toward state central supervision and control. In Mr.

2. Malcolm Moos and Francis Rourke, *The Campus and the State* (Baltimore, Md.: Johns Hopkins Press, 1959); Francis Rourke and G. E. Brooks, *The Managerial Revolution in Higher Education* (Baltimore, Md.: Johns Hopkins Press, 1966); Lyman A. Glenny, *Autonomy of Public Colleges: The Challenge of Coordination* (New York: McGraw-Hill Book Co., 1959).

3. Robert Berdahl confirms these earlier findings in his *Statewide Coordination of Higher Education* (Washington: American Council on Education, 1971).

4. L. A. Glenny, "Politics and Current Patterns in Coordinating Higher Education," in *Campus and Capitol*, ed. John Minter (Boulder, Colo.: Western Interstate Commission on Higher Education, 1966).

5. See Ernest Palola, *Higher Education by Design: The Sociology of Planning* (Berkeley: Center for Research and Development in Higher Education, 1970) for the results of that author's interviews in 1968 with legislators in several states, including Illinois, New York, and California, which were also in the Eulau survey.

Eulau's survey, legislators appear to have reported outmoded practices or myths which their concrete actions belied.

Faculties as Legislatures

DAVID C. KNAPP

PROFESSOR EULAU'S PAPER suggests that the response to the question "Higher education for everybody?" will come at least in part through the interaction of legislatures and universities—two institutions that function in accordance with a conflict model of politics. Although ample evidence supports their likeness as conflict models, the universities differ in preferring bureaucratic to legislative decision making and in transforming the norm of passivity in oversight, as Eulau terms it, into two other norms that foster decisions by bureaucracy rather than legislation.

Eulau distinguishes the conflict model from the competitive, noting that the latter assumes agreement on goals and the former does not. That conflict politics pervade the university, much as they do the legislature, is not, I think, open to question. Indeed, in every novel of academic life that I have seen, from C. P. Snow's *The Masters* on, the central theme is essentially a case study of a struggle for personal or group power. Interestingly enough, power itself most frequently preoccupies the novelist, not the uses to which power may be put in defining and fulfilling university goals. This emphasis is, in my judgment, no accident or mere literary license, but rather an accurate commentary on the nature of the internal politics of academic institutions—at least in the recent past. And even though a "new politics" is emerging, it is the old model that remains dominant and that will provide the mechanism for answering the questions with which we are here concerned.

Many academicians—perhaps most—are interested less in institution-wide goals and policies than in their own individual goals and conditions of existence. Generally speaking, academic man wants to be left alone in his field of interest, and only when general institutional policy intrudes on his autonomous sphere does he manifest concern. Hence, even though faculty may assert that academic policy making through representative legislative bodies is their prerogative, they usually accord the process at best a secondary order of value in their professional lives. Attendance at faculty meetings is usually scant, and those who actually act on their prerogatives and involve themselves in policy making are often regarded with disdain by their colleagues.

These observations lead to my basic hypothesis: The conflict model of politics in universities is employed to foster bureaucratic rather than legislative decision making, and it is the bureaucratic power of the individual or the group that is of central concern. Thus, despite the extensive paraphernalia for legislative self-government—representative bodies, standing committees, and hallowed procedures—faculty members abjure the legislative function if they can possibly do so. The explanation of this phenomenon lies in the combination of three factors.

First, as indicated above, faculty members are interested in basic institutional policy only if it presents to them a clear and present danger. Hence, the much described preoccupation with parking regulations, and only passing interest in standards for admission. Second, because legislative action takes time, and time is the faculty member's most valuable resource, he often would prefer to have others make decisions for him— even an administrator or board of trustees—*provided* he can reserve the right to reverse decisions if they are found to infringe on what he considers his own sphere of freedom and action. Third, and perhaps most important for our purposes here, the legislative function is psychologically disturbing, for it is not only a way of resolving conflict, but also a process that brings conflict to the fore.

This conflict is of two kinds. For many faculty members, discussion of goal-oriented policies requires, on the one hand, an examination of the relationship of self to institution, an exercise which any autonomous professional—faculty member, physician, or lawyer—finds painful and resists. On the other hand, policy making brings basic philosophical cleavages to the surface and requires that abstract purposes, on which there may be general accord, be translated into concrete policies, on which accord is missing. Hence, if the legislative process is invoked, it will mean that a policy of general applicability and one interpretation will prevail for all—for engineer quite as much as humanist. The desire then is to avoid the adoption of a single, general solution, and the stratagem employed is to throw the problem to the bureaucracy, which can more readily achieve accommodation to several group interests simultaneously.

These considerations suggest that the most significant behavioral norm for faculty members on policy matters is *issue avoidance* through recourse to bureaucratic decision making by administrators in the hierarchy or ad hoc committees. Issues are, of course, sometimes brought to representative bodies for resolution in the legislative manner, but they are not always the most important ones and they appear more infrequently than the many academic legislative trappings would suggest. The norm of issue avoidance prevents university issues from reaching the legislative body, where they belong; Eulau's norm of passivity in oversight protects the legislature from having to deal with bureaucratic issues that do *not* belong in the legislature.

In a university's bureaucratic politics, three of Dr. Eulau's norms are employed regularly. The *norm of authority* is fully operative, especially the authority of the "expert committee" and of administrators speaking in their own areas of special competence or on the basis of information "privileged" to their positions. So also is the *norm of comparison,* as Ivy League faculties look to other Ivy Leaguers and Big Ten faculties look to other Big Ten institutions for guidance on the respectability of alternative courses of action. (Imagine the dilemma of institutions that need to look at both.) For many faculty members, if Harvard has done it, the decision has been made for them as well. It is in the arena of comparison, I suspect, that one can identify some of the reason for the gulf between academicians and legislators on issues of higher education, for the former are less impressed by criteria of "relative indulgence" and "relative deprivation" than the latter.

The *norm of responsiveness* plays the same role in faculty decision making as in the legislative politics of higher education, but probably for a different reason. If the faculty member has thought conceptually about his legislative role at all, he would likely agree more with Edmund Burke than John Stuart Mill. He regards the legislator as one who votes his own conscience rather than the will of his constituents. Notwithstanding, faculty members do take into account the interests of a variety of constituents—departmental colleagues, others in the discipline they represent, and to an extent their students. Especially in applied fields, faculty members are concerned with the possible reactions of accrediting associations or business and political groups with which they associate in their work. Differences in reference groups, as well as in the conception of the legislative role, may also help to explain some legislative-university differences on educational policy.

To these norms, I add a fifth—that of *procedural consensus.* On the basis of fairly limited observation, I conclude that the procedural and semantic debates in which faculties seem to delight are in fact a device for avoiding basic cleavages on goals and values by gaining agreement on means and for throwing fundamental issues into the bureaucracy for resolution and group accommodation.

The dilemma of the mode of decision making I describe here is that decisions "happen" rather than get made, even on issues that affect the long-term viability of a college or university. Moreover, because decisions "happen" in what often has the appearance of a closed rather than open political system, the faculty are brought into direct conflict with the advocates of the "new politics" on the campus, especially on the issue of "higher education for everybody."

Those students, faculty, and social groups that are most interested in opening up educational opportunity, and in providing educational experience that they define as relevant, do not favor the avoidance of issues and hidden systems of decision making. Rather, they demand the direct confrontation of issues and clean-cut decisions openly arrived at. This difference in style accounts for much of the turmoil on the campus in the recent past. And this difference in style, as well as different reference points of comparison and responsiveness, will exacerbate legislative-university relations in responding to issues of full educational opportunity.

DANIEL P. MOYNIHAN

On Universal Higher Education

A NYONE WHO ATTEMPTS A SERIOUS STATEMENT ABOUT HIGHER EDUCATION at this moment courts serious trouble. In mid-1969, writing in the *American Scholar*, I invoked Joyce's formula: "silence, exile, cunning."[1] Nothing in the interval has changed my mind. Today I respond not to any sense of opportunity, but merely to dull Duty, Virtue's residue, Reason's remnant.

Duty is a conception that is all the more elusive for being familiar. It denotes something more than obligation, but nonetheless begins there. One service performed in return for another. In this instance I have not the least difficulty in perceiving and acknowledging just where my indebtedness lies. For two decades I have had access on the most generous bases to the worlds of government, of social science, and of university administration. Something is owed in return for that experience. My purpose then is to address, from the point of view of government, a subject of concern to education: "Higher Education for Everybody?"

That government must be a party to any such decision is unlikely to be disputed. Elite education can be paid for by elites. Universal education must be paid for by taxes. That is that, save to note that, given this ineluctability, political science ought to explore this relationship and perhaps even help facilitate it, especially now. Few things are more depressing to a social scientist than crisis-mongering—especially of the sort we have witnessed over the past decade or so, when social scientists themselves have been the principal culprits. But there *are* such things as genuine crises, and one has come along in higher education. The present situation was fairly described in the opening statement of the *Report of the President's Commission on Campus Unrest:* "The crisis on American campuses has no parallel in the history of the nation."

Of course, a crisis for the campus is by no means necessarily a crisis for the society at large. It is easy to confuse or to equate the two. But crisis there is, and this has considerable consequences for the question of whether and how we are to move from our present situation of mass higher education to a universal practice.

1. Daniel P. Moynihan, "Politics as the Art of the Impossible," *American Scholar*, Autumn 1969, p. 575.

UNIVERSAL HIGHER EDUCATION

When, six years ago, Earl J. McGrath assembled a group to consider this subject, we started with the assumption that our society was working its way toward universal higher education. This was certainly my assumption, and I began my contribution to the subsequent book with the assertion that the time had come to get on with the detailed business of specifying exactly what we would need to do, because clearly we were going to do it.

> A point is reached in the development of any major social standard when the ability to conceive must be succeeded by the capacity to measure. That point is clearly at hand with regard to the question of universal opportunity for higher education.
>
> American society has been working toward this standard for some generations now; in a sense, from the outset. The average level of education has steadily advanced; we have in the past two decades reached the point where a very large number of persons go on from secondary to higher education. With the resulting advantage both to the nation and to the individuals firmly established in terms of productivity, life income expectations, and the like, the comparative disadvantage of those who do not go on has become equally evident, whereupon the dynamics of a democratic and to some degree egalitarian society take hold and produce the demand that these opportunities be available to all.[2]

Earlier that year I had drafted the portions of the Democratic party platform concerned with education. It was, I believe, accurate to state there that the 1964 platform marked, in the 124-year sequence,

> the transition from merely encouraging higher education to, in effect, insisting on it. The preceding platform had declared the belief "that America can meet its educational obligations" but had not really defined what those obligations might be. Rather, the 1960 document called for a series of specific categories of Federal assistance, leaving it for the future to determine just how much money and how many people would be involved. The 1964 platform, in contrast, said little about forms of assistance, but was explicit as to the objectives to be attained thereby.
>
> "*Our task* [the 1964 platform declared] *is to make the national purpose serve the human purpose: that every person shall have the opportunity to become all that he or she is capable of becoming.*
>
> "*We believe that knowledge is essential to individual freedom and to the conduct of a free society. We believe that education is the surest and most profitable investment a nation can make.*

2. Daniel P. Moynihan, "The Impact on Manpower Development and the Employment of Youth," in *Universal Higher Education*, ed. Earl J. McGrath (New York: McGraw-Hill Book Co., 1966), p. 65.

"Regardless of family financial status, therefore, education should be open to every boy or girl in America up to the highest level which he or she is able to master." [3]

It would hardly be fair to state that we have abandoned such goals, but surely what seemed an untroubled trajectory, a rather straightforward logarithmic projection, seems somehow less certain now. The course of events, the data continue pretty much as projected, but it is the projections that come into question. Is it really likely that we will continue as we have?

What happened to call seeming certainty into question?

This subject has been widely and, on occasion, intelligently discussed. My aim is not so much to add to the discussion as to stress two points which are familiar enough in themselves but appear to be of special consequence to the subject of universal higher education. First, great dissatisfaction with mass education has arisen within the world of education itself, thereby necessarily casting a cloud on the prospect of proceeding from where we are to a situation which, by simple extrapolation, would presumably be even worse. Second, the growing politization of higher education creates problems concerning continued public support for an ever larger and presumably even more influential higher education community.

DISCONTENT WITH HIGHER EDUCATION

For present purposes the sources of discontent need not be considered in detail. Put simply, discontent exists, and it has assumed forms that are immediately threatening to the life of the university as such. Witnesses abound. Nathan Pusey, in his report to the Harvard Board of Overseers, described 1968–69 as " a dismal year" which in time will appear "to have been very costly." Gardner Ackley described 1969–70 as

a tragic year in the life of the University of Michigan—a year that has begun the destruction of this university as a great center of learning—destroyed not so much by outside forces as by the actions of its own faculty and administration.[4]

Prognoses for 1970–71 are equally pessimistic, although not, of course, necessarily accurate. In substance, the system isn't working very well, and a large number of persons in the system appear to want it profoundly changed. Hardly to be assumed then is an untroubled expansion of the present system, where about half the relevant age groups obtain some postsecondary education, to a stage where all, or almost all, do so. The

3. The 1964 Democratic Party Platform (cited in ibid., p. 66).
4. In *Congressional Record.*

most generally agreed point is that the proportion of young persons who really would want and could benefit from higher education carried on at traditional levels of intellect and discipline is limited. (There is a presumed genetic limitation, perhaps also a cultural one.) Judgments will differ on just how large or small that proportion might be, but almost everyone agrees it is considerably lower than the proportion of youth who are students in higher education at this moment. Glazer writes:

> Higher education is not suited to training or apprenticeship, except for training and apprenticeship in learning itself. As a result, the colleges and universities filled with people who had no particular interest in what the institution had to offer, but had to undergo some unpleasant rite to take up decent and satisfying work.[5]

In this light, an untroubled expansion of the present system to the point where everyone receives some kind of postsecondary education seems an unlikelihood.

The limits thus suggested are not imposed merely by a generalized public perception that all is not well on campus. To some degree the self-destructiveness of the higher education community has proceeded to the point where its capacity for expansion is limited. A good man is always hard to find, and to find one for a serious position in academic administration or leadership is becoming very difficult indeed. Stephen K. Bailey has been most forthright on this not especially pleasant matter.

> As I watch the melancholy list grow of friends who have resigned (voluntarily or under duress) from college presidencies and school superintendencies during the past few years (or, more tragically, have dropped dead of heart attacks or have committed suicide), I begin to wonder how many contemporary educational leaders will survive the current educational revolution.
>
> Revolutions are insatiable maws—with cavernous appetite for men's lives and fortunes. The most civilized are a peculiar delicacy of the revolutionary appetite, for, unconsumed, they stand in the way of the necessary oversimplifications of the revolutionary mind. And they are readily betrayed into revolutionary hands by the old guard, who always find perceptive consciences a threat and an embarrassment to the status quo.[6]

POLITIZATION

Bailey's concern goes to the second of the two points I see as most relevant to the question of universal higher education, that is, the growing politization of the academic world. He speaks of the revolutionary appe-

5. Nathan Glazer, "The Six Roots of Campus Trouble," *Harvard Bulletin*, Sept. 21, 1970, p. 29.

6. Bailey, speech cited in *Wall Street Journal*, Sept. 3, 1970.

tite, the revolutionary mind. He is speaking about the rise on campus of activities directed toward shaping the character, not simply of the university community itself, but of the society at large.

Politization in higher education is relatively recent, an outcome of what Glazer has termed "the Berkeley invention"—the joining of general political issues with specific university issues—and relates in at least two ways to the issue of universal higher education. First, it has resulted in considerable measure from the rapid and recent expansion of higher education, such that sheer size gave political consequence to the views of dominant university opinions. Second, these opinions are increasingly opposed to those of the larger society.

The issue is an adversary culture firmly entrenched in higher education. The nature of this culture, the extent of its strength, and its grip on the universities, as well as other institutions of acculturation, have come as a surprise to many. The patrician tradition and leadership of the most prestigious universities seems to have been painfully vulnerable in its initial encounters with this new reality. It seems to me that the individuals involved by and large could not understand or could not believe what suddenly was before their eyes, and in varying degrees panicked, collaborated, or simply collapsed. They displayed what I fear has been a problem in higher education: its leaders have not been especially well educated. For all the spectacular minds that from time to time have been put in charge of our great institutions, on balance the leadership has been social and administrative—the right family or the right work habits—rather than intellectual.

We have paid and are paying a price for this failing in leadership. For example, in the early postwar period the radical impulse in politics moved over into the culture, where it prospered as almost never before. Students fell silent about politics, and university administrators concluded that some strange malady or profound discontinuity had occurred. When in the course of the 1960s the radical impulse returned to politics, this time greatly strengthened and legitimized by the culture, administrators again concluded they were being confronted with something utterly new, altogether without precedent. We began to hear about the "youth culture." I for one disagree. To me, the present state of campus politics and manners represents a clear continuity with earlier forms, allowing only for changes of scale. For years Lionel Trilling has been describing, defining, and projecting what he first termed "the adversary culture." Surely there are persons in authority in academia capable of understanding that Trilling is a most serious man, that—unlike some others perhaps—he really is trying to tell us something. Surely there are those capable of perceiving the polemical advantage of depicting a minority movement as a generational transformation. There is no justification for having been taken so utterly unawares.

Some things have, of course, changed. For some time—years, not months—it has been evident that an almost classic form of nihilism has been taking root in upper-class culture in the United States. I so argued in a paper first given in 1968, citing the analysis by Michael Polanyi of the bases of nihilist belief, and his superbly important aside that the nihilist argument, given its premises, had not been answered. A subsequent version of the paper was duly published,[7] and I later learned from Polanyi that my discussion was the first time anyone had referred to his earlier analysis. So far as I am aware, it was also the last time, for not a murmur arose in response to my effort. How many university youngsters will have to blow up how many buildings before anyone begins to take Polanyi seriously is a question I will accordingly not seek to answer. The point is that this knowledge was available to us had we cared to use it; quite simply, that work was not really taken seriously.

Nor has anyone grounds for being surprised at the increasing political ambitions and activities of the campus community. Writing in *Foreign Affairs* more than three years ago, Kristol explained why political activism on campus would come about and what it would likely mean. It would happen because the higher education community had become large and important enough to serve as a viable base for intellectuals seeking "that species of power we call moral authority." A new class would seem to have emerged.

> The politics of this new class is novel in that its locus of struggle is the college campus. One is shocked at this—we are used to thinking that politics ought not to intrude on the campus. But we shall no doubt get accustomed to the idea. Meanwhile, there is going to be a great deal of unpleasant turbulence. The academic community in the United States today has evolved into a new political constituency. College students, like their teachers, are "new men" who find the traditional student role too restrictive. Students and faculty therefore find it easy to combine their numbers and their energies for the purpose of social and political action. The first objective—already accomplished in large measure —is to weaken control of the administration and to dispossess it of its authoritative powers over campus activities. From this point the movement into politics proper—including elections—is about as predictable as anything can be.[8]

7. Moynihan, "Politics as the Art of the Impossible," pp. 573–83.
8. Irving Kristol, "American Intellectuals and Foreign Policy," *Foreign Affairs*, July 1967, p. 608.

Kristol was less confident concerning the consequences of this emergence save that they were not likely to be especially helpful.

> Just what direction this movement into politics will follow it is too early to say with certainty. Presumably, it will be toward "the left," since this is the historical orientation of the intellectual class as a whole. It is even possible that the movement will not be calmed until the United States has witnessed the transformation of its two-party system to make room for a mass party of the ideological left, as in most European countries—except that its "grass roots" will be on the campus rather than in the factory. But what is certain is that the national prestige and the international position of the United States are being adversely affected by this *secession des clercs.* Imperial powers need social equilibrium at home if they are to act effectively in the world. It was possible to think, in the years immediately after World War II, that the United States had indeed achieved this kind of equilibrium—that consensus and equipoise at home would permit our statesmen to formulate and pursue a coherent foreign policy. But the "academic revolution" of the 1950s and 1960s raises this issue again, in a most problematic and urgent way.[9]

Our concern here is not with the consequences for foreign policy, but, rather, what effect this academic revolution will have on the disposition of the public to support a continued movement toward universal higher education. It is impossible to know, and hazardous to speculate on, the answer to this question. Surely, however, the presumption would be that public support will diminish, especially to the degree that the "academic" position is seen as hostile to the course of the larger polity in ways that are both hard to follow and hard to explain.

There is, for example, an anomaly in the present situation in which so much of what university intellectuals detest about American foreign policy is so indisputably the product of American intellectuals. A consultant to the Special Committee on Campus Tensions, which was established in 1969 by the American Council on Education, put this point with a certain acerbity.

> It wasn't the Mississippi tenant farmer who ordered the troops to Vietnam. More likely, and more specifically, it was the former professors/ Harvard Junior Fellows—those who had maximum chance to develop intellectually.[10]

Robert Nisbet has ascribed such assertion of competence to a "special kind of hubris that attacked the social sciences in this country in the 1950's." I share this view. One could wish for a period of mild repentance.

9. Ibid.
10. Marcus G. Raskin, "What Is the New University?" in *Perspectives on Campus Tensions*, ed. David C. Nichols (Washington: American Council on Education, 1970), p. 32.

Instead the experience seems to have produced in many circles a kind of frustrated outrage of the kind Lenin might have described as an "infantile disorder," but which increasingly we are told is a virtuous rage to off the pigs and generally to punish working-class groups, who are doubtless guilty of much wrongdoing but surely cannot be accused of having taken game theory too far in the evolution of the doctrine of counterinsurgency. Here, a further, and to my thinking, fundamental point arises concerning the increasing politization of the university community: it is not likely to raise the quality, in the sense of the generally perceived effectiveness, of our politics. Kristol writes that "No modern nation has ever constructed a foreign policy that was acceptable to its intellectuals."[11] Perhaps there is a corollary, that no group of modern intellectuals, when they have managed to get hold of a nation's foreign policy, has produced one satisfactory to the people at large. I don't know why this should be so—if indeed it is—but I suspect it involves an exaggerated notion of the power of intellectual analysis to master the political process. Nor do I wholly comprehend the increasing tendency among intellectuals to be intolerant of deviations from prevailing doctrine, even contemptuous of dissent. Thirty years ago Orwell wrote: "The common man is still living in the mental world of Dickens, but nearly every modern intellectual has gone over to some or other form of totalitarianism." And as recently as the close of 1970, Podhoretz repeats this observation, deploring "the barbaric hostility to freedom of thought which by the late 1960's had become one of the hallmarks of [the radical] ethos."[12] It was the practice of the university radicals of that period to compare the America of the Johnson administration to Hitler's Germany. Certainly, only a serious abandonment of standards of evidence could make any such comparison even remotely credible. This was absurd. What one fears is not absurd is the growing conviction among critics of the left that the present era *can* be compared to the Weimar era in Germany, when the same devaluation and detestation of everything the polity was able to achieve was also the mark of the high intellectuals. One is struck, for example, by the echoes in our own times of Laqueur's account of Kurt Tucholsky and his circle.

> These were not insensitive men but they had no real roots themselves and, therefore, they lacked the sensorium for the patriotic feeling of their fellow-citizens. They were incapable of understanding anyone who reacted differently from the way they did.[13]

11. Kristol, "American Intellectuals and Foreign Policy."
12. Norman Podhoretz, "Laws, Kings, and Cures," *Commentary*, October 1970, p. 30.
13. Walter Z. Laqueur, "The Tucholsky Complaint," *Commentary*, October 1969, p. 79.

For surely the manner persists. Aaron Wildavsky writes:

> In the relation of the white elite to public issues there is a desire to condemn. There is a will to believe the worst. There is a compulsion to make events speak to the necessity of revolutionary change.

Is this not almost a formula for lowering the level of esteem in which the elite institutions of advanced thought are held by the great mass of citizenry whose ideological life tends toward the unadventurous? It is exactly that, and it is necessary to stay a moment with this point.

THE ELITE MINORITY

Higher education in America, for all its size, remains a privilege. It is to some extent a generational privilege, separating old from young. But it is also a privilege among the young. Half get it. Half do not. Of those who do, far the most attractive arrangements are made for the children of the well-to-do and for another, not less lucky, group of persons who happen to be very smart. Of those who do not, the disadvantage is all the greater because they are so conspicuously excluded.

The elite quality of higher education is not likely to change. The social composition of the "high quality" American university is to the American social structure as a masked ball is to a mass movement. To be sure, one of the very best covers for class privilege is a passionate public concern with the underprivileged. Yet the sheer minority status of students and persons with higher education, and the fact of their vastly better prospects when compared with the rest of society, make it difficult to suppose their political demands will ever in our time acquire the legitimacy that democracies associate with majority opinion. Those seeking to induce the public to pay for universal higher education might do well to remember that only 11 percent of the adult population of the United States graduated from a four-year college, and despite the recent growth in college attendance, in 1985 that figure will have risen only to 14–15 percent. Put differently, 89 percent of American voters may or may not share the values and political inclinations associated with a college degree, but at all events they do not have the degree.

Thus, the more politicized the universities become, the less public support they can expect—at least, so I believe. David Riesman, Nathan Glazer, and others have usefully questioned the notion that the economy or the government or the society at large genuinely "needs" to have a large number of young persons receiving higher education. We tend to cloak our idealist actions in pragmatic guise. The society pays for education because it is thought to be advantageous to those who get it. If the society should ever widely perceive that it itself is threatened in the process, we may expect genuinely pragmatic considerations to come into play.

The Scranton Commission said as much:

> As a practical matter, it would be naïve for the universities that frequently or intensely involve themselves in controversial political issue to expect to retain the full financial and attitudinal support of a society to which they may seem to be laying political siege.[14]

A general change in public attitude, should it come, is likely to make an extraordinarily unpleasant impression on higher education communities, which continue to enjoy among themselves a slightly beleaguered aura when in fact they are exceptionally free of outside pressures. In a study made for the Carnegie Commission on Higher Education only two years ago, Eulau found that "legislative oversight of higher education is characterized by a norm of passivity."[15] Constituents made few demands, and it was, in any event, assumed that the educators knew best. This assumption is eroding. In September 1970 at Berkeley, Paul Seabury (professor of political science) spoke of the university's "ominous and progressive estrangement from the people of California."[16]

There is a poignant quality to the growing estrangement between the society and the higher education community, for the encounter is so unequal. The silent majority, if one accepts that term, is silent not least because of its difficulty in saying things in terms that will win a respectful hearing among those who judge such matters. Like Orwell's working class, it lives in a world not far removed from Victorian virtues. I for one find those virtues—confidence in the nation, love of the nation, a willingness to sacrifice for it—priceless. But the symbols of those beliefs are tattered, even at times tawdry. It is not fair. But it is true. Bell has recently stated the facts with an understanding but painful candor.

> While minority life-styles and cultures have often conflicted with those of the majority, what is striking today is that the *majority* has no intellectually respectable culture of its own—no major figures in literature (the best is James Gould Cozzens), painting (except, perhaps, Andrew Wyeth), or poetry—to counterpose to the adversary culture. In this sense, bourgeois culture has been shattered.[17]

14. *Report of the President's Commission on Campus Unrest* (Washington: Government Printing Office, 1970), p. 190.
15. Heinz Eulau, "Political Norms Affecting Decisions Concerning Higher Education," in *Higher Education for Everybody?* Background Papers for Participants in the 53rd Annual Meeting of the American Council on Education (Washington: The Council, 1970, o.p.), p. 69.
16. In a press interview.
17. Daniel Bell, "The Cultural Contradictions of Capitalism," *Commentary*, October 1969, p. 79.

If this polarization, this conflict is true, increasingly higher education will come to stand for the humiliation of traditional America and there will likely be some faltering in our apparent progress toward universal higher education. I expect there will be. But it need be no more than a faltering if we will be a bit more rigorous and also perhaps a bit more honest about the situation we are in, and try to respond accordingly.

THE ADMINISTRATION'S PROGRAM

President Nixon's Message to the Congress on Higher Education, sent in March 1970, had as its intent and, he hoped, its outcome progress toward universal opportunity for higher education.

The issue of universal higher education is a matter—I believe our data are now firm on this point—of primary concern to two groups: young persons from poor families, and those whose natural endowment is not such as would likely benefit from traditional forms of higher education. The President's message began by addressing itself to both these groups. His statement was unequivocal.

> No qualified student who wants to go to college should be barred by lack of money. That has long been a great American goal; I propose that we achieve it now.
>
> Something is basically unequal about opportunity for higher education when a young person whose family earns more than $15,000 a year is nine times more likely to attend college than a young person whose family earns less than $3,000.
>
> Something is basically wrong with Federal policy toward higher education when it has failed to correct this inequity, and when Government programs spending $5.3 billion yearly have largely been disjointed, ill-directed and without a coherent long-range plan.
>
> Something is wrong with our higher education policy when—on the threshold of a decade in which enrollments will increase almost 50%—not nearly enough attention is focused on the 2-year community colleges so important to the careers of so many young people.

The President went on to propose the Higher Education Opportunity Act of 1970, a series of measures that would greatly expand loan funds available to students in higher education, but with the unprecedented provision that the overall federal program would be administered so that there would be, in effect, no such thing as a student from a poor family. Federal subsidies would be used in such a way that the resources available to poor students would be brought up to the level of middle-income students. Put another way, the economic disadvantage of the bottom half of the income distribution is eliminated (to the degree that a federal subsidy program can do so). There would be, in effect, no bottom half.

At the same time, students from the upper half of the income distribution would be assured the availability of loan funds, not so heavily subsidized as in the past, but still carrying the important discount associated with a federal guarantee. The President stated:

> With the passage of this legislation, every low-income student entering an accredited college would be eligible for a combination of Federal grants and subsidized loans sufficient to give him the same ability to pay as a student from a family earning $10,000.
>
> With the passage of this legislation every qualified student would be able to augment his own resources with Federally guaranteed loans, but Federal subsidies would be directed to students who need them most.

This proposal is without a precedent in American history. Its activation would establish the conditions of universal higher education, and leave the outcome to the free choice of the young persons involved. (It is important to be firm on the point of free choice. Not everyone will want to continue his education beyond high school or even through high school. I would be most dubious about the wisdom of a society that did any more than point out the likely advantages, make it possible to continue, and leave it to the individual to decide.)

Passage of the Higher Education Opportunity Act of 1970 would, in effect, establish the national goal of universal higher education. It is time we did just that.

The President simultaneously proposed a Career Education Program, funded at $100 million in fiscal 1972

> to assist States and institutions in meeting the additional costs of starting new programs to teach critically needed skills in community colleges and technical institutes.

This additional provision seems an indispensable adjunct to any large expansion of the numbers of persons receiving postsecondary education.

Lack of Response

What, then, impedes the passage of this historic legislation? For surely, nothing whatever has happened in the Congress, and—more important—the proposal has been greeted with near silence on the campuses. The Scranton Commission was specific and enthusiastic in its endorsement of the legislation. Clark Kerr, who heads the Carnegie Commission on Higher Education, has spoken warmly of the President's message and noted how closely his proposals parallel some that the Carnegie Commission has made. But, on balance, the response must be described as indifference in the Congress and embarrassed silence or even suspicion in the world of higher education.

There are some who have said the university elite has been silent about this bill because it likes to talk about equal opportunity, but wants nothing to do with it. I reject any such notion. The record of higher education in America is manifestly otherwise, in light of its accomplishments with the resources available to it.

I see another reason; that is, the universities are so preoccupied with internal problems, with the difficulty of managing what now exists, that they cannot for the moment give much thought to the larger problem of expansion. At this moment, to those responsible for higher education, the central issue is not expansion, but rather of maintaining what now exists. Hardly a major educational institution in the nation—and likely soon, many of our smaller and more specialized institutions—does not now face a crisis of governance and a crisis of finance.

The crisis of finance in higher education inevitably involves the federal government. The task of statesmanship in the decade ahead will be to ensure that involvement with the financing of higher education shall not lead to involvement with governance. This outcome will not be easily achieved. The federal government provides almost a quarter of the funds that go to support higher education and a far greater proportion of the monies available for research. This situation has considerable historical precedent: Washington raised the subject in his first Inaugural Address. But only in the past three decades has federal involvement risen to critical levels, and the problem become, as with so many federal initiatives, the vast proliferation of programs without the formulation of a coherent policy.

POLICY FIRST

The administration has sought to correct the imbalances of federal support. We have sought to put policy first, and to require program to follow therefrom.

Hence the President first spoke on the subject of higher education in March 1969, after barely nine weeks in office. In the context of the turbulence and alarm and recrimination that has so much characterized higher education in all its governmental relations in recent years, it is useful to recall that statement. The President began with the assertion that the crisis, which I have been discussing, was clearly upon us. The essence of the crisis was the preservation of intellectual freedom and the avoidance of politization.

> Freedom—intellectual freedom—is in danger in America. The nature and content of that danger is as clear as any one thing could be. Violence —physical violence, physical intimidation—is seemingly on its way to becoming an accepted, or at all events a normal and not to be avoided element in the clash of opinion within university confines. Increasingly it is

clear that this violence is directed to a clearly perceived and altogether too conceivable objective: not only to politicize the student bodies of our educational institutions, but to politicize the institutions as well. Anyone with the least understanding of the history of freedom will know that this has invariably meant not only political disaster to those nations that have submitted to such forces of obfuscation and repression, but cultural calamity as well. It is not too strong a statement to declare that this is the way civilizations begin to die.

The process is altogether too familiar to those who would survey the wreckage of history. Assault and counterassault, one extreme leading to the opposite extreme; the voices of reason and calm discredited. As Yeats foresaw: "Things fall apart; the centre cannot hold. . . ." None of us has the right to suppose it cannot happen here.

Thereupon the President asserted the fundamental point of federal policy, that intellectual freedom within the colleges and universities of the land is something that can be preserved only by internal efforts, that it cannot be imposed by external force.

The first thing to do at such moments is to reassert first principles. The Federal Government cannot, should not—must not—enforce such principles. That is fundamentally the task and the responsibility of the university community. But any may state what these principles are, for they are as widely understood as they are cherished.

First, that universities and colleges are places of excellence in which men are judged by achievement and merit in defined areas. The independence and competence of the faculty, the commitment, and equally the competence of the student body, are matters not to be compromised. The singular fact of American society—the fact which very likely distinguishes us most markedly from any other nation on earth—is that in the untroubled pursuit of an application of this principle we have created the largest, most democratic, most open system of higher learning in history. None need fear the continued application of those principles; but all most dread their erosion. The second principle—and I would argue, the only other—is that violence or the threat of violence may never be permitted to influence the actions or judgments of the university community. Once it does, the community, almost by definition, ceases to be a university.

The substance of this statement has continued to be the policy of the administration, despite the alarm and recrimination that have from time to time appeared on all sides.

CATEGORICAL AID

Mr. Nixon's statement was made early in his administration. What followed has been a prolonged and, as would be expected, complex effort to translate policy into program. Here the administration emerged with a fundamental conclusion: Increasingly it appears to us that reliance on categorical aid programs, as the principal source of federal support for higher education, is fundamentally subversive of the principle of non-interference. A categorical aid program is by definition a form of federal interference in the internal affairs and priorities of the university.

A measure of history is required here, of which the first element is the growth of higher education associated with the growth of categorical aid programs. Between 1945 and 1970, enrollments more than quadrupled. The ratio of college and university students to the total population of the country nearly tripled, such that 3.3 percent of all Americans were enrolled for degree credit in postsecondary institutions. The total annual cost multiplied twentyfold; the amount of the federal share went from one-sixth to almost one-fourth of the total budgets of higher education. This over a period when the nation's population rose less than 50 percent (from 140 million to 200 million), when the gross national product rose less than fivefold, and when the total budget of the federal government only doubled. Higher education has been one of the fastest growing sectors of our national life. In 1945, it accounted for approximately 0.5 percent of the GNP; by last year, it had more than quintupled, rising to 2.6 percent of the gross national product.

Let us turn now to the *nature* of the federal government's role in higher education as it has evolved since the Morrill Act. Here I shall borrow heavily from an excellent summary prepared for the Carnegie Commission by Ronald A. Wolk.[18] Until World War II, federal aid to higher education was all but nonexistent. In the academic year 1939–40, federal sources provided about 5 percent of the total income of institutions of higher education. As I noted, by 1945 that share had grown to 16 percent. This extraordinary rise—from an almost inconsequential share to a very important one over five years' time—reflects the mammoth wartime research and development effort (in which universities shared dramatically) and the GI bill which, in Wolk's words, "paved the way for the most dramatic enrollment explosion in the history of higher education."

Aside from the large numbers of students whose way was now, for the first time, paid by the federal government, the principal beneficiary of government spending in universities during the war was large-scale academic science. Although scientific research received its first federal boost from the Morrill Act itself, the principal effect was on agricultural research. Although this support helped ensure the beginning of science and scientific research as we have come to understand them, they were

18. Wolk, *Alternative Methods of Federal Funding for Higher Education* (Berkeley: Carnegie Commission on Higher Education, 1968), especially pp. 2, 10–12.

relatively minor operations until World War II. The enormous expansion of chemistry, physics, biology, engineering, and their derivative fields came from the federal government. It is absolutely essential to remember, however, that *the federal government wanted this expansion.* The universities were put to work on behalf of goals and activities deemed by government officials to be in the national interest.

In his message of March 1970, the President was about as open about the nature of federal support as I would think a chief executive ought to be.

> For three decades now the Federal Government has been hiring universities to do work it wanted done. In far the greatest measure, this work has been in the national interest, and the Nation is in the debt of those universities that so brilliantly performed it. But the time has come for the Federal Government to help academic communities to pursue excellence and reform in fields of their own choosing as well, and by means of their own choice.

The extent to which it has been the federal government that has done the choosing of late simply cannot be overestimated. Wolk reminds us that

> Some $15 million in federal funds went to higher education for research in 1940—almost exclusively for agricultural research. In 1944 alone, a single agency (the Office of Scientific Research and Development) spent $90 million on contracts with the Universities.

Despite the postwar cutbacks, the federal investment in university-sponsored research and development continued to grow, and after the launching of Sputnik it grew very quickly indeed.

> In 1955–56, the federal government spent about $355 million on academic research and development; a decade later, the amount reached $1.3 billion.

I emphasize *scientific* research because it is probably the biggest example of the effect of federal support on higher education: mammoth and rapid expansion, so big and so fast as to be quite exhilarating for all concerned, but accompanied by a clear case of federal domination of the directions in which higher education moved. The government was still hiring the universities to do its bidding. In retrospect, this is perfectly clear. At the time, the huge amounts and rapid expansion made it appear to many academics that the federal government was underwriting them to do as they liked. But that latitude was an illusion; the fact was that the Congress and the executive deemed the expansion and improvement of American science to be in the national interest; and that is what they hired universities to do, no matter how lax the rules may have seemed at the time.

STUDENT AID

Much the same may be said of student aid. It has come in three waves, all within the last quarter-century. First was the GI bill, demonstrating the nation's gratitude to its veterans and its commitment to educate and employ them after the war they won. In the 1950s came the National Defense Education Act, which gave money to people to go to college because the government felt an acute need to upgrade American education, especially school teaching; hence the teacher forgiveness provisions of the NDEA. And in the 1960s, of course, has come a wide assortment of programs that provide federal aid for disadvantaged students to attend college, again because the government, reflecting a national concern, decided that their opportunity for further education constituted an important national purpose.

At no point in these processes would I judge that the higher education community had control over its own destiny, at least insofar as its destiny was shaped by federal funds. I think we in the academic community tended to absorb and assimilate each new federal intrusion, concluding after the fact that we must have wanted it, and not bridling at requests that might have seemed outrageous had they not been accompanied by large sums of the taxpayers' money. There are exceptions, of course, such as Harvard's refusal to undertake classified research; but only the wealthy could afford to preserve their virtue in the light of generous and repeated propositions.

Categorical aid is just about all there has been. As Wolk says,

> Virtually all of the $4.6 billion in federal aid to higher education in 1967 could be described as categorical aid, in the sense that the federal government has categorized or designated its funds to be spent in certain areas which it has deemed to be of national concern.

Back in the days when federal aid comprised 5 percent or less of university budgets, the fact that such aid came through categorical programs had, at most, a marginal effect on higher education. But in an era when the federal share approaches a full one-quarter of the institutional budgets, the effect is very powerful indeed and is primarily one of distortion of institutional purposes in pursuit of federally determined objectives.

GOVERNMENTAL PRIORITIES

In light of the somewhat arbitrary character of categorical aid, one is bemused when members of the academic community get upset over

reductions in any one of the many categories of federal aid. Such
reductions (they are more than matched by increases elsewhere, for total
*federal outlays for higher education have risen every single year since
1960*) simply reflect changed national interests, changed *priorities*. When
the higher education community allowed itself to get into the business
of accepting categorical grant money from the federal government, it
accepted the implicit condition that no category was permanent or im-
mutable. When a private institution allows itself to become dependent
on support that is subject to the political process, it entangles itself in a
sequence that it is largely powerless to control. And it certainly runs the
risk of being victimized by the political forces that govern the money;
but one would have to be paranoid indeed to think that the federal
government's changes in emphasis in recent years amounted to victimiza-
tion. Let me repeat: the total federal outlays for higher education have
grown in every one of the last ten years; they have grown dramatically
from *$1.1 billion in 1960 to about $5 billion in 1970;* they have, thus,
sustained a rising curve that has had few dips and no severe or lasting
ones since World War II.

Of course, categorical emphases have shifted, and the overall rate of
growth has slowed in the higher education segment of the federal budget,
as it has for the total budget and almost every other individual portion
of it. During the decade of the 1960s, education was the fastest growing
portion of the federal budget, and many would argue that it was only
catching up to where it should be, was only receiving its due. I do not
disagree. But it would be naïve in the extreme to think that this "catch-
up growth rate" would continue forever, particularly as the rate of growth
in college enrollments has itself slowed. (Degree-credit enrollments in
postsecondary institutions more than doubled from 1957 to 1967; although the projected increase in absolute numbers of students over the
next decade, from 1967 to 1977, is about the same, the growth rate will
be 50 percent rather than 100 percent.)

In a political system, one man's raised priority is another man's reduced
budget; one categorical program increased usually means another one
diminished. It is perfectly understandable why anyone whose favorite
program is cut is irritated, if not desolate. But that is the built-in risk of
organizing institutions around categorical federal support. Not to know
this is not to know how government operates. If many on the academic
side of the exchange did not know much about government, the reverse
ignorance has been equally evident.

Higher education has been deemed important to the government only
to the extent that it has accomplished particular purposes the government
deemed important, and could accomplish them more effectively, faster,

or cheaper than someone else. This statement sounds harsh, for we academics spend a good deal of time reassuring ourselves that universities and especially professors are vitally important to the future of the nation. But there is a crucial distinction to be made. Something that is considered important to the *nation* by its proponents and beneficiaries becomes important to the *government* only insofar as those proponents and beneficiaries can convince the nation as a whole that it *is* important, that it is worth the money, and that it is more worthy of the money than competing claimants for the same funds. Even then, it does not become important in its own right or as its proponents view it; it becomes important to the government only in those terms that the nation has started to perceive as important. The result: another categorical program.

The three great bursts of federal funds and categorical programs follow this pattern. During the second world war, the nation perceived that higher education was important insofar as it could do the research and development necessary to win a modern war and insofar as it could make veterans employable. Sputnik roused the nation to concern over the state of teaching in its schools, particularly in science, and over the state of elementary and secondary education in general. The newly awakened concern with poverty and opportunity in the early 1960s bred a sense that higher education could somehow ease the plight of the poor, the non-white, and the deprived. And in each case, the federal categorical programs that resulted were concentrated on these purposes, not on others. And each time the higher education community not only accepted the money and adopted the purposes, but also came to view the programs and funds as its birthright, as something to which it was somehow entitled, rather than as a necessarily temporary response to a perceived condition.

THE NATIONAL FOUNDATION FOR HIGHER EDUCATION

The administration's response to this long continued method of support, which had so clearly become unviable, was to propose a fundamental shift in the form of federal assistance to educational institutions, away from categorical aid and toward general purpose grants. A National Foundation for Higher Education was proposed, to be administered by a semiautonomous board and director appointed by the President. It would make grants to individual institutions, to states and communities, and to public and private agencies. The object was not simply to reverse the forms of federal assistance but in the measure possible to redress the imbalances that earlier forms have wrought. The President's message was explicit:

> One of the unique achievements of American higher education in the past century has been the standard of excellence that its leading institu-

tions have set. The most serious threat posed by the present fiscal plight of higher education is the possible loss of that excellence.

But the crisis in higher education at this time is more than simply one of finances. It has to do with the uses to which the resources of higher education are put, as well as to the amount of those resources, and it is past time the Federal Government acknowledged its own responsibility for bringing about, through the forms of support it has given and the conditions of that support, a serious distortion of the activities of our centers of academic excellence.

The purposes the President avowed are ones I would hope most academics might share. His concern was in no sense limited to the large or prestigious institutions. He referred also to

the community college mounting an outstanding program of technical education, the predominantly black college educating future leaders, the university turning toward new programs in ecology or oceanography, education or public administration.

To this end he proposed that the National Foundation have three principal purposes.

- To provide a source of funds for the support of excellence, new ideas and reform in higher education, which could be given out on the basis of the quality of the institutions and programs concerned.
- To strengthen colleges and universities or courses of instruction that play a uniquely valuable role in American higher education or that are faced with special difficulties.
- To provide an organization concerned, on the highest level, with the development of national policy in higher education.

For the Foundation's first year, $200 million was budgeted.

One would like to report that the response of higher education was positive with respect at least to this proposal, but I fear this was not the case either. Here and there approval was expressed. Here and there suspicion. But, on balance, there was no response. Quite serious efforts by the President and members of the Cabinet and White House staff to explain the proposal and to elicit either support or some counterproposal came to nothing. Time after time such discussion would begin on a fairly high—and appropriate—level of general principles and within moments degenerate into a competitive and barely dignified clamor over this or that little categorical program.

Had we thought categorical aid had distorted the relations of the higher education community to the federal government before the program was announced, in the aftermath we were utterly convinced. Corrupted would not be too strong a term. *No one seemed able to think of the whole subject.* Few, even, seemed able to think of the interests of a single whole institution. A major presidential initiative that, right or wrong, was at very least the product of some thought and some analysis was greeted by silence on the part of precisely those institutions that are presumably devoted to thought and analysis.

LEADERSHIP

Had there existed a powerful "higher education lobby" that willy nilly would push through great increases in existing programs, the sequence of events might be more explicable. (It is worth noting that in the course of five years the elementary and secondary school interests have created such a lobby in Washington.) But there was no such lobby, and the result was predictable. Congress did nothing. A newsletter of the American Council on Education reported that the chairman of the Subcommittee on Education of the House had given up efforts to assemble a committee quorum to draft a comprehensive higher education bill. "She said," the report continues, "she saw no chance of passing a higher education bill at this time because of concern over campus unrest."[19] And there we are left.

I have hoped to make clear a conviction that campus unrest is not going to go away. It is and will remain a condition of American society in the present era. (One hopes that campus violence will ebb, and that is surely a possibility. But the gulf between the campus, especially the elite ones, and the rest of the society will persist.) The task of statesmanship would accordingly seem to be to fashion a system of federal (and of course state and local) support for higher education that is insulated as much as possible from the political tempers of the time.

The campuses will almost surely continue to make quite extraordinary demands on the society at large—a condition both predictable and predicted. The culture in this respect is extremely volatile, even in ways unstable, a result not of failure, but of success; not of the suppression of liberty, but of its extension. One recalls Bernard Shaw's prophecy:

> Later on, liberty will not be . . . enough: men will die for human perfection, to which they will sacrifice all their liberty gladly.

This condition we shall live with, threatening to the traditions of the university and society alike. More then is the reason to address ourselves with some urgency to the question of how we are to preserve and expand higher education whilst maintaining a diverse society that will on occasion appear almost a dichotomous one.

19. *Higher Education and National Affairs,* Oct. 2, 1970, p. 12.

Similarly, the society will continue to make enormous demands on higher education. The circumstances that led to the categorical aid system of federal support have not much changed. Indeed, the demands for relevancy in higher education, and the presumption that university professors can do what mayors, governors, and even presidents cannot, are much encountered at this time. Oscar and Mary Handlin have made unmistakably clear that this was the primordial expectation of American higher education. Higher education was to be "immediately useful and practical" if it was to receive public support.[20] Useful in training ministers; useful in training farmers; useful in training technicians; useful in training social engineers. Indeed at times one wonders that education as such survived. All this will continue, albeit one would predict a certain withdrawal of the campuses in the period just ahead. (It was interesting to note the proposal of the Scranton Commission that "In general, we recommend an overall reduction in outside service commitments."[21]) Here again the task of statesmanship will be to devise ways by which the services to institutions, private or public, off the campus, can be carried out in ways that maintain both the independence of the institution and its viability as a stable and creative society.

No small efforts these. Gigantic ones if they are to be combined with steady progress toward a national goal of universal higher education. New kinds of institutions will need to be invented. New forms of institutional governance, new types of teaching, and new subjects to be taught. But to achieve such goals in, let us say, the next thirty years, would hardly involve a greater achievement, or greater change, than that of the past three decades.

In only one respect does the period ahead involve demands on higher education that are in ways novel. The demand is for national leadership. If there is to be fundamental reform in the relations between the national government and higher education, there must be leadership on both sides, there must be negotiations, agreements, oversight, revision. The higher education community is not now organized for any such effort. It has no such men. It seemingly comprehends no such undertakings.

A leap of imagination is required for higher education to become not just a national resource and a national problem, but a national force as well. The effort is contrary to many of the best instincts of precisely those men now in higher education whom one would wish to see take up the challenge. But that is what a challenge involves. Much will depend on the outcome.

20. *The American College and American Culture* (Berkeley: Carnegie Commission on Higher Education, 1970), p. 52.
21. *Report of the President's Commission on Campus Unrest*, p. 193.

Response to Mr. Moynihan

ARTHUR S. FLEMMING

I APPRECIATE THE OPPORTUNITY to make a statement in response to the presentation by Dr. Moynihan. He has presented the higher education community both with an opportunity and with a challenge to take advantage of that opportunity.

I was struck by Dr. Moynihan's emphasis on higher education's involvement in adversary processes. Those of us who are associated with higher education are constantly aware of the validity of this emphasis. We recognize that—to quote Dr. Moynihan—there is "an adversary culture firmly entrenched in higher education." We recognize that this situation leads to an increase in political ambitions and activities of those within the academic community, which, in turn, leads to adversary relationships between those who entertain the ambitions and engage in activities and some strong groups within the larger community. As a result, we in higher education are struggling as never before to reconcile the objective of keeping our institutions aloof from political strife with the objective of permitting and even encouraging members of our educational communities to involve themselves in the political process according to their own insights and convictions.

We also recognize that we are involved in adversary relationships with the federal government in working toward the common objective of providing equal opportunity for higher education for all Americans regardless of race or economic circumstance.

We recognize that the federal government's fiscal problems lead to vigorous efforts to get as many items as possible "off the budget." One result of the economy moves is the increased emphasis on loans to students, as contrasted with grants, and the concomitant development of creative approaches to the lending field—approaches reflected in the administration's proposals to Congress. The higher education community too believes that a reordering of priorities could lead to a program for reaching the objective of universal access to postsecondary education but avoid saddling the disadvantaged with heavy debts. That belief has sometimes put us in an uncomfortable adversary relationship with the government. We do not oppose improved loan programs, but we do feel that they must be accompanied by sharply increased grant programs. Dr. Moynihan was considerate when he indicated that our opposition to loans, which we felt would weaken the grant programs, was expressed by silence.

We recognize that we are involved in adversary relationships with the federal government as together we work toward the objective of the federal government's providing higher education with the increased financial support—support that only the federal government can provide—which must come if higher education is to serve the nation's needs appropriately. We recognize the problems and dangers inherent in policies of categorical aid. We appreciate that thousands of officials in the federal government have been sensitive to the problems and dangers and have tried to prevent them from materializing. At the same time we must welcome initiatives for increased emphasis on institutional grants—initiatives such as those reflected in the Nixon administration proposals which have been so effectively presented by Dr. Moynihan.

The financial situation of institutions of higher education is such, however, that at this point new institutional grant programs must be "add-ons" to the funds now being received through categorical aid. Here, again, we find ourselves in an adversary relationship with the federal government on proposals that we fear may lead to the substitution of the institutional approach for the categorical approach. Should this happen, institutions would likely receive less rather than more federal support, or support would no more than level off.

Steps can be taken, however, to turn these adversary relationships into an asset for this nation. A healthy adversary relationship can produce constructive action that otherwise would never come about.

First, as institutions and government deal with each other, both can avoid attributions about competencies and motives of the participants in the adversary proceedings.

Second, we can dedicate ourselves to the task of reconciliation—a task that has been underlined effectively by the Scranton Commission. I welcome Dr. Moynihan's call for the initiation of the process of reconciliation when, in closing, he says:

> If there is to be fundamental reform in the relations between the national government and higher education, there must be leadership on both sides, there must be negotiations, agreements, oversight, revision.

Both the federal government and the community of higher education must become involved in the process of reconciliation. I take issue, however, with the following sentences in Dr. Moynihan's paper that follow this call for reconciliation:

> The higher education community is not now organized for any such effort. It has no such men. It seemingly comprehends no such undertakings.

I am confident that I speak for the Board of Directors of the American

Council on Education when I say that we are prepared for such an undertaking. This Council came into being in World War I in order to perform just such a task. Through the succeeding years, it has continued to undertake comparable responsibilities. It stands ready now to respond to Dr. Moynihan's challenge.

If the federal government will designate the time and place and their participants, we will provide the leaders on our side and shall be prepared to do so as early as next week.

The task should be undertaken with a sense of urgency. Those, on both sides, who are assigned to it should be prepared to spend, not a few hours every now and then, but days at a time, with a definite schedule.

Those assigned to the task should stay with it until there emerge in the major areas that now divide us—not weak-kneed compromises—but commitments that will command the respect of the American people. In this way the institutions of higher education will be able to take full advantage of the opportunities for service which now confront them.

Dr. Moynihan's proposal provides us with a light at the end of the tunnel. I say this, growing out of my own relationships with both government and higher education, and I am confident that Dr. Moynihan's proposal stems from experience in similar relationships.

A drastic change must take place in the relationships between the federal government and higher education. Should the course of events be otherwise, one of the nation's greatest assets, its investment in higher education, will be seriously undermined.

The means for reconciliation must be established. We are prepared to do our part.

PART FOUR

Leadership

SAMUEL B. GOULD

Damn the Torpedoes—Full Speed Ahead!

Having been separated from my official duties for only a brief period, I can be looked upon as being in the early part of a withdrawal period. The pains and difficulties of such a withdrawal are hard to bear at this first stage. Perhaps I can be forgiven then if I unburden myself of some thoughts that have recently occupied my attention.

Embattled Leaders

These are indeed strange times for presidents and chancellors, especially for those who can look back to the so-called "quiet years." Then we had only Joe McCarthy to worry about, or student apathy mixed with a little seasonal mischievousness, or alumni athletic ambitions, or financial brinkmanship, or educational atrophy. We still have some of these, but a good deal more has been added. We have lived in times when weathermen were meteorologists, when young lords were members of the nobility, when panthers were a species of beautiful animal, and when pigs were related to the bucolic life.

As I move through my withdrawal period, there are elements of university life I am already beginning to miss. For example, I miss the glow of physical well-being that comes from leaping back and forth across the generation gap. I miss the deep sense of satisfaction at the end of a long night when all the broken window glass has been swept up, the fires put out, and the damage neatly totaled. I miss the exhilarating challenge of fighting chaos with one hand tied and the other weaponless, while phrases like "due process" and "rights of the individual" echo about. I miss the intellectual stimulation of the daily sparkling correspondence with anonymous admirers and some not so anonymous, but all united and unanimous in agreeing upon the high degree of idiocy and cowardice I have attained.

I miss the surge of creativity felt each day as one prepares tomorrow's statement expressing firmness in the face of every student threat and, at the same time, the most stalwart defense of academic freedom and supreme faith in youth. I miss the eye-watering happiness that comes of walking through the haze settling over the student lounges, where hospitality is king and the pot is always simmering. I miss the brilliant prose

LEADERSHIP

styles of student newspaper columnists and editorial writers as they skill-
fully improvise on four-letter words, making every verb irregular, every
tense imperfect, every noun peculiarly singular and possessive, and always
arriving at amazingly erotic and unlikely conjunctions. I miss the wonderful pause in the day's occupation, otherwise known as the "children's
hour," when the legal injunction has just been served and the offices are
once more quiet, with only the debris left by passionate environmentalists
to mark what has happened.

Finally, and more seriously, I miss the hitching posts of a lifetime, now
suddenly removed, when, in some strange and wonderful way, to be teth-
ered was at the same time to be free to move and act in the world of
learning.

Yes, presidents are living in extraordinary times. There seem to be only
four kinds of presidents left: those in transition, those in flight, those in
desperation, and those who are newly anointed. The ones in transition
have moved from one institution to another in the wistful hope that
things will be better somewhere else. Those in flight have given up hope
altogether and are searching for solace elsewhere, often in studies designed to explain why all these present-day phenomena occur. (The conclusions of these studies can almost always be predicted, by the way; we
need money and more communication, preferably in that order.) Those
in desperation persist in staying at their posts out of a conviction that
somehow the worst of the voyage must be over but are at the same time
haunted by the possibility that there may be still more dangerous rapids
to run. And the newly anointed have mixed feelings of horror and exhilaration. They are fearful, but they are also very certain that they have
learned enough from the stupidities of their predecessors to guarantee
them the heroic role they expect to assume.

But there is still another kind of president. He is a person deeply concerned and troubled over the present state of college and university life.
He is as deeply committed as ever to his task of discovering and utilizing
every idea, every technique, every device that can bring about rapid but
reasoned approaches to change. He represents that kind of heroism which
is the art of hanging on a bit longer. He is the convenient scapegoat for
many of the diatribes of students and faculty and press and community
regardless of where the real responsibility for error lies. His courage and
integrity are tested over and over each day as he struggles to protect academic freedom even when it comes dangerously close to being abused.
I think he is insufficiently recognized and honored for his service to education in one of its most crucial periods. I wish I could say that this
recognition and honor will come, and soon, but much will have to change
before that happy day arrives.

THE FAULT IS NOT IN OUR STARS

The theme of this conference asks the question, "Higher education for everybody?" The background papers are most pertinent and all-inclusive. They deal with the major issues soundly and sometimes provocatively. There is little point in my iterating what they say, a great deal of which I would readily agree to. They speak to the major question candidly, albeit with a more pessimistic tone than I think is warranted. But I would ask the further questions: Does *everybody* include educational leaders? Is it not appropriate that they, too, need a new and higher education for the time that faces us? And if so, on what kinds of truths shall such education be based?

Suppose we ask ourselves a few other blunt questions. What kinds of truths lie behind our troubles these days? Have we recognized them, and do we admit to them? Or are we inclined to turn our eyes away and pretend they are nonexistent? Can it be that our own defensiveness and even our timidity have as much to do with our problems as the societal events that are so overpowering? Do we, ourselves, lack faith in our institutions of learning? Is it possible that, having discovered we can no longer carry on business as usual, we are realizing guiltily that we really know very little about how to make that business appropriately *unusual*? Does our reluctance to change stem from complacency or fear or ignorance or stubbornness or lack of ability or a conviction that everyone else is wrong?

Education in America is the greatest single preoccupation of our time, and yet as educators we seem to recognize no advantages for ourselves in that fact. Never have we had a better opportunity to lead from strength; yet we are retreating out of fear. The numbers of students for whom we are asked to provide, the financial commitments that exceed by so much those of any other country in the world, the increasingly accepted philosophy that bespeaks higher education for everyone who can benefit from it —one could suppose that these societal characteristics proved rather conclusively that the American people believe in education, want more of it for more people, and want to help it become better. Our citizenry are not seeking to do away with colleges and universities because some are not fulfilling their educational potential. To the contrary, they worry lest the present attacks on higher education from zealots of the right or left should endanger the future growth and stability of our educational institutions.

Let us remember that if there are minuses in American higher education, there are many pluses also. These have sometimes been forgotten in the midst of cries from an angry or bewildered populace over the changing life styles of youth and the discourtesies, dissents, or even destructive actions that have resulted. But the solid achievements of education are evident to each person if he is willing to open his eyes without prejudice.

We have knowingly and purposefully created a generation of youth better able than any others to think for themselves. In earlier days we were always severely criticized for *not* doing this; now that it is done, those who urged us on have suddenly discovered that the younger generation does not always agree with them on social, economic, or governmental policy, and expresses its disagreements with disconcerting frankness.

We lead all the nations of the world in educating the highest percentage of college-age youth and in the development of graduate study, professional schools, and research. Imperfect as the education may be, it moves steadily toward the democratic goals of enlightenment and competence for all.

We have made fantastic contributions to the growth of the nation's economy and to its service functions, governmental and private.

And let us remind those who shrill endlessly about repression that we are among the few remaining bulwarks of intellectual independence.

> Among all social institutions today the university allows more dissent, takes freedom of mind and spirit more seriously, and, under considerable sufferance, labors to create an environment closer to the ideal for free expression and for free interchange of ideas and emotions than any other institution in the land. By its very nature, the university gives birth to criticism, scrutiny, and dissent.[1]

These are only a few of the positive factors one could cite. Yet for some strange reason, as educational leaders we appear reluctant to take the initiative and move boldly, even though we have an enormous amount of goodwill supporting us. We equivocate between overfirmness and overpermissiveness, just as the parents of our students do, and we are held responsible not only for our own equivocations but for theirs as well, a circumstance that always causes our responses to be defensive. We take refuge in theoretical dissertations on the causes of campus discontent or violence, but in those areas contributing to such discontent where we have competence and jurisdiction (as in academic and administrative change), we often do as little as possible and take as long as possible to do it. Perhaps one reason for this limited action is that whatever we plan is usually kept within carefully circumscribed limits that are characteristic of our own past experience. This may be the age for bold explorations in outer space, but our educational explorations are still very much in the

---

1. Samuel B. Gould, *Today's Academic Condition* (New York: McGraw-Hill Book Co., 1970), p. 7.

traditional, compartmentalized, earth-bound stage. For example, teacher education has still not found the key to how learning takes place; continuing education remains no more than a stepchild; international education is more talked of and written about than practiced; educational technology is still feared rather than welcomed.

One aspect of our present situation needs very special emphasis. Although we are generally agreed upon the desirability of more involvement by students and faculty in decision making about curriculum, governance, and other matters, we tend to forget that these constituencies have a much lesser concern than do presidents about the progress or even the survival of the university as an educational entity. Indeed, some of them have no concern at all, consider the university outmoded, and would welcome its dissolution. The best structure, in their view, is no structure of any sort. So far as some faculty have thought about it, all that is necessary is someone to find the funds with which to pay salaries and other costs and someone else to disburse them. Anything else representing supervision or leadership is too constraining to be other than a nuisance and even an affront. Students, by and large, are not inclined to worry much about even these financial practicalities. Neither group offers any design for this new approach to academic life but both are considerably committed to it as an idealistic theory. A radical view, perhaps, but it is growing in popularity among many who do not consider themselves radical.

We have created this condition ourselves by our own blind concentration on noneducational affairs. When we ourselves look upon the university as a succession of financial and management challenges rather than as a haven of intellect, when we are personally withdrawn from active involvement with academic planning and leave this for others to develop, we are misconceiving our calling. Not only do we remove ourselves from a central role relating to the institution's purpose, but we also increase our alienation from faculty and students. They cannot be blamed, after all, for mistaking our motives and misinterpreting our function when we constantly offer them the picture of a bureaucratic administrator with no warmer tones of academic concern. In a university, as in any other organization, efficiency is desirable. But no university can afford intellectual sterility, and it is as much a responsibility of presidents to ensure educational growth and vitality as it is to be a good steward of resources.

To call for educational leadership at this crucial time may seem old-fashioned and even irrelevant. But I am convinced that unless such leadership is evident in the head of the institution and unless it manifests itself daily, there is little defense against the moves to politicize a campus or the pressures to water down quality or the geologic attitudes toward change.

MORE TRUTHS FOR THE TROUBLED

Lack of educational leadership at the top is only one of the truths that lie behind our troubles as institutions of learning. There are others, as well. And most of them, with the attendant dissatisfactions they cause, go far beyond the university.

The campus community is in many ways a microcosm of society and reflects the latter's misgivings and disapprovals and fears; yet it is not at all typical of society. It is artificial and largely temporal in its makeup and unbalanced in its age groupings vis-à-vis the world around it; it is understandably and inevitably given to introspection and idealism and thus to rebelliousness; it is the focal point for the swift fulfillment of each individual's expectations regardless of how varied and disparate these may be. From within and without, therefore, it cannot help but be the target for today's student dissatisfactions and those of society itself. Life is too complex and change occurs too rapidly for the situation to be otherwise. The complexity and change, however, are not the sole doing of the university. Other and larger forces contribute their share.

For example, the new element of physical fear that we sense for the first time on our campuses is no more than the physical fear within society itself. The streets of our cities are unsafe to all at night and sometimes even during the day; this same disquieting, even horrifying, phenomenon has become part of university life. Violence is not just a problem; it has become an accepted method of problem solution. And violence on one side naturally begets violence on the other. Success in achieving a goal is in direct relation to the amount of bullying or other strong-arm tactics one can use. Life is increasingly cheap for old and young alike, whether it is to be thrown away in war, in automobiles, in nocturnal muggings, in conscienceless bombings, or in campus confrontations.

Similarly, the impersonality of modern life and its lack of privacy are characteristics not limited to the campus scene, even though they are attacked so vehemently there. The misuses of expanding technology have created a new headache to match each new invention. Our whole society suffers from recurring dislocations as it struggles to keep pace psychologically with its technical or scientific achievements. As Toffler points out, we are indeed in a never-ending state of "future shock."[2] His major emphasis is on the shock from technical progress.

But there is as much or more to be said about the shock from swiftly deteriorating or discarded moral values. And here again in this latter in-

2. Alvin Toffler, *Future Shock* (New York: Random House).

stance the university is given full blame for a hypocritical, permissive, sex-ridden, drug-laden environment while all around it the adult society gives expression to what it considers a new freedom in theater, films, literature, and life style. Any theater or film advertising page or any weekly best-seller book list will document what I am saying.

The most evident truth that plagues us is the steady discrediting of the use of reason as a fundamental approach to life. And once again it can be noted that the rejection of reason by our students has its origins to a considerable extent in what they see going on around them in the world of today. We have entered a period where reason is being challenged, assaulted, and ripped out of more and more of our whole society. This phenomenon may turn out to be the single most fundamental value change of our time.

Wherever we look, we can find ample illustrations. The most highly educated nation in the world is reviving astrology and occultism, and is importing obscurantist pundits from exotic corners of the world to give advice. And it is not the poor and distraught people who are doing this, but some of the most highly educated and affluent. The emphasis is not on the interaction of minds but on the release of emotions and the encouragement of impulse. In cultural circles we have the phenomenon of so-called Impossible Art. The theater seems to concentrate its efforts on new forms of soul- and body-baring that blunt and numb not only the mind but ultimately the senses as well. In films and books, American directors and authors often act like smirking juveniles who have just discovered the titillations of pornography and don't know whether to feel guilty or liberated. In music we find serious musicians discarding their work of creating edifying tonal architecture and toying with random electronic squeaks and roars, while a growing portion of popular music has a decibel volume that not only destroys its occasionally ingenious subtleties and touching lyrics but creates a form of mass catalepsy.

And over the whole scene hangs the miasma of drugs. Millions of persons now escape regularly from the reality, responsibilities, and complexity of life through drugs, preferring to plunge into the lethargic fantasies of their irrational selves. Last year Americans purchased and presumably consumed three and one-half *billion* pep pills and almost as many tranquilizers. We seem to prefer the self-imposed chemical pollution of our bodies to the really tough confrontation of our minds with our huge social problems. With growing hypocrisy, we preach the urgent need for greater intelligence, concern for others, and sustained social action; and then we cop out with a trip into personal gratification or self-pity, replacing constructive efforts with freak-outs, rationality with sensation.

This growing number of forms through which the rational instrument of our mind is being pushed aside in the emerging life styles, this rejection of history and disregard of the future leaving only the *now* as life's essential element, this fever pitch of emotionalism, hedonism, and righteous moralism, however stimulated—these have become distinguishing features of our society.

The major protagonists in pressing for this new philosophy have been our young people. This is nothing new; youth have always been in the forefront of romance, adventure, and challenges to the status quo. What *is* different is the amount of attention paid to their desires by the rest of society. We now have a remarkable adult preoccupation with young people and a corresponding preoccupation of young people with themselves, their own wishes, and their new sense of power. And in spite of all the attention given them, young men and women are complaining with mounting bitterness that they are neglected, misunderstood, and even forgotten as a generation. They claim that modern life depersonalizes them and drains away or represses their freedom and individuality. They argue that the world has given them nothing but botched enterprises, outmoded structures, and imminent death. A portion of them believe with deep conviction that most adults are craftily working to enslave young people's souls.

To escape and to liberate themselves, an increasing number of young people annually flout the accepted mores of society in what seem to be outrageous actions; or they adopt the rhetoric, slogans, and even the tactics of jungle guerrillas or terrorist anarchists. A growing proportion maintain that what they feel in their hearts or in their bellies has a greater truth than all the piles of evidence, accumulation of facts, or rational arguments that others assemble for their scrutiny.

The university, open to new ideas and relatively defenseless, seems an ideal launching pad for the assaults on society and on reason itself. Where else can one talk about and practice exhibitionism or anarchism or any other kind of *ism* with such impunity? What better place is there for getting maximum attention for one's thrusts against society, democracy, and reason while receiving at the same time maximum protection from the legal authorities and the powerful and sometimes equally irrational counterforces?

Thus, the modern university has become a staging area and a battleground. It is both the focal point and the mirror for the new characteristics of our society. What sublime irony! The institution that has steadfastly championed freedom of thought as an inviolable right of man finds itself contributing to its own extermination because it can discover no acceptable way to resist the violent actions that stem from such freedom of thought. The institution that has as its reason for existence the advancement of the life of the mind finds itself increasingly used as the base from which reason is challenged and derided.

Yes, the truths behind our troubles are far-reaching and sobering. And they can put us into utter despair if we lose sight of our own strength, both actual and potential. This we must never do, and, in reorganizing and using this strength, we must remember that it grows from the fulfillment of a university's true purposes, shaped and guided by the times but not directed or manipulated by them.

A Basis for Action Today

What can I tell you by way of valedictory, then? What have I learned from these years that could in any way be helpful? I have no special wisdom to impart, but I have labored for a long time, sometimes blundering and sometimes successful.

First of all, I have learned that the potential of the single child or youth or man is still the center of our collective hope regardless of how we grow institutionally or change our educational patterns.

I have learned that the search for truth grows more rather than less arduous and painful, and that we are only a hair's breadth closer to it and its accompanying wisdom than we were before. I have learned that pedantry remains, as it has over the centuries, a threatening vulture hovering over our institutions, turning vibrant and vital intellects into bleached skeletons when its strikes. But I have also learned that the eagerness to teach, and teach imaginatively, persists and could be a rejuvenating force in the university if it were encouraged.

I have learned that when people, whatever their creed or color, hunger and thirst—whether for power or goods or learning or even merely a place in the sun—their craving will be satisfied not by logic but only by action. And such action on our part must relate to honest, attainable expectations for a human dignity that starts with education.

I have learned that the old saws are indeed correct when they tell us that patience and caution are virtues, but that the strong winds of change cannot be ignored when simple humanity is the issue. I have learned that liberty exercised without self-discipline soon degenerates into license and that governance offered without compassion soon leads to repression. I have learned that power wielded by the young or the old without the accompaniment of reasoned persuasion wreaks havoc on all who use it as well as on those who feel its weight.

I have learned that when reason ceases to be the method of the university and freedom ceases to be its encompassing armor, it is doomed. I have learned that educational initiative is the only worthwhile defense against attack and the only hope for the university of the future. I have learned that when we seek only to be administrators and forget we are educators, we sow no more than a crop of nettles and reap a bitter harvest.

Finally, I have learned that to be fearful out of expediency is to surrender the university swiftly to its enemies, to be vindictive out of rage is to multiply them, and to be steadfast in performing the university's proper tasks in a democratic society is to guarantee the only permanent future it has.

And so I say, damn the torpedoes—full speed ahead! The destiny of the world of thought still rests in the hands of those who choose to be educational leaders, not in those who choose to destroy or denigrate such a world. This is not a time to be turned from the main task. It is a time, rather, to grapple with it boldly, thus to ensure a worthy intellectual heritage for the generations to come.

TERRY SANFORD

Or Time Will Waste Us

IN HIS HISTORICAL PLAY ABOUT RICHARD II, WILLIAM SHAKESPEARE CRE-
ates a provocative portrayal of the English king. One interesting
characteristic of Richard is his apparent inability to reconcile the emotional excesses of his personality with the high calling of his office. In one
minute, he proudly praises his own royal blood; in the next, he deplores
the growing dissent in his kingdom. And in either stance, he dresses his
comments in highly impressive rhetoric.

But as the play goes on, his declamations begin to sound hollow. It
becomes harder to find any real substance undergirding all that proliferous
language. For instance, Richard will seize on a minor event, and balloon
it with the hot air of his rhetoric until he is satisfied that it looks, or at
least sounds, important.

In this critical time of American history, and especially during our
present crisis in higher education, you might guess there are several reasons why I am reminded of King Richard's tragedy. When that play
opens, England is waging a war that requires a continuing outlay of government funds. Incidentally, England herself has not been invaded; but,
to maintain her existing sphere of influence, she has sent troops across
the Irish Sea to suppress a rebel uprising in Ireland.

In the opening scenes of the play, there are suggestions that an under-
current of dissatisfaction is growing in England. Aside from the play's
text, history explains to us that this restlessness grew out of years of agitation for social reforms on behalf of the poor and the disadvantaged. But
England's funds had been diverted instead to finance first a war in France
and in Scotland, and then this Irish war across another sea. In the play's
second act, the king's own uncle at last declares: "England, who was
wont to conquer others, hath made a shameful conquest of itself." And
he dares to criticize Richard openly. The king responds, not by examining
this valuable advice, but by bitterly insulting his uncle. He begins by calling his critic a "lunatic, lean-witted fool," and then goes on to stronger
terms.

The king's references to "treason" and "traitors" become more notice-
able as the play unfolds, and they always apply to the growing dissent and

271

the dissenters in his kingdom. When he finds that the ranks of dissenters are growing larger rather than smaller, he rails against them, calling them "villains, vipers, damned without redemption; dogs, . . . snakes!" Continuing to rely on rhetoric, rather than reform, he allows his position of authority to deteriorate until ultimately he has no more power to lose.

Today there is obvious evidence that dissatisfaction is growing in our society. This restlessness also has evolved from years of agitation for social reforms on behalf of the poor and the disadvantaged. And it, likewise, has been aggravated by the diversion of government funds away from needed reformative programs and toward a counterrevolutionary war across the sea. But the most distressing parallel of all is in the impulsive and abrasive reaction of high governmental leaders to voices of criticism—voices that are trying desperately to awaken this society to the urgency of its present crisis. Much of this warning, although by no means all of it, comes from college and university campuses, for which we should be proud. Almost all of the abrasive reaction is directed toward the campus.

RESPONSE TO SLANDER

We must not allow the institutions of higher education to accept this slander without response. I do not absolve administrators, faculty members, or students from all blame, but I do think that society cannot endure such an unwarranted discrediting of the entire academic community. In the first place, the phenomenon of change and dissent extends across all of society; it is not confined to campuses alone. Second, American society cannot afford a self-inflicted wound that damages the strength it must have for its future.

From an historical view, universities traditionally take a leading role in major transformations of social and political life. It is a tradition that now implies a duty. As our past decade of campus unrest has shown, universities may act as heralds of impending social transformations. Universities collectively are the alarm clock that goes off in the early morning of a new historical era, allowing our society time enough to get dressed and eat breakfast before it goes forward to cope with its own transformations.

Higher education has succeeded, I think, in that service, but it has been paid poorly for its troubles. Indeed, instead of taking advantage of that early warning, society—or at least some of its leaders—would rather lie in bed at high noon pretending that morning has not yet come, and ranting against the alarm clock for not allowing more time to sleep.

In addition to our alarm-clock role of the past decade, I think the coming decade of campus transition will introduce a new role for universities —that of anticipating the transformation of our society. Other components of our society—from managers to masses, from leaders to laymen—can await such transformation and then adapt to it when it comes. But if a university waits, it will become obsolete. What is worse, it will have sent thousands of graduates out into society with education that is out of date before it becomes fully useful. Furthermore, our society must depend on the humanitarian and intellectual resources of our universities to lay the groundwork for such change. No other institutions, no other agencies, not even governments collectively, have the available resources to accept such a challenge.

The campuses of our colleges and universities have served as a harbinger for the compounding American crisis. Our students started by calling society's attention to its shameful mistreatment of its black citizens and other disadvantaged people. Later they identified the myopia of our escalating involvement in Vietnam and pointed to other social and political ills. In addition, many members of our faculties forewarned society of the dangers of environmental pollution and of what could be termed "technological overdependence." All these problems were obviously external to our campuses, but the increased activism and concern of students soon focused on internal conditions as well. The campus had been a harbinger. It was now a crucible for society's distress.

It isn't hard to see in retrospect that we simply were not functionally prepared for such a multipronged assault on our established institutional processes. In the turmoil that ensued from this general assault on our administrations, communication has often been difficult; and communiques themselves have sometimes become garbled in transmission. The resulting frustration and animosities often boil over into disruption and sometimes into violence. And administrators who were there received some rough on-the-job training, reorienting themselves to an entirely new era of higher education. It has been far from easy.

A Basis for Optimism

The temptation in meetings is to compare wounds and to console and comfort one another. Yet more profit will come from resisting that temptation.

We need instead to look back critically at what we have done and what we have not done, what we should have done, and what we may yet be able to do. We need to see both where we fell short and where we may have overreached. We should never expect to be completely satisfied, or to judge ourselves faultless or guiltless. But regardless of reservations, we can draw collective pride from one accomplishment that pervades the field of higher education today. We have accomplished great changes—some relatively drastic—in a very short time. And we did not sacrifice our viability; on the contrary, we enhanced it, ensured it. And we made progress not only in the direction of reforms, but also in our ability to effect reforms, not without effort but with minimum confusion. As James Perkins has pointed out, in summarizing his paper, "In the 1960s higher education was subjected to the most vigorous and violent changes in its history—in size, finances, curriculum, governance, and relations with society." (Dr. Perkins, of course, worries whether higher education should "label the changes it has undergone as reforms or destruction." I, for one, am optimistic that the future will produce a happy answer to his doubt.)

It is important that, instead of repressing the forces of change, we were able to subdue our fears of change. We have in many cases even altered our administrative machinery to make appropriate changes easier to effect. Of course, some student activism is outrageous and even more is vexatious. Although we on campuses never expect to rid ourselves of the vexation, I believe we shall be able to check the outrage and the destruction much more quickly than society will be able to resolve its own off-campus distress, among the young and the old.

I want to dare another optimistic outlook. I am well aware that we will probably be confronted with additional disruption on some campuses this year, and that there may even be violence again. Still I believe that we have finally topped the mountain and are on the downhill side of this phenomenon. I have several reasons for this view.

Administrators have generally learned how to react without overreacting. We have learned how to anticipate trouble spots; how to listen, attentively and with due respect; how to distinguish the deliberate destructionist from the legitimate dissenter. We have learned how to sort out the minority tactics of disruption and violence from the majority purposes of dissent and criticism; and we are now better equipped and firmly set to stop unlawful and destructive acts by students and outsiders.

Students, too, have become reoriented, I believe. They have learned to identify more accurately the agents of wrongdoing and injustice in our society. They have learned that their concerns and objections can be registered in more creative and, therefore, more effective ways. And they have learned that when such desires have been rationally presented to administrators, they will more often be encouraged than discouraged. Furthermore, they realize that excessive action is counterproductive and, thus, not really very smart.

At the least we are moving in these directions.

THE CAMPUS AND THE PUBLIC

There are apparently those in our society who would deny or avoid taking rightful responsibility for any of the off-campus problems which originally triggered campus unrest. Furthermore, they have turned their confused resentment on higher education itself. Led by some of our highest government officials, they have labeled "campus unrest" as a bigger problem than any of its causes, and in so doing, have diverted not only attention but constructive effort away from the root problems.

If there were no more consequences to their tactics than being called names, we could simply treat it as bad manners, bad taste, and bad rhetoric, and let it go at that. These outbursts, however, are far more serious than they might appear on the surface. Lurking beneath this misleading assault is the very dangerous suggestion that some public officials think they should repress expression that does not agree with their own ideas and programs. I see no offensive force yet mounted against this attack.

If these leaders of repression were to be successful in removing dissent from our campuses, what would be the next step? Does such a march against dissent continue until the only truly free agents in our society are those of government?

Various states have proposed various forms of control. More than thirty have already enacted legislation dealing with campus unrest, much of which is constructive, but other states, like California, propose financial repression. The federal government itself set the example for cutting down on the financial support of higher education.

And how have we in higher education reacted to this criticism and to these insidious efforts to repress free dissent on our campuses? We have been generally offended, and have reacted rather defensively. We are, after all, accustomed to remaining aloof from street fighting. Unlike some other institutions of American life, we are reluctant to counterattack, or to call on political or other allies to avenge our injuries. We must get off the defensive, and we must assume the offensive now—not for the sake of our institutional dignity, but for the survival of our society. As dedicated as many of our supporters have remained throughout this crisis, they alone cannot long assume the burden of carrying us financially. And yet, unless our colleges and universities remain solvent and viable, as well as free, we should all fear for the future of American society.

We must remind the public of the ways in which its future is tied inextricably to ours. Where else in American life will we find the combination of accumulated knowledge and humanitarian concerns that will be required to devise effective solutions for the grave problems that confront us? The problems range from housing to hunger, from pollution to poverty to power supplies, from inflation to integration, from inner-city decay to interpersonal relationships, and many, many more. Do the American people have any other institution of any kind anywhere that is equal to that kind of undertaking?

We will not, of course, academically resolve these problems like engineers repairing a bridge. The unique qualification of higher education in this historic challenge is its ability to combine its technical skills with creative ideas in human relations. In other words, we will be about the moral and spiritual, as well as the intellectual and physical, rebuilding of America. Not that we fancy that higher education alone can rebuild America; it will take all the people and all the institutions of our society to achieve that goal. But higher education remains society's best resource for the endeavor.

In his background paper for the American Council meeting, James Miller asked, "Who Needs Higher Education?" He showed that government, business, industry, and private agencies—all the institutions of our society—need it. Because they need it, they must support it, not only financially, but morally as well.

The job of those in higher education is to make the public aware of the opportunity that we all have together to convert our present crisis into a new era of human accomplishment and human accommodation. In the face of the criticism now being thrust at us, however, we cannot effectively approach the public—or any other audience—with hat in hand. We must drop our apologetic, tentative attitude, and take the positive approach. We must be enterprising. Our academic performances and our research achievements can speak for themselves, but in the din and uproar of criticism, their messages won't carry beyond the campus gates. It will be up to us to carry our own message to our greater society.

THE CAMPUS AND THE GOVERNMENT

As we enlist the support of business, of industry, of the church, of every sector of our society, we must also regain the faith and the increased support of government. As our society reorders its national priorities in an effort to resolve constructively all the facets of our present crisis, no other investment of public funds will pay higher dividends to the people than support of higher education.

The future of the nation requires a greater financial investment now. We must not hesitate to assert this claim. We cannot wait for the noise surrounding campus unrest to die down. The cries of help must be relayed by those who understand to those who are in a position to help, or it may be too late. We cannot wait much longer, for example, for substantial additional support for medical education. Further delay will ultimately affect every community in the land.

We cannot wait any longer for substantial expansion of financial assistance for the disadvantaged. If the present proposals are not approved by Congress, then we will have lost all chance of serving another sizable number of high school graduates, who will not pass this way again. And the contributions they might have made, based on the asset of higher education, will be forever lost to society because of this lack of funds. In the meantime the problems of society will be multiplied.

There are dozens of other items, just as urgent, on the agenda that cry for immediate attention. The private universities and colleges can look beyond their most obvious problems today and see the ominous threat of insolvency imperiling their future. That in itself must be the concern of all our institutions, both public and private. As a recent report of the Carnegie Commission on Higher Education shows, "If there were a decline in the ability of private universities to perform their functions, the burdens—financial and otherwise—on the rest of our system of higher education would be vastly increased." And in other sections, the Carnegie report shows the very real possibility of such a development. After describing the current fiscal failures of some private institutions, the report concludes, "If they go much beyond this, their continued operation is placed in jeopardy."

There are other ideas for future support that need to be studied and developed, such as sustaining grants to institutions, both public and private, by the federal government.

We cannot wait for more favorable times to promote increased support. We need positive attention now to shaping a program that uses to the best advantage the vast resources available to the federal government. About the only consensus I can detect is that the federal program is not adequate either in certainty or in dollars.

Roger Bolton's paper has spelled out most of the issues yet to be determined, but they cannot be determined without the involvement of those responsible for and intimately concerned with the institutions of higher education. The issues have an urgent ring, as well as a long-term value, because the federal government is proposing too little too late, and is sacrificing potential benefits that would accrue to the nation as a whole. We in higher education must promote our own alternative proposals.

THE RULE OF REASON

As we shift to the positive approach, let us insist that the "rule of reason" apply off the campus as well as on. It is easy to teach respect for force. That is the technique of dictators. It is far more difficult to teach respect for reason, but this is the task of democracy, and universities must teach it by precept and by example. Our example must be self-restraint and consideration of the ideas and rights of others. It must be based on reason that leads to self-discipline, because the leadership of the nation and leadership for the world must be made up of men and women of reason.

Let us reaffirm that we will deal with destruction and disruption, as we will, but let us reaffirm even more strongly that we will lead our students toward the great adventure of rebuilding America. These are the people who will make the decisions for the improvement of our society. These people, who already influence the election of leaders who make such decisions, offer the best hope for the future. We must be positive, and not negative, in our attitudes toward them.

Let us reenlist the support of parents and alumni, reminding them that we on campuses are not their enemy. Neither are the students. The students they have sent us are their sons and daughters from their homes, from their churches, from their schools. If they expect their hopes to be fulfilled, they must regain their faith both in their children and in higher education.

We should also let it be known that we do not hold the illusion that more funds from Congress, or anywhere else for that matter, will alone prepare higher education for its future. The events of the past few years should have alerted us all to the need for internal readjustment in our institutions, for reordering the practices and purposes of our colleges and universities. That also is our responsibility, and it is our best hope of achieving effective renewal and revitalization.

William Birenbaum has raised these challenges in a way that may be a little frightening to those who administer, teach, or govern. But institutions of higher learning must embody courage as well as wisdom, so that we can grasp the lead in change—even drastic change where needed—with vitality rather than fear. His well-phrased observation that "we have many departments of history, but no departments of the future" speaks precisely to the point I raised earlier that universities must, in the coming decade of transition, anticipate the impending transformation of society. We cannot wait any longer. Time is wasting.

In his final scene on stage in the Shakespearean play, Richard II has been deposed, and is confined to prison, expecting to live out the rest of his days there. He is reminiscing over his downfall, and analyzing its causes. And in that mood, he muses, "I wasted time, and now doth time waste me."

Regardless of the echoes of Richard's earlier arrogant, brash, and self-destructive outbursts abroad in our nation today, higher education must, in its way and with its resources, ensure that our society never suffers such an ultimate fate. If we were to miss this opportunity which history offers us now, it would take American higher education and its larger society another generation or longer to regain the threshold where we stand today. At that possible price, we cannot afford to waste time—not another minute of it.

ARTHUR S. FLEMMING

Closing the Gap
Between the Ideal and Reality

At the heart of our Judeo-Christian tradition is the commandment "Thou shalt love thy neighbor as thyself." This commandment does not require us to like our neighbor. We clearly cannot be commanded to like anyone. That is a feeling that must come from within. This commandment does not require us to approve of everything that our neighbor says or does. The commandment does, however, place upon us a common responsibility never to pass up an opportunity to help our neighbor achieve his highest possibilities.

This spiritual law of life must be at the center of our thinking and planning as we confront the issue: higher education for everybody? If it is, we will start by concluding that as a community of higher education we have failed to take advantage of opportunities that have been presented to us to help our neighbor achieve his highest possibilities. We will not attempt to shift responsibility for our failure to others. We will recognize that as a community of higher education we have played a major role, oftentimes by inaction, in creating a wide gap between one of the professed ideals of this nation and actual performance.

The National Advisory Commission on Civil Disorders identified the ideal when it said:

> By enactment of the Higher Education Act of 1965, the Congress committed this nation to the goal of equal opportunity for higher education for all Americans regardless of race or economic circumstance.

The Commission also identified the gap between the ideal and actual performance when it said:

> While progress has been made, the goal . . . remains for the disadvantaged student an unfulfilled promise.

That statement is just as true today as it was on March 1, 1968.

We know, for example, that there has been no substantial gain in the percentage of high school graduates in the black community who attend postsecondary educational institutions, that there has been a comparable failure in opening up substantially increased higher educational opportunities for American Indians and members of Hispanic groups, and that a substantial percentage of the disadvantaged members of our white society likewise continue to find the doors of opportunity shut.

The shortcoming is a national tragedy. It calls for united action on the part of the community of higher education in order to compensate for our sins of omission.

The American Council on Education should take the initiative and call together the leaders of our associations in the field of higher education. These leaders should develop a plan of action designed to provide an equal opportunity for higher education for all Americans. The plan should be identified clearly as the plan of the higher education community. It should reflect a resolution of any built-in conflicts between types of institutions about the best way of tackling this issue. In this manner the higher education community can present a united front in seeking support from the government and other segments of society.

Why should the higher education community take on such an assignment?

Goals and Programs

First, we should accept the assignment because we have a greater capability than any other group in society to develop a plan that will narrow significantly the gap between the promise our nation has made of equal opportunity for higher education for all Americans and the reality that confronts us today.

We can agree on a goal.

Some have suggested that the goal might be stated as follows: "To provide equal access to postsecondary education programs for those who desire them and are able to profit by them." Others have suggested the goal be recognized as that of universal access, namely, that anyone who has graduated from high school shall have a place available for him in higher education. Other statements have been and will be suggested.

The leaders of our higher education associations have the capability of agreeing on a formulation of a goal that will command respect and support. If they do, we will demonstrate that in one major area it is possible for the higher education community to agree on its mission: to enter into a new convenant with the people of this nation.

We can agree on a program designed to achieve our goal.

We can agree, for example, on admission policies that will open the door of each type of postsecondary educational institution to large numbers of ethnic groups for whom the doors are now closed. Contributions to the attainment of the goal must be made by all types of institutions.

These policies should rest on the assumption that only one question need be answered in deciding on admissions: Does the applicant have the potential to profit from an experience in a particular institution?

Admission policies should also rest on the assumption that whenever and for whatever reasons admission policies discriminate against significant numbers of disadvantaged persons, two groups are hurt. First, the educational institution is depriving those who are barred from the institution of the opportunity for a genuine educational experience. Second, it is denying those who have been admitted the kind of educational experience that is so desperately needed in these days.

We can agree on national policies in the area of student financial aid that will have to be implemented if our agreed-upon goal is to be achieved.

We can agree on an order of magnitude of cost for each of the next five years if our program is to be implemented and our goal is to be reached.

Other issues will have to be resolved in order to develop a well-rounded program. The point is, however, that we have the capability of developing and reaching agreement on such a program. It is important for us to be in the position where the country is reacting to our program rather than our reacting to a program developed by others. Furthermore, it is important for the country to know that we have ironed out the issues that are internal to the community of higher education rather than expecting government, for example, to make decisions about the responsibilities of different types of institutions.

FUNDS

We can obtain the financial resources needed to implement our program.

We can demonstrate our determination to achieve our goal by giving up some of our highly specialized missions in order to provide resources for our broader mission. In brief, we can make choices that reflect the values we espouse.

We can, with a unity that will command respect, appeal to private foundations for major support of our program.

We can decide, with a unity that will command respect, to organize an all-out campaign for doubling in 1971–72 and doubling again in 1972–73 the federal funds for the Educational Opportunity Grant Program and the federal programs providing for special services for the disadvantaged. Today less than half of the funds authorized for Educational Opportunity Grants are being appropriated, and yet it is clear that this is the one program that can close significantly the gap between the ideal of equal opportunity and our present performance. Special services programs for the disadvantaged, such as Upward Bound, are receiving funds far below authorizations, and yet two and one-half years ago the Kerner Commission noted that estimates then indicated that this program could usefully serve 600,000 poverty area students as against the approximately 25,000 that are now being served.

Why shouldn't we marshal our political resources and make it clear that talk about equal opportunity in higher education for all Americans is like sounding brass and tinkling cymbal unless the federal government is willing to increase sharply its appropriations for Educational Opportunity Grants? Why shouldn't we accord this program the top priority in requesting federal funds for the support of higher education? If we had done so in the past—if we had backed up positions taken by the American Council on Education with all-out grass-roots activity—the doors of opportunity would have been opened for many disadvantaged persons for whom they are now forever closed.

A campaign for federal financial support for our action program should command the support of the President and the Congress. How else can the nation achieve the goal identified by President Nixon in his March 19, 1970, Message on Higher Education of seven out of ten persons of college age furthering their education beyond high school by 1976, as contrasted with the present five out of ten? How else can the nation achieve the goal set by the Congress in the Higher Education Act of 1965, of equal opportunity for higher education for all Americans regardless of race or economic circumstance?

Reforms

The second reason why we should accept the assignment of developing and supporting a plan of action is that an all-out dedication to the cause of universal access to postsecondary education will provide new incentives for needed reforms in our system of higher education.

The considerations, including the spiritual, that lead to such a dedication when combined with the presence of rapidly increasing numbers of the disadvantaged in the community of higher education will result in the creation of a far more favorable climate for action on such issues as, to cite a few examples:

· Educational programing to determine, as Dr. Furniss puts it, "how these patterns may be adapted to students rather than how students may be adapted to production programs that now exist."
· Individualized learning, namely, helping the student determine his educational objectives, then helping him determine how he can best utilize resources both inside and outside the college to achieve his objectives, and then helping him establish guideposts to mark his progress or lack of progress.

- Developing effective programs for encouraging and helping students to put knowledge, as Dr. Pusey puts it, "to work for moral, social and political ends."
- Developing support for research programs involving both faculty and students that will contribute directly to the teaching and learning processes.
- Identifying and meeting the needs of those who are attending institutions of higher learning involuntarily by reason of pressures placed upon them by society.
- Determining methods for measuring institutional effectiveness on the basis of the progress made by individual students toward the realization of their potential.
- Making provision for intermittent periods of work directly related to the student's educational objectives.
- Opening up opportunities for increasing numbers of minority groups to occupy faculty and administrative positions.
- Pooling the resources of like and unlike colleges in a given area in order to meet more effectively the needs of students in the respective institutions.
- Increasing involvement, without politicizing the institution as an institution, of members of the educational community in working out solutions for the social, political, and economic issues of the community.
- Developing personnel policies that will remove from teaching positions those who no longer make meaningful contributions to the teaching and learning processes.

In brief, if higher education responds to the challenge to close the gap between the ideal of equality of opportunity in higher education and our actual performance, it can bring about profound changes in the way we approach our total job. It will provide us with that inner strength that will lead us to make major changes in order to serve far more effectively than we now do those individuals who make up our respective educational communities.

These changes could save us from a serious undermining of our entire system of higher education; without them our future is not assured.

The National Commission on Causes and Prevention of Violence was right when, in its concluding paragraph of the chapter on "Campus Disorder," it said:

> One effective way for the rest of us to help reduce campus disorders is to focus on the unfinished task of striving toward the goals of human life that all of us share and that young people admire and respect.

We have an unfinished task on our own doorstep.

The Unpardonable Sin

There are those who warn us against responding to the demand for universal access to higher education. They say: We will add to our financial burdens. We will transfer to the campus more of the tensions that confront the larger community. Individual institutions will find themselves subjected increasingly to the decisions of planning authorities at both the federal and the state levels. In meeting the demands of the disadvantaged, we may squeeze out students from middle-income groups (as though we were talking about subtracting resources from that group instead of obtaining additional resources for the disadvantaged).

As I have pondered these objections, I have reminded myself of this observation by John Knox, the theologian:

> When we once set ourselves to resist the truth, we can always find excellent reasons for objecting to all possible representations of it or arguments for it.

The truth is that men and women have the right of equal opportunity for higher education regardless of race or economic circumstance. A system of higher education that expects to grow in strength must work in season and out of season to make that right a living reality. As Albert Bowker, the head of the New York City system of higher education, put it, "The unpardonable sin is not to try."

Philip N. Harder is the first vice-president of the First National Bank of Minneapolis. He is just completing a one-year term as head of the Minneapolis Urban Coalition. In an interview in the *Minneapolis Tribune* commenting on the problems confronting that city, he said:

> I think the Kerner Commission was right—white racism is the main problem. There are aspects of prejudice that we all have.
>
> At the start, you can get into a kind of white-suburban, guilt-complex thing. Later you come to the point of view that "I don't give a damn what caused it; it's wrong and it's got to be changed."

That the promise of equal opportunity for higher education for all Americans, regardless of race or economic circumstance, is an unfulfilled promise is wrong. It's got to be changed. We have it within our power to change it. Let's get to work.

AMERICAN COUNCIL ON EDUCATION

LOGAN WILSON, *President*

The American Council on Education, founded in 1918, is a *council* of educational organizations and institutions. Its purpose is to advance education and educational methods through comprehensive voluntary and cooperative action on the part of American educational associations, organizations, and institutions.